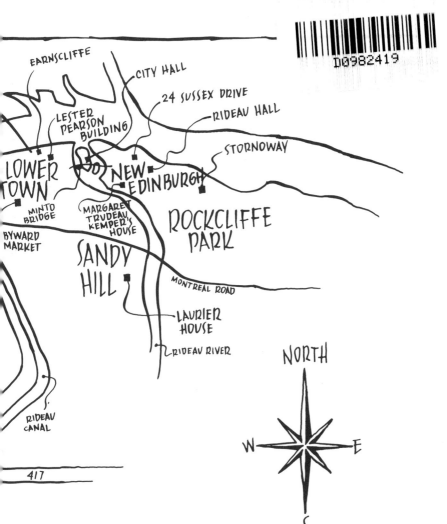

CITY OF OTTAWA

OTTAWA
INSIDE OUT

Power, prestige and scandal in the nation's capital

STEVIE CAMERON

KEY PORTER BOOKS

For David and Tassie and Amy

Canadian Cataloguing in Publication Data

Cameron, Stevie
  Inside Ottawa

ISBN 1-55013-150-8

1. Power (Social sciences).   2. Social status – Ontario – Ottawa.   I. Title.

HN110.08C35 1989   305′.0971384   C89-094089-4

Typesetting: Southam Business Information and Communications Group Inc.
Printed and bound in Canada

Key Porter Books Limited
70 The Esplanade
Toronto, Ontario
Canada M5E 1R2

89 90 91 92 93 5 4 3 2 1

Contents

Acknowledgements

Whether they knew it or not, many people helped with this book. Several gave me lengthy interviews or suggested important references. Others pointed me in directions I might not have thought of. But a few are simply people I have known over the years, whose friendship made Ottawa a fascinating place in which to live and whose insights have helped me as a reporter to cover the city, both for the Ottawa *Citizen* and more recently for the *Globe and Mail*, with some real understanding. In particular I would like to thank the following people:

Bev Koester, Carroll Niles, David and Diana Kirkwood, Mary Ann Griffith, Nancy and Henry Richardson, Reeves and Hilary Haggan, Jim Watson, Joan Henderson, Rosa Pereira, Cecilia Humphreys, Shelley Ehrenworth, Arthur Kroeger, Nancy Gall, Margo Roston, John Grice, Marie Dorion, Barbara Mirsky, Lloyd Francis, Marie Bender, Mark Daniels, David McNaughton, John Swain, Kurt Waldele, Jean-Pierre Muller, Russell MacLellan, Stuart Langford, Roger Phillips, Donna Kearns, Paddye Mann, Ed Riedel, Carol Reesor, Bill Knight, Penny and David Collenette, Pierre Fortier, Bill Lee, Lucille and Ed Broadbent, Tom Axworthy, Bob Rabinovitch, Tim Porteous, Frank Iacobucci, André Tessier, Kim Pollock, Dan Donovan, Glen Kealey and Diana Crosbie.

There are one or two people I cannot name in this list of acknowledgements; they know who they are, and for their help I will always be grateful.

But along with the ones I can name, I must particularly thank Jim Littleton, whose advice and insight helped me dive into the Ottawa underworld of spies and intelligence agencies.

I must also thank Gordon Osbaldeston for many hours, over the past two years, of long conversations (spiked with much laughter) that have helped me understand his world of the *haute* mandarinate.

Although I did not interview them specifically for this book, I owe Bill Neville and Finlay MacDonald a big debt for their insights over the years into how Ottawa works.

John Sawatsky continues to be the most generous friend any writer could ask for; not only did he share information but he gave me invaluable advice on physically organizing a project as large as this book.

I must thank Nick Hills, who first gave me the opportunity to write about politics in Ottawa and who gave me the plum assignment of the summer of 1984, Pierre Trudeau's patronage appointments.

With Nick, there was Paddy Sherman, my publisher at the *Citizen* who also believed I would make a good political reporter and assigned me to the *Citizen*'s investigative report-ing team in 1984. A year later he gave me my own column. And a year after that I joined the *Globe and Mail*, thanks to Geoffrey Stevens, the former managing editor who always stood by me whenever the flak flew. I miss him. No one ever had a better editor than I did in Shirley Sharzer, and I miss her too.

Without Peter Benesh, my dear friend through many wars, the book would have foundered. Peter set up my computer, rescued chapters from the netherworld of MS-DOS and was always there with his acute insight into Ottawa's unique world.

And I must thank my hand-holders. Nancy Colbert, my agent and friend, who steered this project through. Jan Walter, who understood and who waited. Phyllis Bruce, who listened a lot and whose enthusiasm made all the difference. My wonderful editor, Anne Holloway, whose sensitivity, patience and good nature were severely tried.

The Ontario Arts Council helped this project with a generous grant; again, I am most grateful.

And finally there is my husband, David, who dragged me kicking and screaming to Ottawa and made politics and government as much a part of my life as it was of his. His steadfast support, whether it was in explaining an arcane document or just walking the dogs when it was my turn, made this book possible.

Introduction

To understand Ottawa, you must know more than how bills are passed in the House or how the Public Service Commission hires bureaucrats or where the new National Gallery is. You must understand the city's history, its social life, its neighbourhoods, its unique French-English culture. The city and the Hill can be won, but not without an appreciation or at least an understanding of cherished traditions and old battles. This book is an odd collection of questions I would answer for close friends who move to Ottawa to work and live. Where should you live? Hang out? Shop? How do you get ahead? Who do you have to know? Can you trust the press? Who are the new lobbyists and how do they operate? How does the House work? Are there poor people in Ottawa?

As a journalist, I'm also aware of all the political junkies across the country who love politics but who can't get the behind-the-scenes story of how things really work, who really counts, what the city is really like. I've always figured my job was simple: to tell people what I know – within the laws of good taste and libel. Readers should know what the insiders know, and that's what I have tried to do here.

Some people will say that this book represents a foolish nostalgia for a time that is over, for the good old days of the Trudeau government. It doesn't, but I am alarmed about the way the city has changed. Paranoia has infected the bureaucracy. High ethical standards of political conduct now seem like quaint old customs. Expressions like "parliamentary tradition" and "ministerial accountability" are about as current as yellowed antimacassars on old armchairs. Partisan Tories think the city looks down on Brian Mulroney because he's an electrician's son from Baie Comeau. That's not so; there are plenty of successful people in Ottawa who worked their way up from humble roots in small towns. The city looks down on him because they are not sure they can trust him.

This book is only a lopsided view of the city. I've never been in a cabinet meeting, so I don't pretend to explain how they work. I don't spend a lot of time dealing with senators or senate issues; they are important, but I leave that job to someone else. Ottawa has an interesting cultural life with talented artists, musicians, actors and writers; I was lucky to be included in this world, but again, there wasn't room in this book. No one is more aware of the gaps than I am. But I was allowed the privilege of writing from one point of view and choosing the things about Ottawa that amuse me or enrage me or move me. Maybe there is more history and less gossip in this book than readers would like, but it is the history that gives me hope that this wonderful and fascinating city will survive any government we can throw at it.

• •

PART ONE

INSIDE OTTAWA

1

And on Your Right ...

When new members of Parliament and their spouses first
arrive in Ottawa, the administrators of the House of Commons take them on a bus tour as part of their orientation.
When tourists come to town, they get on the double-decker
buses and roll around the city looking at the tulips and
Parliament Hill. And when old friends come to visit, they
too want a tour, but they want something different. While
they always want to start with Parliament Hill, it isn't long
before they ask sheepishly, "Couldn't we just drive by where
Margaret Trudeau lives?" or inquire diffidently, "Isn't this
about where Stornoway is?" or even break down and wail,
"Okay: *enough* history. Show me all the big houses in
Rockcliffe and start at 24 Sussex. Show me Pierre Trudeau's
pool."

Whatever kind of tour you take, it has to start with the
House of Commons. Guides will show you around the Centre
Block (the middle section with the Peace Tower), pointing out
the exquisite Library of Parliament at the far end of the Hall of
Honour and the Green Chamber, the splendid room presided
over by the Speaker where parliamentarians meet for debate.

They will tell you the prime minister's office is on the second floor in front of the Chamber. They will point out the Memorial Chamber where the beautifully illuminated Books of Remembrance list every Canadian soldier who died in the world wars and other wars. They will show you how the elevator up to the top of the Peace Tower ascends at a slant. They will take you to see the Red Chamber where the Senate sits.

But the guides won't show you the best stuff, the rooms you really want to see. The guides won't show you the Speaker's Corridor, which houses the Speaker's panelled offices, his elegant little apartment and his green and gold private dining room, which looks as if it had been designed by Pre-Raphaelite painter William Morris. They won't let you try out the Speaker's chair in the Chamber, with its hydraulic lift installed for former Speaker Jeanne Sauvé, whose legs were too short to reach the ground. You won't get to see into the prime minister's office, the Opposition leader's office or even into an MP's or senator's office. You won't get a glimpse of the MPs' private Reading Room, a large, panelled library stocked with newspapers from all over Canada, murder mysteries, spy thrillers and Jackie Collins' novels.

You won't be shown the Parliamentary Dining Room on the sixth floor, with its private dining rooms and antechambers, a dining room that has a subculture all its own. Anyone wanting a discreet conversation avoids a seat under one of the arched domes in the centre of the room because the acoustics are so tricky that even whispered conversations can be overheard. Those wanting secrecy hug the edges. And newcomers learn quickly not to expect a seat in an alcove; these are permanently reserved for special groups. For example, although the prime minister almost never eats here, the alcove to your immediate left as you enter the dining room is set aside for him. Senators on their own head for the Senate alcove on the right; there is also one each for Liberal MPs and NDPers.

The guides won't show you the spaces under the rafters, beyond the men's washroom on the sixth floor, where former

NDP MP Stanley Knowles keeps his filing cabinets. You won't get to see the ridiculous double post office in the basement where an invisible line down the middle divides the Senate Post Office from the House Post Office, where the mail bags are kept separate, where staff line up in separate lines to send parcels and letters that are weighed by separate staff on separate scales.

Even the Hot Room, the long, untidy third-floor room at the back of the Centre Block where many Press Gallery reporters work, is off-limits to the public. So are the television studios, hanging out over the Chamber but cleverly hidden behind decorative woodwork and glass, which are equipped with the latest high-tech equipment to broadcast House proceedings.

Visitors are not allowed into the West Block of the House at all. This is the wing that houses members' offices, some large committee rooms and the parliamentary cafeteria – not as grand as the dining room, but very popular. This means visitors can't see the daily 8:15 Breakfast Club, the gang of right-wing MPs, political aides and even a few journalists who once sat around gossiping and leaking damaging stories about the people Brian Mulroney could do without, people like John Bosley and Joe Clark.

Charter members of this table included Nova Scotia Tory backbencher Robert Coates; Alberta Tory Gordon Towers from Red Deer; Oakville Tory Otto Jelinek, now minister of national revenue; Toronto *Sun* columnist Doug Fisher; former Broadcast News radio chief Fred Ennis, now an Ottawa consultant with a regular gossip column in the Ottawa *Sun*; Commons' Sergeant-at-Arms Gus Cloutier; and Patrick MacAdam, the former Mulroney aide who served the PM as caucus liaison before winning a coveted (and much criticized) patronage job as a senior diplomat in London. The job did not work out as everyone had planned, and MacAdam had to be brought home again. Now, after a year of flogging Korean-made fax machines with another table patron, Rick Logan, he has joined the well-known Tory lobbying firm, Government

Consultants International. Logan is a former aide to former defence minister and Tory MP Robert Coates. It was Logan, along with Coates' press secretary Jeff Matthews, who went with two strippers into the back room of a bar in Lahr, West Germany, during an official visit in the fall of 1984, just a few weeks after the government came into power. Journalist Bill Fox was another member of the infamous breakfast club in the early 1980s; this is where he and other journalists gathered so many of the dump-Joe-Clark stories that were so harmful to the Tory leader. After the Tories came into power, the breakfast club membership changed as some of the coterie became too powerful and too busy to drop by, but to this day you can occasionally see the boys gathered around their mugs of coffee at 8:15, spinning their webs.

Although visitors who come on weekends or during the summer parliamentary recess can see one of the best little museums in Canada in the House of Commons' East Block, most, sadly, miss it. This gorgeously restored area, finished in 1981 after four years of what officials called "the most ambitious restoration and renovation undertaken by Public Works Canada," contains Sir John A. Macdonald's office, Sir George-Étienne Cartier's office, the office of the third governor general, Lord Dufferin, and the original Privy Council Office. These rooms, along with Laurier House, Mackenzie King's residence in Sandy Hill, are the most interesting museums in the city, notwithstanding the more grandiose National Museums. Together with the Library, the East Block was the only part of the Parliament Buildings not destroyed by fire in 1916, so most of the rooms are just as they were in 1872 when the country was first dealing with the crisis of building a railway to the Pacific.

Sir John A. Macdonald's office is in the southwest corner of the East Block; after his death it was never again used by a prime minister, but in the mid-twentieth century ministers of external affairs such as Louis St. Laurent and Lester Pearson camped there. During the 1982 Economic Summit, French President Francois Mitterrand was assigned this room, while

Ronald Reagan was down the hall in Lord Dufferin's old office. Macdonald's office has a nineteenth-century chill; the only heating comes from a coal fireplace, which was always lit before Sir John arrived in the mornings. Light came from a "gasolier" hanging over his desk. A map of Canada in 1871 hangs on the wall; the carpet is a replica of the one that was here then. A spittoon sits on the floor, and his tartan and top hat are hung casually on pegs by the door.

On the desk lies the fateful paper condemning Louis Riel, the Order-in-Council stating "that the law be allowed to take its course of Louis Riel, convicted of high treason." Beside it is the telegram that confirmed the execution had taken place.

Once, Macdonald was sick for a month with a gall bladder attack; believing it would be too dangerous to move him, his doctor made him stay in the office, where there was only a brown leather button-back chaise longue for a bed. Lady Macdonald nursed him, but it wasn't easy; the only water in the room came from a little corner sink, fed by a cold-water gravity tank in the roof. It is still there and it still works. A curtain hangs by it, which Macdonald could pull round for a quick change and a chilly sponge-bath.

Down the hall is the office of Sir George-Étienne Cartier, a Father of Confederation and minister of militia and defence in 1872, who took over as leader of the government while Macdonald recovered from his illness. Sir George was largely responsible for the creation of the provinces of Manitoba and British Columbia, as well as for the purchase of the Hudson's Bay Company territories, but was later involved in the Pacific scandal with Sir Hector Langevin and Macdonald himself.

Lord Dufferin's office was the headquarters for all governors general from 1866 until 1942, when they moved their offices to Rideau Hall. The red carpet and the porte-cochère outside are by tradition used only by the governor general or by the reigning monarch, although Ronald Reagan was permitted to use them during the Economic Summit. True to the year 1872, the room boasts burgundy velvet hangings, heavily fringed in gold, which cloak the pointed arches of the Gothic windows. Voluptuous burgundy velvet chairs invite whispered confidences. The partners' desk, the red leather chairs, the bookcase were all used by Dufferin. As he requested before his death, former governor general Jules Léger lay here in state before his funeral in Quebec City in 1980.

The Privy Council Office, resplendent in its Gothic revival grandeur, was used for Privy Council meetings from the days of Sir John A. to Trudeau. Now these meetings are held in the Centre Block cabinet office. Between 1865 and 1867, the executive council of the United Provinces of Canada met here. Lit by a big gasolier with counterweights that move it up and down, the room is dominated by a massive table, a reproduction made at Upper Canada Village in Morrisburg, Ontario. (The original is in the Regina public library.) The table is unusual because of the pyramid of slotted shelves that runs down the middle, designed for ministers to tuck in notes, files, letters and documents as they worked. The Clerk of the Privy Council sat like a schoolchild at a diminutive desk in the corner and took notes.

Two prime ministers, Mackenzie King and John Diefenbaker, would not permit smoking in the chamber. A door in the corner opens into a little antechamber with a fireplace and button-back chaise longue where ministers would sneak away to grab a furtive cigarette.

What the guides won't tell you is that for many years Robert Coates had a splendid suite of offices in this part of the East Block, a suite stuffed with antique furniture like its historic neighbours and far too grand for a lowly Opposition back-bencher, a suite NDP Leader Ed Broadbent could only dream of, a suite now in the grip of Health Minister Perrin Beatty. What was Coates' pull? Simply his close friendship with Sergeant-at-Arms Gus Cloutier, the man who doles out furniture and favours to chosen MPs.

Right across the street from the East Block, facing Parliament, is the Langevin Block. In Ottawa, when people talk about the PMO they don't mean the prime minister's office in the Centre Block of the House of Commons. What they are talking about are the 140 or so powerful people who work for the prime minister and the deputy prime minister, most of them in the Langevin. Here the key players include the prime minister's principal secretary, his chief of staff, his press secretary and his senior policy advisors as well as the government's top public servant, Paul Tellier, the Clerk of the Privy Council, and his senior staff.

The pecking order of the prime minister's staff is manifest in the offices each commands. His principal secretary and chief of staff are next door, with offices facing the Hill. Lesser mortals are consigned to space at the back, overlooking the alley between the Langevin Block and the office buildings that face Sparks Street. Mila Mulroney's suite, 129S, is on the first floor at the back, near the western entrance. And the press office is right by the front door, on the right; as one former Trudeau staff member said years ago, "When the lights are on here late at night, you know something's cooking; they're getting an announcement ready."

With the advent of Don Mazankowski's growing fiefdom some Privy Council Office staff have been driven into the ignominy of the drab buildings behind on Sparks Street, turning the Langevin Block into the Doges Palace of Ottawa, with bridges and tunnels connecting it to its lesser satellites.

Built between 1883 and 1889, the Langevin was named after Sir Hector Langevin, a former mayor of Quebec and twice minister of public works, from 1869 to 1873 and again from 1879 to 1891, in Sir John A. Macdonald's government. Like so many other public works ministers (most recently, one thinks of Roch LaSalle), Sir Hector could not resist the temptations of an office dedicated to porkbarrel politics and he twice resigned over scandals to do with government contracts.

The Ottawa Press Building, at 150 Wellington, just west of the U.S. Embassy (which you can recognize by its steel anti-tank barriers and its flag), is a favourite with visitors lucky enough to have friends who are members. Most of the nine floors are devoted to offices for newspapers and magazines or broadcasting studios, but the second floor is the Press Club, which offers a daily dose of strong liquor, wretched food and hot gossip to an assortment of reporters, cameramen, producers and editors as well as the hundreds of "associate" members in the city's public relations community. Bureaucrats and politicians sometimes eat here, but they make enough money to buy their lunches at better places. It is heart-warming, however, to see Ottawa's most cherished senior citizen, diplomat and diarist Charles Ritchie, eating here regularly, at a table full of old friends.

Wellington Street is the city's grandest thoroughfare, although in the winter it is a ferocious wind tunnel of blowing snow and black ice. In the summer it is not much better: pogo stands and *frites* trucks line the curbs, filling the air with the smell of vinegar and frying fat. Between the Press Club and the U.S. Embassy is the Victoria Building, full of grumpy senators trying to negotiate offices in the Centre Block. Just west of the Press Building is one of the House of Commons buildings few tourists know about, the Wellington Building, or, as it is known around the Hill, the South Block. This was the old Metropolitan Life Insurance building, and it now houses the main administrative offices of the House as well as the furniture repair shops and the leader of the Opposition's office.

Continuing along Wellington on the south side, just across Bank Street from the South Block is the Bank of Canada complex, a glass palace that houses other government offices such as those of regional industrial expansion and tourism. (Driving past it for the first time, my Cape Breton sister-in-law mused aloud that given all that glass it was a good thing this wasn't a gravel road.) The concrete facade of the original bank building is oddly wedged in the middle of all the glass. Kitty-corner from the South Block, on the north side of Wellington Street, is the Confederation Building, a huge old office building that houses dozens of MPs. (Behind it and down a winding road at the bottom of the hill near the river is the dreaded Pit, the parking lot assigned to Untouchables, like journalists, who can't get better spaces up higher around the Commons buildings.)

Farther west on Wellington Street, just beyond the Department of Justice, the Supreme Court, a chilly and forbidding slab of a building, squats glumly, repelling the curious. Aside from the strange Veterans' Affairs Building, which straddles Lyon Street with an odd stone arch and which houses the Canadian Security and Intelligence Service, the only other government building of note along Wellington is the truly appalling National Library, a monstrous structure built in the 1960s on one of the city's most dramatic sites, a cliff overlooking the Ottawa River and the city of Hull.

A block or two south of Wellington Street, you'll find the thriving lobbying community starting to congregate in luxurious new offices. Government Consultants International, the well-connected Tory firm, throws its considerable weight around from offices on the thirteenth floor at 50 O'Connor, one of the city's most impressive new highrise office towers. Boeing, which runs its own Ottawa lobbying operation right across the hall from GCI, fought a long hard battle against its neighbour in an attempt to win the Air Canada contract for new planes. But GCI's clients, Airbus Industries, got it, so one can't help but wonder if things occasionally get tense in the hallways or washrooms. (Jean Chrétien practises law with Lang Michener Lash Johnston in a swanky suite just a few floors down from GCI.) And 50 O'Connor is also home to the local branch of Hy's restaurants, which opened everywhere in Canada in the 1960s and 1970s but waited until 1986 to open in Ottawa. Hy's is where all sorts of odd people who haven't quite reached the top levels of power in Ottawa meet for lunch; as one person described it, "Hy's at noon looks like the waiting room for the Rideau Club." The Rideau Club, the city's most exclusive social club, faces Bank Street, at the other end of the 50 O'Connor tower development.

But there is another whole group of lobbyists nearby who can't afford space in 50 O'Connor; they're the one-man bucket shops, many operating out of 130 Albert, a building that has been home to all sorts of scamps and scoundrels over the years. Reporters have learned that when they go off to interview some dubious characters in the lobbying business – characters doing the same kind of business as the fellows at 50 O'Connor but wearing cheaper suits – they're sure to be at 130 Albert, next door to the Four Seasons. I once asked one of these small-fry operators, a man who did a great deal of business in Korea, how he avoided a competitor and mortal enemy in the elevator every day. He grinned wolfishly and said, "Easy. My office is in the basement; I just go down the stairs."

After exploring Wellington Street and taking a diversionary junket to visit the lobbyists, you should return to Confederation Square at the eastern end. Passing the Château Laurier hotel on the left, turn left down Sussex Drive. All the way along on the right is the beautifully restored streetscape of nineteenth-century shop fronts, a project supervised by meticulous National Capital Commission architects. As you go north on Sussex Drive, you will be tempted, probably irresistibly so, by the shops and restaurants of the Byward Market on your right. Give in to your desires; not for nothing is the market the heart of Ottawa, while the Hill might be considered its soul. Further north on Sussex Drive, on the left, are the spectacular new National Gallery, the National War Museum and the Royal Mint, all worth several visits.

A new favourite sight for all Ottawans is the old Perpendicular-style nineteenth-century chapel of the Rideau Street Convent, a triumph of *trompe l'oeil* – wood painted to look like marble – now lovingly restored inside the National Gallery. When the Rideau Street Convent was demolished in 1972, Ottawa lost Bruyère College, the small college run by the strict Grey Nuns, or the Sisters of Charity as they are more properly known, where most young upper-class French-Canadian women had been educated. And it almost lost the chapel as well, but a group of smart and far-sighted people, led by such women as former National Gallery director Jean Sutherland

Boggs and Ottawa homemaker Leonora McCarney, began a fundraising drive to save it.

Moving along Sussex Drive, you'll pass the modern red-brick Japanese Embassy just as Sussex Drive turns right towards Rockcliffe. Soon the new Saudi Arabian Embassy will be here as well. Just as you reach the Macdonald-Cartier Bridge to Hull, you pass Earnscliffe, a three-storey stone house built in 1857, the home of Sir John A. Macdonald from 1871 until his death in 1891 and now the residence of the British High Commissioner.

Earnscliffe was built for John MacKinnon, the partner and son-in-law of Thomas McKay, a wealthy builder who had emigrated to Canada as a stonemason from Scotland. McKay built a magnificent house for himself in New Edinburgh, which is now Rideau Hall, the home of the governor general. MacKinnon did not have any of his father-in-law's financial acumen and died deeply in debt, leaving his widow penniless. Another McKay son-in-law, Thomas Coltrin Keefer, bought the house and let Annie MacKinnon go on living there until she moved to her mother's house, called Rockcliffe Manor. Today, that house, the loveliest in all of Ottawa, is the residence of the papal nuncio, the Vatican's ambassador to Canada.

Earnscliffe's next owner, in 1868, was an English business-man, Thomas Reynolds; when ill health forced him to return to England he rented it to Sir John in 1871. Twelve years later Sir John was able to buy the house. After his death, his family kept it for a few years and then sold it. Finally, in 1928 the British bought it when no one in Ottawa was able to convince the government that Canada should own it. The British are de-lighted to have such a prize and they madden visiting Cana-dians by piously pointing out that they have kept Sir John's bedroom as it was, with most of the original furniture.

But if the British were being entirely candid, they would admit that the house rattles as the traffic rumbles across the Macdonald-Cartier Bridge and that they have little privacy from gawkers going by in cars. They'd confess that the house needs work and that from a security point of view they are sitting ducks. Canadians have not given up hope of extracting Earnscliffe from the British, but if it ever happens the price will be dizzying.

Right across Sussex Drive from Earnscliffe is the Lester Pearson Building, a great grey monstrosity that has housed the Department of External Affairs since 1974. When it was put up in the 1960s, critics used to say it was built here so the foreign service officers could walk to work from their homes in Rockcliffe and New Edinburgh. Some of the city's most exclusive functions take place in External's sixth-floor private dining rooms, where old-fashioned protocol reigns supreme: the menu cards and place cards are richly embossed in gold, and the silver, crystal, china, napery, flowers and food are equalled only at the tables at Rideau Hall, the Speaker's dining room and 24 Sussex Drive.

Across Sussex from External Affairs is the original National Research Council building, but most of the NRC now works out of a vast modern complex in the city's east end. Farther along you'll come upon Ottawa City Hall, a miserable office building plunked on Green Island, one of the city's most charming sites. On Saturdays, from 10 a.m. until sunset, the neighbourhood endures a steady cacophony of honking as one wedding party after another drives around the back of City Hall for its picture-taking session.

Just before you get to 24 Sussex, on the left you'll see a Stalinist building that looks as if it might house a generating plant; this is the Art Deco residence of the French ambassador. Like 24 Sussex, it sits on the edge of the cliff overlooking the Ottawa River, but from the outside it has none of the other house's charm. Inside it is a different story; the rooms are large, filled with light and lavishly decorated. The dining room is especially notorious. In the 1930s, a French artist painted frescos of cavorting youths and maidens on its walls. The work was later painted over by prudes and only uncovered in the early 1980s by art experts, who had to pick off the coverup flake by flake. Underneath were the fresh young faces and supple young bodies of some of Ottawa's best families in the

1930s. Apparently, the young people had been quite happy to pose for the artist, although those who are alive today are not keen to have their identities known. Even some well-known mandarins of the time are to be found dotted here and there among the portraits.

Just past the French Embassy is the prime minister's residence, which you can recognize by the curious tourists trying to peer in through the wrought-iron fence and the thick bushes. The governor general's residence, Government House, or Rideau Hall, is just across the street. It used to be possible to drive visitors through the front gates of the governor general's property and up to the front of Rideau Hall and then around the side and out a back driveway. It used to be possible to skate on the Rideau Hall rink or slide your toboggan down the specially constructed toboggan run. It used to be possible to take toddlers over to the grounds and lie on the grass and watch the clouds change shape overhead. All that changed in 1985 when Government House closed its gates to the public. Only by signing up for a guided tour can you enter the grounds now, and only in strictly regulated groups. Ottawans are already campaigning to have Jeanne Sauvé's successor reopen the grounds.

Almost no one knows that the government also has an official guest house for VIPs, a place named after its address, 7 Rideau Gate, which is across the street from 24 Sussex and tucked demurely between Hamilton Southam's beautiful red-brick house and the imposing South African Embassy. An elegant, almost severe stone house with a classic little circular drive and the usual Rockcliffe-style canvas awning over the front door, 7 Rideau Gate looks correct and dull and prosperous. Some of Ottawa's most marvellous scandals, however, are tucked behind its prim front door. There was the African visitor who brought a prostitute home one night and took her up to his room, only to be interrupted and severely reprimanded by Andrée Brown, the official hostess. As the woman crept away, Mrs. Brown told the distinguished visitor that his room was intended for one person, not two.

Following the grand tradition of the other official

residences, 7 Rideau Gate is undergoing an extensive eighteen-month renovation and redecoration, its first since the government bought it from the Ahearn family in 1966. That was when the government was starting to worry about all the foreign VIPs arriving the next year for Expo 67 in Montreal. Many planned to make courtesy calls in Ottawa and there was a shortage of places to put them. Government House is only for heads of state, people like kings and queens and vice-regal representatives; elected heads of government, lesser mortals like presidents, premiers and prime ministers as well as cabinet ministers were usually put into hotels. For Expo, the government wanted to do things in style.

The house, which has five bedrooms, each with its own bathroom and two with small salons as well, can sleep up to nine people at a time and hosts about twenty-five foreign visitors a year. (In contrast, Blair House, the Americans' official guest house in Washington across the street from the White House, has 114 rooms.) Seven Rideau Gate was used in February 1988 as President George Bush's headquarters during the brief visit he made to Ottawa. The rest of the year the house is used for meetings, conferences, breakfasts, lunches, teas, cocktail parties and receptions. It can cope with up to fourteen people for dinner, thirty for a buffet and fifty for cocktails. About three dinners a week are held here.

One time, a French visitor arrived and asked to be wakened for breakfast at 6:30 a.m. with his favourite meal: veal stew served with boiled potatoes and carrots. The official hostess, who normally lives off the premises but who sleeps in a small suite at the back of the house when foreign visitors are in residence, had to set her alarm for 3:30 to get up to start the meal; the chef arrived at 4:00.

Full of antiques, Aynsley china (four sets, one for each meal and one tea service), silver, crystal and traditional furniture, this lovely old house feels like home to most visitors. "Everyone loves it," says Sheila Watson, the official hostess from 1986 to 1989. "Margaret Thatcher was a fantastic guest; she took the time to ask about the wallpaper and the paintings and she wanted to know the history of the house." One guest in particular stands out in Watson's memory: Israel's prime minister, Shimon Peres. "He is an amazingly normal person, with a heart as big as a barn door," she remembers. "He had a TV interview as soon as he got here, so he walked in, had his makeup put on, talked to Barbara Frum and then as soon as it was over, took his shoes and tie off. I poured him a cognac and he padded around the house quite happily."

Although the National Capital Commission owns the house, its use is determined by the protocol department at External Affairs, and insiders say they do not like to broadcast its availability in case the riffraff try to get in. While the rules say it can be used by the prime minister, cabinet ministers, MPs, deputy ministers, associate deputy ministers, assistant deputy ministers, directors general, Supreme Court judges and federal court judges, very few of them know this.

The only people who use it regularly are the prime minister, a few of his senior officials and a few members of the judiciary. NDP Leader Ed Broadbent's office had no idea he could use it, nor did any other NDP MPs. Liberal Leader John Turner's principal secretary, Peter Connolly, said he knew Mr. Turner could use it but didn't; he preferred to entertain and to hold meetings and interviews at Stornoway. Mr. Mulroney, the first prime minister to use it frequently, holds confidential meetings there as well as his year-end television interviews. According to an NCC official, Mr. Mulroney regards 24 Sussex as his family home and likes to keep it as private as possible.

Farther along Sussex Drive, in a park bordering the Ottawa River, you will come to the Lookout, where you should park and gaze at the spectacular view. Here the Gatineau River curves down from the Gatineau Hills, bringing hundreds of yards of logs at a time in loose booms that slide into the Ottawa River. You can see something of the spray of the Rideau Falls blowing up as the Rideau River empties into the Ottawa.

If you turn around at the Lookout and retrace your steps along Sussex back to Parliament Hill, you will be diverted along Mackenzie Street, now infamous as the place men like to go to pick up young boys. As soon as dusk falls the boys, thin and shivering in the cold, come out to lean against the parking meters or huddle in the east door of the Château Laurier, waiting for the men who drive along slowly until they see something they like. Every few months, the local papers report a stabbing or a mugging or a murder that happened after a man picked up a boy on Mackenzie.

The best thing to see in Sandy Hill, the historic area just across Rideau Street from Lower Town and the Byward Market, is Laurier House, the former home of Sir Wilfrid and Lady Laurier and then of Mackenzie King, and today the most personal, fascinating and least-visited museum in the city. Laurier House is a large yellow-brick house on the corner of Chapel and Laurier bought by Sir Wilfrid in 1897, the year after he became prime minister. Sir Wilfrid and Lady Laurier lived there in a grand Edwardian style until he died in 1919; Lady Laurier stayed on until she died in 1921. She left the house to Mackenzie King, who was elected prime minister in 1921. He did not move in until 1923, but he stayed there until his own death in 1950, using for himself the same bedroom in which Laurier died. King left the house to the nation, to be turned into a museum. Today the museum is a Liberal shrine, devoted to the memories of three past prime ministers, Laurier, King and Lester Pearson, but the personality pervading the house is undoubtedly that of King.

The first floor contains King memorabilia, and the large exhibition room to the left of the front door as you enter is lined with cabinets of his mementoes. The most poignant is the gold cigarette box King bought in London in 1937 when he attended the coronation of King George VI. Engraved on the lid are the words "A gift to myself . . ." to commemorate the hundred years between Queen Victoria's coronation in 1837 and that of King George. Upstairs on the second floor are two Laurier rooms, one showing off a small glass case holding a "receipt" for a knitting pattern for a child's sweater and the four gold knitting needles Sir Wilfrid gave his wife on their fiftieth wedding anniversary. Not a very romantic man, Sir

Wilfrid, unless you count the time he spent with Emilie Lavergne, reputed to be his mistress.

If you are lucky you may get the exuberant French-Canadian guard who loves to steer visitors around the house and make sure they don't miss a thing. Peterborough, Ontario, judge Wendy Robson's favourite memory of Laurier House is having this guard usher her into the second-floor drawing room and say in his heavy accent, "And dis is de room where dey used to come and, you know, shoot de shit."

Although he never lived here, Laurier House also contains Lester Pearson's "rumpus room," installed after the former prime minister's death in 1972. The mind boggles to think of the work involved in meticulously recreating a mid-fifties rumpus room in the old Laurier house. But here it is in all its plywood-panelled glory, a triumph of dreck. Pearson willed all his prime-ministerial memorabilia to the nation, including his Nobel prize, which reposes here amid the basement furniture.

The third floor, Mackenzie King's personal quarters, is the one everyone comes for. King was so pleased with them that he made every foreign visitor trudge upstairs for a viewing, including Shirley Temple, Winston Churchill and King George VI. This floor was once the maids' quarters and the rooms are far more modest than the lofty chambers below, but they are cosy and comfortable, rather like a child's nursery. There's his little breakfast room with the sprigged china and the morning paper laid out beside his cereal and coffee cup. There's his bathroom, all the towels neatly in place, where he anxiously weighed himself. King's favourite room was the book-lined living room, a deep snuggery of a place with his mother's portrait reigning in one corner, right beside the crystal ball he used for his seances. There are pictures of his dog, Pat, and even little sculptures of him, as well as a small box in which he kept the collars of Pat's predecessors, Pat I and Pat II. Every spare inch of wall space is full of pictures of King with the mighty: King with his first patron, John D. Rockefeller; King with Churchill and Roosevelt and Stalin; King with King George VI and Queen Elizabeth; King with his Cabinet.

When you leave Sandy Hill, you should drive south along Colonel By Drive as it curves along beside the Rideau Canal. You'll pass the ugly monolith of the National Defence Headquarters, which straddles a road leading on to the Drive, and several of the main buildings of the University of Ottawa before you reach the odd new condominiums built on the old Morrison Lamothe Bakery site by William Teron, who had his heyday as a millionaire developer in Ottawa during the Trudeau years. These condominiums, among the most expensive in the city, were built from precast concrete units and look more like offices than houses. Teron has had nothing but grief from them; the latest chapter, which unfolded in 1988, was that dozens of tradesmen were suing him for nonpayment of bills relating to their work here.

You'll pass Bower Street, where Jean and Aline Chrétien live in an interesting contemporary house filled with Inuit art and sculpture, collected from his days as minister of Indian affairs and northern development, and wind under the old Grey Nuns convent, where the nuns used to toll the bell to let the neighbourhood know when they had run out of food.

The Rideau Canal is one of Ottawa's most famous attractions. The houses are large and impressive and the gardens that line the banks are beautifully maintained by the National Capital Commission, especially in the spring when they are the pride of the Tulip Festival. All year long joggers pound along the sidewalk and all winter long skaters, from toddlers to old folks, glide up and down the frozen canal, stopping to warm themselves at NCC shacks or to buy a hot sugared chunk of fried dough called a Beaver Tail from vendors along the route. But beware: nowhere will you find as mean a wind as the one that screams down the canal on a sunny winter Sunday afternoon; go at night and you risk frostbite. The ice is boobytrapped with yawning cracks and crevices, and malevolent snowplows race up and down the ice, scattering skaters in their wakes.

The roads along the canal take you south to Dow's Lake and Carling Avenue, and if you follow Carling west to Island Park Drive and then turn north, you'll eventually cross the Ottawa

River to Quebec. This road joins the Aylmer Road, where two great local institutions are just a few hundred yards away from one another. To the west and on the south side of the road is The Country Club, a pretty, private family club with a pool and a dining room overlooking the river. To the east, on the north side of the Aylmer Road, is the Royal Ottawa Golf Club, the more exclusive of the two. The Aylmer Road, like Island Park Drive, has seen better days when only great houses graced its banks; now subdivisions crowd the lush acres of the Italian ambassador's residence and the few remaining old estates. At night, as they have for generations, drunken teenagers gun their cars up and down this highway.

Driving east, the closer you get to Hull the tackier everything gets. Brash poutine stands and weatherbeaten Dairy Queens vie for space with service stations. It's much more interesting to take the Gatineau Hills Parkway north before you get into Hull, and drive up through this wonderful park, passing signs for Meech Lake and the ski hills of Camp Fortune. Snake over to Highway 105 along the Gatineau River until you get to the well-known Tulip Valley Motel, the scene of many an amorous assignation for the Ottawa press corps. Take the right-hand fork off the main highway here and continue north along the scenic country road that hugs the river bank, through little communities like Cascades, to Wakefield. Wakefield, full of white clapboard houses with deep gables, is like a village from an old Bing Crosby movie. Halfway through the picturesque village you should turn left up the hill to the old grist mill above the village; just beyond it, in a small, quiet cemetery, lie the graves of three old friends who wanted to be buried here, together, on this hill overlooking the Gatineau River. They are the "Ottawa Men," as historian Jack Granatstein called them, the great mandarins of the 1930s and 1940s – Lester Pearson, Norman Robertson and Hume Wrong.

2

· ·

Everything Happens at Parties

Sandra Gwyn once noted that an era in Ottawa ended on Saturday, May 26, 1979, when U.S. Ambassador Thomas Enders and his wife, Gaetana, married off their daughter Alice before four hundred high-powered guests in Ottawa's Notre Dame cathedral and brought everyone back to the embassy residence for a dinner-dance. It was just after the 1979 victory of Joe Clark's Conservatives, and the guests included a chastened Pierre Trudeau and many defeated Liberals as well as a few elated new Tory ministers like Flora MacDonald. The wedding was the last social hurrah of the Trudeau era. After the May 1979 defeat, many Liberals retired or disappeared into the business or academic communities, and the Enderses themselves, who had burrowed so deeply into the Ottawa world, moved on to a posting in Brussels. Even after they came back in 1980, the Liberals knew in their bones that they were slipping and sliding, that soon it would all be over.

But the real end of the era, or at least the end of another era, came – fittingly enough – with a party for Sandra Gwyn herself in December 1984. She had just published *The Private*

Capital, and to celebrate, her publishers and her husband, Richard, invited two hundred friends to the Royal Ottawa Golf Club. The party's theme was An Edwardian At-Home, and most of the guests, including *Saturday Night* editor Robert Fulford and publisher Jack McClelland, arrived in period costume. A horse-drawn sleigh, piled high with fur robes, met the guests in the parking lot and swept them up to the front door, where a group of suffragettes dressed in long, severe black skirts and prim white blouses, led by the Status of Women's director, Maureen O'Neil, were picketing for women's rights. Inside, the Palm Court Orchestra played as guests danced old-fashioned waltzes and gathered around a lavish buffet.

By that night in December, the Mulroney Tories had been in power since September 4, but precious few were there, though many had been invited. True or not, the word quickly went through the crowd that Tory ministers had been told by Mulroney's people to stay away from the party because it would be nothing but Liberals and their mandarin buddies. The only minister who came was John Crosbie with his wife, Jane; Sandra Gwyn, after all, was a fellow Newfoundlander, and for Newfoundlanders like the Crosbies blood is always thicker than politics.

The best party most people ever remembered had a sweet melancholy to it. The Gwyns, two of Ottawa's most popular and talented writers, were moving to London, England, after twenty-five years in the city, and many of the Liberals were also scattering again, several of them for good. There was some black humour among the bureaucrats who rightly suspected they were on the Tory hit list.

Since then the private capital has shut down and the only large and lavish parties these days are state ceremonials or public functions or charity pay-as-you-go events or lobbyists' Christmas free-for-alls. The opening of the new National Gallery. A fundraising gala for the Children's Hospital of Eastern Ontario. The Press Gallery Dinner. The Prime Minister's Christmas party for the Tory caucus in the Hall of Honour in the House of Commons. Government Consultants International's Christmas Screech-in. Charity galas are being cancelled because people are weary of them, and three local professional theatre companies that depended on such events have quietly folded. Even embassies, the last bastion for freeloaders, are pulling back frugally. One startling exception was provided recently by the Dutch ambassador's wife, who invited guests to a black-tie affair and asked them to bring their dogs. The dogs received party favours.

Ottawa used to be more fun. Now it is dreary and extremely careful. No one has parties like Allan and Sondra Gotlieb threw in the 1960s and 1970s, before they moved to Washington, or like Bernard and Sylvia Ostry gave in their Aylmer Road home before they too moved on to grander jobs and busier lives. Then there were the Gwyns' parties, always held in their cosy Cole Avenue house, jammed with antiques, cats, Christopher and Mary Pratt's pictures, good food and intriguing guests.

Why does the city feel sour today? Partly because the Mulroneys and the Sauvés, the two couples everyone expected would add glitter and glamour, have not cooperated. Tory MPs have been told by Mulroney to stick close to their ridings, and the political and the bureaucratic spheres are still circling each other warily after five years of Tory rule. "Mulroney does not want his people to mix with us," explained the wife of a powerful and socially prominent Ottawa businessman, a powerhouse in her own right. "He controls them and we believe he has told them not to mingle with the locals." Other social leaders quietly confirm her statement. One of the few PC commuters who has thrown herself into Ottawa life is the ebullient and clever senator from Winnipeg, Mira Spivak; another is Nova Scotia senator Finlay MacDonald.

To be fair, it is always difficult for a prime minister to mingle socially with the locals, no matter how exalted their rank. Pierre Trudeau rarely mixed with Ottawa society, and even Joe Clark hurt his old friends' feelings by leaving them out of festivities at 24 Sussex Drive after he became prime minister. In the last four years, however, the Mulroneys seem to have gone out of their way to avoid Ottawa society. Mila Mulroney has made it clear that she prefers Montreal and her friends there. Even when they throw large pay-to-enter parties at 24 Sussex Drive, as they did at the 1987 $5,000-a-person cocktail party and hockey game to raise money for Mila Mulroney's charity, cystic fibrosis, guests are usually directed into large tents erected on the grounds, not into the house.

People resent being treated this way, as Liberal Leader John Turner found to his cost in 1986, when he hosted a series of summer garden parties at Stornoway. Loyal Liberals who had flown in at their own expense from all over Canada were justifiably peeved at being herded into tents and discouraged from entering the house even to use the bathrooms.

The Mulroneys rarely do much private entertaining – not surprising when one considers the kind of schedules a prime minister has – but when they do, it is usually a discreet little cocktail reception. Ottawans are rarely invited; the guests are almost always the old cronies from St. Francis Xavier and Laval university days or from Montreal's business community.

Every year Mila Mulroney throws her husband a birthday party. Most of the guests come up from Montreal; a few come from Toronto. Three years ago, buddy Brian Gallery arrived for the birthday boy's party with his wife and a group of pals from Montreal, including Tory lawyer Richard Holden, in the Canadian National Railways chairman's private railcar, hitched on to the back of a regular VIA train. Gallery, who runs a shipping magazine and is president of one of the Tory's fundraising 500 Clubs in Montreal, had been appointed acting chairman of CN and was enjoying the perks of the job. Maurice LeClair, CN's former chairman, used the car only for business trips.

If you want to know who really counts with Brian and Mila Mulroney, you'll find them on the A list culled from Brian's fiftieth birthday party in March 1989:

Mulroney's closest friend, Toronto lawyer Sam Wakim,

with his wife, Marty. Lobbyist Fred Doucet with his wife, Helena. (They were married in the living room at 24 Sussex Drive.) Lobbyist Frank Moores and his wife, Beth. Lobbyist Gary Ouellet. Lobbyist Bill Fox and his wife, Bonnie Brownlee, who is Mila Mulroney's executive assistant and constant companion. Senator Michel Cogger. Senator Guy Charbonneau, Speaker of the Senate and Tory "patron" of Quebec. Senator Jean Bazin. Principal Secretary Stanley Hartt. Deputy Prime Minister Don Mazankowski. Environment Minister Lucien Bouchard. Canadian ambassador to the U.S. Derek Burney and his wife, Joan. Fern Roberge, the manager of the Ritz Carlton Hotel in Montreal, Mila Mulroney's home-away-from-home on her frequent shopping trips to Montreal.

Another guest was Ottawa alderman and former aide to Robert Coates, Mike McSweeney, sometimes known as the capital's Jerry Zipkin. Zipkin is the gnomic figure who escorted Nancy Reagan around when the former U.S. president was not available. McSweeney takes the Mulroney children to movies and other places. He took them to the 1988 performance of "Aladdin," for example, and escorted them and Mila Mulroney to the grandstand during Ottawa's summer Exhibition. His devotion to the Mulroneys has earned him plenty of ink in Margo Roston's *Citizen* columns, a little too much even for his taste; on one occasion the usually cheerful McSweeney complained that he was tired of being made fun of. But McSweeney will have earned his footnote in history: besides being the first family's favourite extra man, he was their driver and aide on the 1983 "rusty station wagon campaign." This was the down-home tour undertaken when Mulroney was seeking the Tory leadership, the campaign in which he ditched some of his 1976 glitz-and-champagne style for beer and basement rumpus rooms. (Although he continued to use private planes and helicopters in 1983 his handlers carefully hid them.)

Like the Mulroneys, the Sauvés have disappointed social

Ottawa. Most of their entertaining has been the formal protocol-ridden receptions and dinners that accompany different awards ceremonies. Last year the annual press skating party was cancelled, the excuse being that the winter was too mild for good ice. It's got to the point where Ottawans actually talk nostalgically about "the good old days" when the Schreyers were at Rideau Hall throwing one whoop-de-doo after another, with rock-and-roll bands and platters of perogies. In those days, stuffy social climbers snickered behind their hankies at the folksy Schreyer style, but they resent Jeanne Sauvé's airs and graces even more. Perhaps they mistake her natural dignity for snobbishness or perhaps part of the resentment comes from the way she replaced almost all the Anglo staff at Rideau Hall with Francophones. But the majority of Ottawans dislike her for one reason alone: in 1986 she closed Rideau Hall's grounds to the public.

Sauvé has been a hard-working, graceful and dignified governor general. She was the Speaker of the House of Commons who cleaned up an unimaginable mess of corrupt practices there, and she has been a successful member of Parliament and minister of communications. Sadly, those very real accomplishments, in the minds of Ottawans, pale beside the act of closing the gates. For Ottawa, the eighty-eight acres here were a public garden. No one abused the privilege, so the only times they were closed was when the Queen was in residence or an American president was staying there. Yes, once in a while a stranger would take liberties and enter the house when a guard wasn't watching properly; once a stranger was found wandering in the Sauvés' private quarters. The same thing happened to the Queen in her private bedroom at Buckingham Palace. Yes, security should be stepped up. But at Rideau Hall, the governor general has always enjoyed several acres of a large private garden that surrounds two sides of the house, a garden equipped with tennis courts and shrubberies and a rose garden. At the back there are also two beautiful greenhouses, which offer bloom and warmth even in winter.

Who ordered the gates shut and the public turned away? The National Capital Commission or Government House? Whose people whisper that it was Madame Sauvé who played the principal role? Whose loyal staff point the finger at the NCC's Jean Pigott and the RCMP? Whoever it was, they made a right mess of the whole thing and it became a public relations disaster.

Although the city has written off the Mulroneys and the Sauvés as duds, a shy, roly-poly figure usually dressed in black robes and a weird hat or in thick wool knee socks, a kilt and a velvet jacket has made up for their inadequacies. House of Commons Speaker John Fraser has become Ottawa's hottest official host while his press secretary, Jim Watson, is in the running for the hottest unofficial host. These two guys just love parties.

Fraser's entertaining, done with great attention to detail and protocol (he has a rule that his office will not have functions without members of all parties present), is eclectic to say the least. He permits the Canadian Football League to host a Grey Cup party on the Hill each year, but they pay the bill themselves. Fraser also hosts an annual Robbie Burns dinner, at which he gets to wear his beloved kilt. He has invited the Press Gallery executive to his farm at Kingsmere once a year for dinner.

When John and Cate Fraser entertain in the country they do it informally, employing a neighbour as cook, but when they host a formal dinner at the House, it is a full fig affair. The china, gold-tasselled menus and place cards all bear the coat of arms of the Speaker, and footmen and maids proceed with extraordinary formality. The parliamentary chef is cautioned to prepare elegant but simple meals; extravagance does not sit well with Fraser.

Occasionally the official dinners turn surprisingly madcap. On September 17, 1987, Fraser held a dinner for the British actor Peter Ustinov and the members of the board of a fundraising drive at Carleton University. After the meal Fraser took the party into the House Chamber, where he climbed into his chair and showed how its hydraulic lift could move him up and down. As he did this, Ustinov dropped to his knees and bobbed up and down, keeping time with an African chant.

Jim Watson's parties are more risqué. Watson was a young Carleton University graduate looking for work in 1984 when he talked Speaker John Bosley into hiring him. After Bosley left the job, Watson moved to Otto Jelinek's office as press secretary. In 1987 Fraser coaxed him back into the Speaker's office again because Watson was well-liked, independent-minded and respected by everyone on the Hill. Many of the most successful parties thrown by Fraser are credited to the lively imagination of Jim Watson – who is too smart to admit this is true. People are still talking about a party he threw for 175 people in December 1988 with a friend, Graham Covington. It was just after the federal election, and Watson's saucy theme was "Trust Us" – guests wore pins decorated with caricatures of the three federal leaders. Not only did John and Cate Fraser show up, so did the president of Carleton University, William Beckel, several Cabinet ministers, Opposition MPs and senior journalists. Watson is worried that his social success might give some people the wrong idea. "I don't want to be known as the lounge-lizard of Ottawa, someone who is always out, or who will go to anything, anywhere," he frets.

Watson, the professional party-watcher, offers a surprising candidate for the social butterfly of the Cabinet. "Next to the PM, the minister of fitness and amateur sport gets the most invitations to the semi-pro events, celebrity tournaments and so on. Next would come the minister of multiculturalism." At one time Otto Jelinek, now revenue minister, held both portfolios; one presumes he was on the hop all day and all night. "He loves celebrity events," admitted Watson, "so he would go to a lot."

Like any small town, Ottawa does have an Old Guard, the

"FOOFs" – Fine Old Ontario Families – a small group of people who have been here forever and who pretend to ignore the comings and goings of various administrations. Years ago the young wives of new MPs called the FOOFs "cliff dwellers." Many were descended from the early lumber barons like Ezra Butler Eddy and Philomen Wright, the founder of Hull, who made their millions on the logs that splashed down the Ottawa and Gatineau rivers to Montreal. These families, which also included the Curriers, Edwards, McKays and Keefers to name just a few, built enormous houses in Sandy Hill, in Centre Town near the Parliament Buildings and along Sussex Drive in what was then countryside.

Lumber king Joseph Currier built 24 Sussex Drive for his third wife, Hannah Wright, Philomen Wright's daughter. Currier began the construction in 1866 and finished it two years later, christening it Gorffwysfa – Welsh for "place of peace." Five hundred people, including Sir John and Lady Macdonald, came to the housewarming. In 1902 Mr. Currier's son sold the property to another lumber baron and politician, William Cameron Edwards, for $30,000; the Edwardses lived peacefully in the house until 1943.

That was when the government decided it might be desirable to expropriate the house even though no one was quite sure how they would use it. The Edwards family fought valiantly against the expropriation for three years, maintaining that they did not have the intention of commercializing the property as the government accused them. In 1946 the government won, but still had no idea what to do with the house, and by 1947 it was abandoned. Only after it had been leased to the Australian government for a few years did the government decide to gut it and rebuild the interior as an official residence for our prime ministers. The prime minister of the day, Louis St. Laurent, wanted nothing to do with the place. All he asked was to go on living in the old Roxborough Hotel on Elgin Street, which was demolished in 1966, and only agreed to move into 24 Sussex Drive on the understanding that he would pay rent as he had at the Roxborough. The prime minister paid rent until 1971, when the government decided to give him, and the Opposition leader, a free roof over their heads.

If they hang in there long enough, Ottawa's new families settle into the old Establishment, but it may take several generations. One family widely regarded as "old Ottawa" is the Perley-Robertson family, but their pedigree shows that they came long after families like the Scotts, Clemows, Cassells, Sparkses, Slaters, Sherwoods and Southams. The Perley-Robertsons arrived only in 1904, when Sir George Perley was elected member of Parliament for the riding of Argenteuil in Quebec. His daughter, Ethel Perley-Robertson, bought a house on Acacia Avenue in Rockcliffe in 1923 and called it Stornoway after the Perleys' ancestral home in Scotland. At that time the owners, Ascanio Joseph Major and his wife, Corinne, who had bought the land from Charles Keefer and built the house in 1913, found it too far from downtown Ottawa.

In 1942 the Perley-Robertsons loaned the house, furnished, to Princess Juliana of the Netherlands and to her husband and two daughters because the Dutch royal family had come to Canada in 1940 after the invasion of the Netherlands by the Germans. When the Perley-Robertsons took Stornoway back after the war, they found the house too big and sold it to the Royal Trust Company, which was holding funds from both Liberals and Conservatives to buy a home for the leader of the Opposition. In 1970, because it was too expensive for the trust to keep up, the government purchased the property for one dollar. Despite the millions of dollars poured into Stornoway since it was acquired by the government, its inhabitants and the Official Residences Council, which keeps an eye on it, keep saying it is almost unfit for human habitation.

One prominent local family had humble beginnings in the bakery business. Cecil Morrison, who died in 1979, was an Ottawa baker who built up a prosperous business, Morrison

Lamothe. Mr. Morrison brought up his three daughters, Jean, Grete and Gay, in the business and today the three still control the family company. The eldest daughter, Jean Pigott, a Tory MP for the former riding of Ottawa-Carleton from 1976 to 1979, is now the chairman of the National Capital Commission, making her the country's most important landlady. She is responsible for the thousands of acres of government-owned land in the National Capital Region as well as for all the buildings and grounds of the official residences.

The next sister, Grete Hale, runs Morrison Lamothe and is grooming two Pigott sons to run it when she retires. She and her husband, Reg, an amateur historian and dedicated war games fanatic with an impressive collection of kilts and military costumes, still live in the family house. The third sister, Gay Cook, runs a cooking school in the kitchen at Bayne House.

For many years the old Morrison house was the informal headquarters of the Moral Rearmament Movement in Canada. MRA, as it was known, was a powerful international movement with its heyday between the 1930s and the 1960s, when its leaders dreamed of a new world order of peace and prosperity. Considered elitist and right-wing, it has now faded from sight. More formal headquarters were maintained in a large stone house on Fairview Road in Rockcliffe Park, where officials held men-only black-tie dinner parties, to recruit candidates to the movement. Morrison had met MRA's founder, Frank Buchman, at a meeting at the Château Laurier during the Depression. Times were hard, Morrison was almost bankrupt and Buchman's message of renewing the moral fibre of nations seemed like the answer. MRA was interested in the influential, the leaders and the politicians and the opinion-makers in the community, and it recruited its converts through high-level social connections.

Morrison's daughters all worked for the family business as young girls and threw themselves into MRA work as well. Their father's cause became their cause. Grete and Reg Hale were based with the movement's world headquarters in

Switzerland for twenty years while Hale edited its international newspaper; Jean worked for an MRA soup kitchen in Los Angeles for seven years; Gay and her husband, Bob Cook, were with Up With People, its entertainment wing in Arizona, for about ten years.

When Mr. Morrison wanted to hand over the company to his children in 1967, Jean came back to Canada. She was the president until she was elected an MP in 1976. Grete has been in charge of the family food business ever since. After Jean was defeated by Jean-Luc Pepin in the 1978 election, she went to work for Prime Minister Joe Clark as his patronage chief, reorganizing and computerizing the appointments process. Because Clark was slow in rewarding the party faithful who had waited so many years for their time in the sun, and was defeated before a substantial number were happily lodged in their Senate seats and boards and directorships, many Tories unfairly blamed Jean. They knew that on December 13, 1979, the day the government fell, there were 186 names waiting on her desk to be appointed. They didn't know it was Clark who refused to let the appointments go through.

Jean went back to Morrison Lamothe for a few years as chairman of the board and worked on other projects until it was time for the 1983 Conservative leadership. This time, fed up with Clark, she campaigned for John Crosbie. After Mulroney won the election, he put her in charge of the National Capital Commission, where she's been ever since, trying to make her dream of Ottawa as a world-class capital city a reality.

Bayne House has offered hospitality to many friends. When Pat Carney was first elected as a Tory MP from Vancouver, she lived with the Hales for months until she found a townhouse of her own. When Carol Goar was appointed the Toronto *Star*'s national columnist, Grete invited the city's leading women to a party to celebrate. Grete, in particular, has been close to many Tory leaders' wives, especially Olive Diefenbaker and Maureen McTeer. Back in the late 1970s, when McTeer was coping with official entertainment at Stornoway as the wife of newly elected party leader Joe Clark, it was Grete Hale and Jean Pigott who quietly organized, as volunteers, all the catering through their Morrison Lamothe facilities.

One of the sisters' most memorable stories, one they tell themselves with laughter and tears, is about a birthday party they held for Maureen McTeer in February 1979. Mr. Morrison, a bed-ridden invalid whose wife had died many years before, was living with the Hales. Just before the guests arrived for Maureen's birthday lunch, Grete discovered that her beloved father had quietly died.

It was too late to call people to cancel the lunch; the cars were already starting to turn up the drive. The sisters looked at each other and decided to do what their father would have wanted: carry on. They shut their father's door, squared their shoulders and marched downstairs to greet their guests. The party progressed, everyone laughed and sang "Happy Birthday." "And how's your dear father?" the women asked the sisters. "As well as can be expected," they replied. Only when the last guest had left, in the late afternoon, did they let themselves fall apart.

The biggest trick to understanding Ottawa's social life, indeed to understanding Ottawa itself, is knowing how people connect. Take just a small part of a small neighbourhood as a microcosm of the city. Drop into MacTavish and Robinson on Beechwood, Rockcliffe's shopping street, where you'll usually find Malcolm MacTavish and Mowat Robinson weighing out fresh pasta for assistant deputy ministers living in nearby New Edinburgh or for the chefs of Rockcliffe diplomats. MacTavish and Mowat, playing store so successfully, both grew up in Rockcliffe, are related through marriage and, on the social scale, outrank most of their customers.

MacTavish, an Ottawa Southam, is a cousin of aristocratic millionaire Hamilton Southam. Southam, a former diplomat who was the first director general of the National Arts Centre, now chairs the Official Residences Council, the genteel but toothless body set up by Prime Minister Brian Mulroney in 1986 to suggest unenforceable guidelines for decorating the leaders' houses.

To carry on with the Southam family, because it illustrates nicely the theory that everything connects, Robert Southam was once the publisher of the *Citizen*; he and his wife, Annie, live in Rockcliffe Park, just a few blocks away from Hamilton. Another Southam, Sheila MacTavish Cudney Eberts, Malcolm's sister and a talented designer who occasionally accepts commissions to decorate people's houses, married Bob Eberts, a successful young real estate agent. Bob's former wife, Ann Eberts, traded a career as a kitchen designer for the high and mighty for one with an Ottawa business newspaper, but it was when she was doing the city's best kitchens that she befriended the dashing Tory senator Finlay MacDonald, who had a new house and kitchen to fret about. Through MacDonald, she met his friends, Dalton and Wendy Camp, who had also bought a new house in the expensive complex just behind Government House, and Ann's advice on their kitchen was welcome.

Wendy Camp, who likes Ottawa much better than her husband does (he moved back to New Brunswick in June 1989), is now selling real estate, throwing herself into cultural volunteering and making plenty of friends. She is a candidate to succeed Diana Kirkwood some day as the city's most fashionable real estate agent. One of Ann Eberts' closest friends is Margaret Sinclair Trudeau Kemper; Ann was Margaret's witness at her wedding to Fried Kemper.

Most of these people live within a few blocks of each other in New Edinburgh. They do not fit into one circle; each is a member of many circles, but in Ottawa all circles overlap.

Knowing who all the old Ottawa families are and how people connect is only part of the job of conquering Ottawa. A newcomer also has to learn the city's unwritten rules. The surest way to fall flat on your face in Ottawa is to call the local paper when your child invites a prime minister's offspring to a birthday party. Someone did this once with a Trudeau child, and while Pierre Trudeau probably never knew or cared, other parents were outraged. In fact, using your children to advance your career is not smart. During the Trudeau years, when his children attended Rockcliffe Park Public School, there were always about seven hundred people squashed into the gym for the Christmas concert, despite the fact that the school only had something like three hundred kids. You had to come half an hour ahead to get a seat. But if anyone had taken advantage of such close access to the prime minister, there to watch his sons Justin, Sasha and Michel in what was surely the world's longest variety show – it even included a tribute to the school janitor – that parent would have been in Siberia socially forever.

After the Trudeaus separated, Margaret sat with a group of her women friends during the concerts. Pierre would usually sit beside his close friend Michael Pitfield, then the Clerk of the Privy Council, who rarely took off his navy blue serge deputy minister's overcoat while he too waited for his children to perform. Other senior mandarins, also buttoned up in navy overcoats, would hover nearby. Parents steadfastly avoided eye contact with the prime minister. Usually he left after his children had performed, forgoing the tribute to the janitor and the coffee hour. A few serge overcoats always slipped out right after him, hoping to give the impression that they were off to a meeting at 24 Sussex Drive.

Another good way to fail in Ottawa is to drink too much, too loudly. Spreading a social disease, as one influential person did not long ago, is also not a good way to win friends. Telling racist and sexist jokes is ill-advised. One Conservative cabinet minister who did so went unmourned when he lost his job for other reasons.

More than most communities Ottawa has a large transient population. Many people move in for few years as politicians or to get experience in the government before going to a job in business. Canny lawyers, for example, like to work in the tax section of the Finance Department before they go off to head up the tax department of their law firm. Some, especially academics, come for just a year or two to work on a royal commission or a task force. Others come on the executive interchange program, in which business and government swap senior management for two years. The military and the diplomatic communities are programmed to move regularly. So the city is always turning over new people. Some love it; others spend all their time bewailing the lack of foreign movies and good restaurants and flee to Montreal as often as they can.

For those who have to size the place up quickly and make their mark quickly, a mentor is indispensable. He or she may have encouraged the newcomer to come to Ottawa and now tells everyone that he is the best thing to hit the department in a generation. The mentor is also a social door-opener. Ottawa is small enough that it takes only one or two people who are willing to throw the newcomer a party or issue an invitation to a special event. In the past, there were plenty of people, usually talented and successful women married to powerful men, who could launch newcomers into Ottawa. Three of the best were Diana Kirkwood, Sandra Gwyn, and Sondra Gotlieb. Today real estate agent Di Kirkwood is the only real hostess left, but she is occupied with building a country home with her husband, David, who is now retired. Sandra Gwyn and Sondra Gotlieb no longer live in Ottawa. Today there are only a few people who can lever the newcomer into Ottawa social life with the same deft touch. They include Joan Henderson, Starr Solomon and Finlay MacDonald.

Some people on the way up in Toronto hire publicists to get their names in the Toronto papers and magazines and spend fortunes on throwing tasteless parties. Ottawa looks down its nose at people who do that. *Any* publicity is the kiss of death for a rising bureaucrat. Getting your name in Margo Roston's social column in the Ottawa *Citizen* does not guarantee social success.

The only reason Roston can dredge up enough information

for her column each week is that she herself is Old Ottawa and is welcome everywhere. Her grandmother, Lillian Freiman, was a legendary figure who started the Red Cross in Ottawa and is a major character in *Willy*, Heather Robertson's novel about Mackenzie King. Roston's parents, Lawrence and Audrey Freiman, owned Freiman's, a small chain of department stores eventually bought by the Hudson's Bay Company. The Freimans were the ones who – until the appointment of Edward Schreyer – always arranged Palm Beach accommodation for the reigning governor general.

Schreyer shocked Old Ottawa by preferring the lowbrow pleasures of Fort Lauderdale to the ritzier enclaves of Palm Beach, and it was particularly hard on his private secretary, Esmond Butler, who had been accustomed to staying in Palm Beach with the Vaniers, the Micheners and the Légers. Schreyer told him he was not needed in attendance in Fort Lauderdale, so Butler regularly took himself off to Palm Beach until their Excellencies were ready to return to Ottawa.

Ottawa is, above all, a family town. People are big on skating parties, tobogganing, skiing. School Christmas concerts and school end-of-year closings are popular draws. Many people like to have family carolling parties in their neighbourhoods. But most of the Mulroney Tories – parliamentarians and policy advisors – are commuters. They enter every Monday morning through the gates of the Ottawa airport, they drive the locals crazy all week by throwing their weight around, and they depart every Friday morning to go back to their little towns across Canada. Their decision to commute was deliberate and there was some sense to it. When Mulroney took office in 1984, he believed the Liberals had become too close to the bureaucracy and too removed from the grassroots across the country. Mulroney did not want his new ministers to become part of the Ottawa Establishment, and he has certainly succeeded in achieving that goal. But even in Liberal years, few senior bureaucrats mixed with cabinet ministers.

If someone comes to Ottawa as a new deputy minister, new

head of the Canada Council or the Economic Council of Canada, new bureau chief of the Toronto *Star* or *Globe and Mail*, new senior correspondent for the CBC, or as a promising new star for one of the political parties, welcome is assured. The invitations will be stacked deep on the mantel.

Ordinary MPs, contrary to their expectations, are not overwhelmed with invitations except by third-string embassies who cannot get larger fry to come. Newly elected in 1988, Jim Karygiannis, Liberal MP for Toronto's Scarborough-Agincourt, told a Toronto *Star* reporter that he would be leaving his family behind to take care of the family shoe store, and that he was a little apprehensive about the sophisticated world he was moving into. "I've heard a lot about the cocktail party circuit in Ottawa," he said darkly, adding that he would eschew its temptations by applying himself primly to the needs of his constituents.

The truth is that for backbench MPs like Mr. Karygiannis, the social pickings are slim. The diplomatic community is the only group with a cocktail party circuit, but you have to be pretty picky about the dips you hang out with. The parties you get invited to are often the ones you should stay away from. Political colleagues won't help. Other MPs are also living in horrible little bachelor flats in apartment-hotels or sharing apartments with colleagues to keep the costs down. Some MPs try to live in their offices, and a few get away with it for a while, but it is frowned on. If the Speaker finds out, the homeless MP is asked to move along, like an indigent bum.

Members who have settled in the city are not enthusiastic about acting as den mothers to lonesome parliamentarians looking for a little action. The only stable community in the city's political world are the bureaucrats, who are wary of MPs, for good reasons. Several bureaucrats who were known to be friendly with Liberals were fired or sidelined by the Tories.

In Ottawa people entertain at home, where the thermostat should be set at 72 degrees and the plastic removed from the lampshades. You need a few old Crown Derby dinner plates (cracks and chips quite acceptable), some antique Persian rugs scattered around – the more holes the better – and a good system of sorting out the toe rubbers.

A generous liquor cabinet is important. Variety is not necessary; in fact if anyone catches you sipping Baby Duck or crème de menthe, you're finished. People who can't cook, learn. Or they hire a caterer. Meals don't have to be pretentious, multi-tiered courses of rare duck breast, smoked salmon and enoki mushrooms, but they must be the best of their kind. Some hosts coast on a great chili recipe; one of the best chilis in Ottawa is to be found at Federal Court Judge Pat Mahoney's house, although Mary Mahoney, a talented local businesswoman, is a good cook at any level of cuisine. A reputation can be ruined by defrosted chicken, frozen vegetables and iceberg lettuce salads, served with whip'n'serve chocolate mousse and instant coffee. No one will come back.

On the whole, however, Ottawa is a tolerant town. Poverty, interesting marital situations (a plethora of ex-wives, perhaps), bisexuality, homosexuality and other sexual inclinations are perfectly acceptable unless they involve children or animals. One former Cabinet minister said to like nubile young girls is quietly avoided. The city breathed a sigh of relief when one MP, a pious individual who talked a good line of social justice, was defeated; he was a ruthless and notorious sexual harasser of hapless secretaries on the Hill. Instead of being drummed out of the boys' club in shame by his colleagues or the Speaker, he was tolerated in the House with good-natured shrugs for many years.

Talented eccentrics, people like National Gallery curator Charles Hill, who sported thick, glossy shoulder-length braids for years, can thrive in Ottawa, but the collective lip will curl over nasty table manners, dirty fingernails and rudeness to waiters and to Air Canada attendants. Although Ottawa is Gossip Central for the rest of Canada, betrayals – real indiscretions – are never forgiven.

Old-fashioned courtesies are essential; without them the

tough political realities of the city would make social life impossible. No matter how unpleasant the meeting may have been in the Privy Council Office in the morning, the unwritten rule is that the gloves go back on in private life. The players, no matter how much they hate each other, will meet in the aisles of the IGA or around the table of a small dinner party or at an Arts Centre concert and be unfailingly polite.

Ottawa is a big town for thank-you notes written on creamy plain paper. It wouldn't do to use cards with flowery messages or cutie-pie notes with happy faces or Garfield cartoons. Ottawans also support the principle of bringing a decent wine or some flowers when they are invited for dinner. Hilary Haggan, arguably the best cook in town, will bring you some homemade jam or chili sauce. Lucky you.

Women here dress down, not up. This is not a town that tolerates synthetic fibres, but eyebrows will rise slightly if you pull on skin-tight black leather pants with a backless blouse for a cocktail party. Men might as well slink back to Toronto if they are seen at a black-tie function in a coloured dinner jacket or pastel shirt. Ottawa mandarins think they are being daring when they wear a wing collar with their dinner jacket. One rule for men is to buy a real bow tie and learn to tie it. Snap-ons and pre-tied are not acceptable; they don't have that little giveaway angle of the real thing. Brown suits are worrisome and generally avoided. Ditto brown shoes, except on weekends with twill pants and tweed jackets.

Corduroy suits were quite acceptable in the Trudeau years because Himself wore them. Today, the Mulroneyites lean to navy double-breasted numbers. When he isn't buying his suits at Holt Renfrew, Mulroney picks up suits at $2,500 a pop at Bijan, the exclusive Persian tailor who has by-appointment-only shops in Manhattan and on Rodeo Drive in Beverly Hills. Bijan is famous for the gold-plated guns he sells to select clients, and once in 1985 he told a *Globe* reporter he had sold twenty suits "to the new young prime minister of a friendly neighbouring country."

What about clubs? Do they matter? Sort of. The Rideau Club, after years of mouldering along, is now back in favour and has a waiting list because of its stunning quarters at the top of the Metropolitan Life building. The other club most people like to join is Le Cercle Universitaire in Sandy Hill. Some people like the Country Club in Aylmer for tennis and swimming; others patronize the Royal Ottawa or the Hunt Club.

The hardest club to get into is the famous mandarins' retreat, the Five Lakes Fishing Club in the Gatineau Hills. It was set up in the 1940s by a group of like-minded deputy ministers who could not afford their own cottages. They pooled their resources and bought a large rustic cottage on a private lake. For years the club was run by a small group of men; women, Jews and French-Canadians were not welcome. That all changed in the 1960s and now there are plenty of each category, but the executive is not above snubbing certain people. For example, Privy Council Clerks are almost automatically asked to join, but club members, jealous of Michael Pitfield's rapid rise, refused to extend an invitation to him. While most of the members are high-ranking bureaucrats, there are a few civilians, like heart specialist Bill Williams and his wife, Sheila, an artist.

Five Lakes is a pleasant place, but a little too cosy. Members hunker down in spartan rooms without much soundproofing between them. And forget the fishing. Every year the club assigns members to stock the lakes with baby trout; every year the loons eat them.

Started in 1985 by a few senior aides to Tory ministers, people like Art Lyon and David Crapper, the Gatineau Hills Gentleman's Club is a Red Tory stronghold. You won't find a whole lot of Mulroney cronies in it but you will find such Tories as Marjory LeBreton, the deputy chief of staff in the PMO, and publicist and former journalist Walter Grey. At the club's annual dinner (its only function each year) in a public school gymnasium in Old Chelsea, just north of Hull, the food is execrable, the speeches superb and invitations scarce as hens' teeth.

The toughest clubs to crack in Ottawa are undoubtedly SPERM and OVUM, black-tie dinner clubs established by Bill Taylor, an anthropologist and the former head of both the Museum of Man and the Social Sciences and Humanities Research Council, John Robertson, the former owner of the Robertson Galleries, and flügelhorn-playing criminologist Bill Outerbridge, the former head of the National Parole Board. Only the wittiest get asked to dine with members of SPERM, the Society for the Preservation of the Excellent Rye Manhattan; only the cleverest are invited to the gatherings of the Organization for the Very Unusual Martini.

PART TWO

TO THE VICTOR . . .

3

· ·

Fat Cat City

People who don't live in Ottawa regard the city with a sullen mixture of resentment and envy. They think of it as fat cat city, a company town where thousands of pinstriped politicians and bureaucrats stream out of their offices at 3:30 every day, go to an endless round of diplomatic cocktail parties and dream up ways to bedevil the rest of Canada with red tape and higher taxes. It's a favourite target for the business community, whose members cherish happy fantasies that if they were just let in there for a few months, they could roll up their shirtsleeves, put the place on a sound financial footing and make it run like IBM. But the truth is that while Ottawa is a small company town, it is also an extraordinarily complicated, multilayered, sophisticated place where beautiful manners matter more than money and where gossip is the local currency.

When critical outsiders move out of their corporate boardrooms and into the Ottawa bureaucracy, their bossy self-confidence starts to evaporate under the complex and multiple demands they never faced on Bay Street, where the only thing that counted was the bottom line. A chief executive officer has to report only to a chairman and a board of directors. A deputy minister is accountable to four bosses: his or her Cabinet minister, the prime minister, the Treasury Board and the Public Service Commission. Deputies must also comply with criteria set down by the Official Languages Commissioner, the Human Rights Commissioner and the auditor general.

And behind all that is a vigilant press and a watchful public. We all remember what happened in Ottawa in 1985 when the new Tory government put the bottom line before indexed pensions for old people. The result was Solange Denis, a fierce old woman who planted herself firmly in Brian Mulroney's path on national television and won everyone's heart. "You lied to us!" she shrilled, to the cheers of a nation. "You made us vote for you, then it's 'Goodbye Charlie Brown.'" A mortified Mulroney told his finance minister, Michael Wilson, to back down on de-indexing the pensions. It is the Solange Denises of the world who can so suddenly confound the best experts in government and make the city so complicated.

In the effort to blend each politician's desire for re-election with each community's needs and then to try to make both fit into government policy, the bottom line usually winds up being the only flexible part of the issue. You can imagine the Toronto banker or the Montreal tax lawyer who has sagely advised the government on loopholes and tax credits watching an old woman on the television news blow it all away. Perhaps then they understand the words "public service" for the first time.

"In Ottawa one always assumes anything is possible," said Financial Trustco Capital's president, Edmund Clark, a former senior Treasury Board official who was fired by the Mulroney government in 1985 for his role, years earlier when he worked for Mickey Cohen at Energy, Mines and Resources, in designing the Tories' favourite bugaboo, the National Energy Program. "Ottawa is driven by ideas," Clark continued. "Energy is devoted to great internal debates about the right thing to do. Then they do it. I know it sounds mushy, but the good people who deal in public policy really want to make Canada a better place to live. You work every night and every weekend, not because you're power-driven but because you feel you're cheating the Canadian public if you can't solve the big problems. You're morally oppressed. You feel you owe it to the public not to go on holidays until you solve the problem. In Toronto, you say you're going to take three weeks off and all that happens is you don't earn as much money."

Plenty of talented, well-educated, bilingual public servants, Clark pointed out, work fourteen-hour days, come into the office on weekends, cancel holidays to brief their ministers and master Byzantine political intrigues that make Bay Street look like kindergarten. Secretaries who have none of their bosses' perks and power to make up for the hours are almost always right there with them. If you phone a deputy minister's office at seven at night, chances are good his or her secretary will answer the phone. When Ed Clark moved to Toronto in January 1985 and started looking for work, he was always amused to have people warn him, "This is not a nine-to-five job."

Frank Iacobucci, a former vice-president of the University of Toronto who went to Ottawa in 1985 as deputy minister of justice and who is now chief justice of the Federal Court of Canada, said he was shocked to find out how hard the city's senior people work. Although his U of T workload was heavy, he found the Ottawa pace much more fast-moving. "There's no question Ottawa has a mystique," he said. "To me it's like the Vatican in a way; it's the centre of political life. And Ottawa has a more impressive number of interesting people per capita than any other place I can think of. But they're restricted, all consumed with government work."

Stanley Hartt left his Montreal law firm, Stikeman Elliott, in 1985 to come to Ottawa as deputy minister of finance. He told his friends he was working twice as hard for half the money and having four times as much fun. But after two years, the nuisance of making half the money became too much and he went back to his law firm. Nevertheless, less than a year later he came back to Ottawa to work as Brian Mulroney's chief of staff. Few people in Canada's business community understand why someone like Hartt would give up his position as one of Stikeman's high flyers, making $450,000, to come to Ottawa for about $130,000 but one explanation, from a friend, makes the reason clear. His father was a member of Parliament who died suddenly, and Hartt believes strongly in serving in the civil service. "There is this huge cultural gap," Ed Clark explained. "The business community doesn't understand Ottawa."

That's true, agrees Liberal Senator Michael Kirby, a former secretary to the Cabinet for federal-provincial relations, an architect of the 1982 Constitution and now a partner in Toronto's Goldfarb Consultants. "In Ottawa they're hooked on power; in Toronto they're hooked on money."

In Ottawa, money has never mattered as much as information and power. Even people who do not have powerful jobs can be considered powerful if they have good information. Ottawans trade information all the time and they do it everywhere: in the Beechwood IGA on Saturday morning, in the Towne Cinema lineup, at Jolicoeur Hardware over the paint brushes, in Domus picking up extra wine glasses for a dinner party. Secrets are hard to keep in this town, and people trade in them shamelessly. The cardinal rule is simple: To get anything, you have to give. It's like baseball cards. Sniffing the wind for a deputy minister or a Cabinet shuffle? Call someone who owes you a big favour for the first trader, the first big name. Then use that name with a second person who might know something; if that person knows the name already, and that's all you have to trade, you won't get anything else – unless that person needs an ego boost and he can get it by revealing inside knowledge you lack. Now you have a couple of names to trade and you're getting somewhere. Now you can call on people you know less well and, after dancing around a while, you can usually swap your names, thriftily eked out one at a time, in return for some new ones. Skilled players need only an hour or two to put together the list.

Small dinner parties are the best places to play this game,

but at breakfast you can see intelligence being picked up in the Four Seasons restaurant, especially at Senator Keith Davey's corner table, and at noon there is the National Arts Centre Café, where the best fun is watching people delicately negotiating new jobs. If you're sharp, you'll catch the moment, just before coffee, when the resumé is slipped across the table.

Because swapping information is such an essential part of the Ottawa game, the city leaks like a sieve. "The only way to prove you're on the inside is to leak information," claims Michael Kirby. "But if you're a secretary to the Cabinet or a deputy minister, you don't have to leak because everybody knows you've got the information." While gossiping is everyone's favourite pastime, until you know all the players and how everyone connects, it's better to keep your lip zipped.

People in Ottawa have long memories and they like to get even, even if it takes years. An assistant deputy minister whose pet program was cut off at the knees by selective spending cuts will never forget or forgive the rival assistant deputy minister who wrested that money away. Someday, somehow, the angry bureaucrat will get even. He will strike like a snake whenever he gets the chance, vetoing his enemy's club application or, even worse, leaking a damaging item about his enemy (usually some tidbit about an expense account, or an incidence of bureaucratic patronage) to a local columnist for the city's delectation over breakfast.

One wonders, for example, how long the acrimony will last over the April 1989 budget cuts when it is so clear that western megaprojects and agricultural programs important to Don Mazankowski, an Albertan who is both the deputy prime minister and the minister of agriculture, were spared while so many other ones dear to the hearts of other ministers and other deputies were killed.

More than 800,000 people live in the greater Ottawa-Hull area, including neighbouring municipalities. About 70,000 of these are federal public servants, but this number does not include the thousands who work for the military and Crown corporations.

Few Canadians in other parts of the country realize that here in fat cat city there are poor people and soup kitchens run out of church basements providing five thousand meals a day to the hungry. Fourteen per cent of families survive under the poverty line and the unemployment rate hovers at about 6.2 per cent. Besides the usual shabby cluster of men's hostels, an old school in Lower Town is home to dozens of men and women, vagrants who are sent outside in the morning and huddle by the front door until they can get back in again. Drugs are sold in school playgrounds and Asian youth gangs have recently taken to terrorizing local citizens. Every once in a while Lebanese restaurateurs work out ancient grudges by firebombing each other's restaurants along Elgin Street.

Ottawa neighbourhoods can be divided into three main geographical areas: central, which has a mix of French- and English-speaking people; west, which is, on the whole, English-speaking; and east, which has a very high proportion of French-speaking Ottawans, especially in Vanier. The strong presence of the French language often surprises newcomers. While they know that in Hull everyone speaks French, they don't expect French to be the mother tongue for about 20 per cent of the people in Ottawa or to find Vanier almost entirely French. Nor do newcomers expect to find communities in West Quebec like Wakefield and Shawville where most people speak English.

Statistics Canada figures show that English is the mother tongue of 60 per cent of the people in Ottawa, that 20 per cent speak French and the remaining 20 per cent speak other languages. Immigrants quickly learn English or French and often both. Francophones are almost all bilingual as are some Anglophones. Anglophone teenagers and young people who underwent French immersion education speak French; Anglophone senior public servants all speak French or they wouldn't be senior public servants. That's not to say there is an easy social mix of French and English. At most top-level parties, there are usually six or seven English speakers to every Francophone. The flip side is that senior Francophones are just as exclusive and cliquish: Anglos find upper-echelon French-Canadian social circles extremely hard to break into, and they are never completely accepted.

In Ottawa, the most important people are not so much the politicians; rather, they are the top public servants – the Clerk of the Privy Council and the deputy ministers – who, along with heads of agencies, boards and commissions, run the place like feudal barons. While top public servants serve, as the expression goes, "at pleasure" of the prime minister (meaning they can be moved or fired at will), they've honed their survival skills to a fine edge and they outlast the politicians by stealth, sobriety, charm and submission of ego. Circling around these stars, these deputies and cabinet ministers, is a supporting cast of senior advisors, consultants, lobbyists, journalists, pollsters and political organizers. What outsiders don't know until they've been here a while is how little diplomats and the military matter in the grand scheme of things. No one pays much attention to them, and only a rare few – usually just the American ambassador and the chief of defence staff – penetrate to the heart of the real power games in Ottawa.

No one in this graceful city likes pushy parvenus, wealthy or powerful people who demand obeisance on the strength of their money or Cabinet rank. Such people are quietly and firmly ignored. They wind up at each other's parties, not at the parties that count. While some do slip through the net, most of the people who rise to the top are courteous, funny, clever and have a prodigious appetite for hard work. Their talent is masked by humility, their money by good taste. This is not a town of frenzied boomers, acquiring and spending at a terrifying clip. Sure, there are some very wealthy people in this city. A few, like Hamilton Southam, inherited it and increased it by investment. Others, like developers William Teron and Robert Campeau, made fortunes putting up housing tracts and office buildings for Pierre Trudeau's Liberals and then decamped for Toronto when the Tory boom was lowered.

But most people here make, more or less, the same kind of

money. The average family income is $44,000 (compared with $40,500 for Toronto). Two-income families can expect, in the fullness of time, to live on a leafy street in a pleasant detached house with a driveway and a basketball hoop over the garage. The average cost of a house is $123,000 (compared with around $270,000 in Toronto). If a family does reasonably well, they'll be able to afford a small heritage house in the Sussex Drive end of New Edinburgh near Margaret Trudeau Kemper's house, or a blood-red brick monstrosity in the Glebe, or a log house with a great view on the banks of the Gatineau River. A lucky break like a modest inheritance might just push them into a gracious centre-halled house in Rockcliffe or into a historic stone farmhouse on a hundred acres in the nearby countryside.

Hong Kong magnates are not yet parking their money in Ottawa real estate. The capital is not a banking centre, a futures market, a commodities exchange. They don't slaughter hogs, pour steel, store grain here. Ottawa is, quite simply, a one-company town and the company is the government. Although only 27 per cent of the population works for the government, the rest of the community depends on the steady employment of that 27 per cent to keep them going. The second biggest industry is tourism. Despite the rotten weather and endless winters, four million tourists visit the city every year.

When the Mulroney government came into power in September 1984, it was with such a deep suspicion of the public service that they forgot that most local voters had gleefully voted Tory. In 1980 Eastern Ontario, which includes the ten ridings in and around Ottawa, had elected eight Liberals and four Conservatives and no New Democrats. In 1984 those ridings dumped six of the eight Liberals, sending instead five Tories and one New Democrat to Parliament in their place. Even Hull and West Quebec across the river, an area that had voted Liberal since Confederation, tossed out most of their Grits.

Ignoring this tangible proof of support, the Mulroney government has tried with considerable success to politicize the public service; the unsurprising result is a severe morale problem. The community that had carried through new Tory policies, policies running from the dismantling of the National Energy Program and the Foreign Investment Review Agency to the sell-off of DeHavilland and entry into a free trade agreement with the United States, the community that drafted and carried through the legislation for its masters, the community that knew the Tories better than anyone else, finally judged them and found them wanting.

In the November 1988 federal election Ottawa ousted all its Tory members, replacing them with Liberals. (The only one in eastern Ontario to survive was Paul Dick in the country riding of Lanark.) Why? There is no end to the reasons.

Public service staff cuts and privatization policies had led to an increase in the government's use of consultants, often well-connected Tory consultants. Public servants recoiled from the explosion of "government relations" firms with well-connected lobbyists patrolling the corridors of power on behalf of their contract-hungry clients.

Under the Tories, public servants had learned that they could be only cheerleaders. They knew that if they questioned decisions made by their political masters, no matter how valid their concerns were, they were considered suspects. That was why, when the free trade negotiations were under way with the United States, no bureaucrat dared question the negotiations. Even at small social gatherings, public servants were circumspect, avoiding any criticism of the deal, just in case their remarks were carried back to their ministers.

Witch hunts became common, especially when politicians believed that a bureaucrat had spoken to a reporter on a sensitive issue. PMO staff, and occasionally privy council staff, called public servants in verbal bluffs, telling them that they knew the bureaucrats had spoken to certain reporters. When this first started happening the public service did not know what to do. Not realizing a bluff was going on, sometimes a terrified public servant would confirm it, believing the reporter had admitted who his source was. Or, if he was innocent, he would deny the allegation and the inquisition would move on to the next victim. Today bureaucrats have learned how to bluff back. They admit nothing. But they do not talk easily to the press, and many honestly believe their phones are tapped.

Incompetent patronage appointments, especially in the first three years of the new government, burdened many agencies, boards and commissions with people who had no idea why they were there or how to do the job they were there to do. Some appointments exposed the contempt with which certain agencies were viewed by the Tories. Just one example was the December 21, 1984, appointment of Denyse Patry, Mulroney's former secretary at the Iron Ore Company of Canada office in Sept-Îles, to the board of Canada's top cultural funding agency, the Canada Council. Her curriculum vitae listed her qualifications for the job; the best she could come up with was that she founded the Sept-Îles branch of Weight Watchers. Another Canada Council appointee, on November 29, 1984, was Louise Dionne, a friend of Gary Mulroney's, the prime minister's brother and riding manager. Dionne, who owns a Sept-Îles dress shop, is also a sister of External Relations Minister Monique Landry.

Patronage appointments to senior public service jobs abounded, especially in the External Affairs Department, where dismayed foreign service officers who had built their careers around their postings saw one Tory crony after another winging off to a plum diplomatic job. Although Mulroney tried to draw attention from the trend by appointing people such as New Democrat Stephen Lewis to the United Nations and Liberal Lloyd Francis to Portugal, nothing could make up for the sour taste created by the posting of former political aide Patrick MacAdam to a senior job in London, Lucien Bouchard, then an inexperienced Chicoutimi lawyer, to Paris or Montreal Tory fundraiser Joan Winser as consul general to Los Angeles.

Public servants had also been made to take the rap for decisions and mistakes they did not make. In 1987 the government attempted to blame senior public servants in the department of regional industrial expansion for departmental overspending. In June 1987, NDP MP Lorne Nystrom revealed that DRIE was only two months into its fiscal year but that it had already overspent its budget by $100 million. Michel Coté, the minister responsible at that time, hired Price Waterhouse, at a cost of $116,000, to do an analysis of the budget. Its report described horrendous financial mismanagement but avoided blaming the political masters.

But the blame had to go somewhere and the bureaucrats in DRIE were convenient targets. They were bitter that neither Coté nor his predecessor, Sinclair Stevens, had listened to officials' warnings about the budget. When urgent political demands for DRIE funds came in from powerful ministers and the PMO, the industry ministers accepted them without question. "We were getting a call every half-hour from the PMO, telling us who had to get a grant here or who had to get one there," said one former official who left in disgust. "They wouldn't accept any explanation that we had run out of money."

"The Price Waterhouse report just whitewashed the government," said another former senior DRIE official. "Every grant there is approved by a minister. Anything over $1 million goes to a minister of state, anything over $5 million goes to the minister and anything over $20 million goes to Treasury Board. All these decisions were approved by ministers and Sinc would never listen to us. Coté was the same. The department started warning the government they were running out of money, but they couldn't stop giving to their friends. I assumed a nationally known accounting firm would do a fair audit, but there was not a single reference to a ministerial decision. Why? Price Waterhouse had a lively appreciation of further favours to come."

Insiders say that Ottawa has changed in the last five years. It's not just that it is being run by a strong and determined

Tory government after so many decades of almost solid Liberal rule. A pervasive and deep belief exists throughout the city and throughout the government that values and ethics have become too elastic. As one insider in the business community puts it, "The morality of business today is that anything is okay as long as you don't get caught. Now that appears to be the morality of the federal government too."

It's not that the Liberals were angels. Their patronage system was deeply rooted and stretched into every hamlet of the country, as the Tories' does now. They bent contracts towards political supporters. The Liberals had their own corrupt MPs and senators and their own schemes for squandering public funds in powerful Liberal ridings. The Liberals found it difficult to advance women and to be fair to minority groups and to share power. When the Grits finally left Ottawa, they were an exhausted party, bereft of ideas, imagination and energy. The Tories deserved to win. Ottawa thought so too.

But Mulroney did not live up to his promise when he promised to change the Liberal system. He made it worse. And never in Canada's history have there been as many police investigations into wrongdoing by MPs and Cabinet ministers, as many kickback charges, as many Cabinet resignations. In mid-June, 1989, RCMP Commissioner Norman Inkster admitted to the House of Commons' justice committee that the RCMP's special federal crimes investigative unit that looks into wrongdoing by federal politicians had twenty-two investigations under way. By the end of June 1989, two more were added to the list as Tory MPs Gabriel Fontaine and Jean-Luc Joncas fell under RCMP investigation for irregularities in their office expenses. Rumours flew around the Hill that several more Tory MPs could follow.

Mulroney likes to pretend the scandals ended in the middle of his first term, but they have never stopped and they have infected the city with a new sense of shame. Here is just the briefest list of some of them, from 1985 until the spring of 1989, a sample of major scandals and minor improprieties.

Starting with the well-known Cabinet disgraces and their accompanying resignations, we find:

February 12, 1985 – Defence Minister Robert Coates resigns after the Ottawa *Citizen* published a story about him visiting a sleazy strip bar in Lahr, West Germany, during an official trip. Coates' libel suit against the *Citizen* and its owners, Southam News, which cost the newspaper more than $1 million in legal fees, was settled out of court. (The paper never apologized or retracted anything, but they did publish a statement, saying that the story never intended to suggest that the Coates affair had constituted a breach of national security.) The costs frightened many media proprietors, creating what is known as "libel chill," which means that even when you can prove it, think twice before publishing a story because defending it can be ruinously expensive. Coates' costs were covered by a secret trust fund set up by buddies led by Halifax lobbyist Gerry Doucet.

September 17, 1985 – CBC Television's "fifth estate" reveals that Tory Fisheries Minister John Fraser, concerned about potential job losses, permitted the sale of tainted tuna from Star-Kist, a New Brunswick fish plant, against the advice of his bureaucrats and fisheries inspectors. (The tuna problems had been known to the government for nearly a year.) Fraser was fired on September 23, 1985.

September 25, 1985 – Communications Minister Marcel Masse resigns over allegations of federal election spending irregularities. Although he was later reinstated, his former employers at Lavalin Industries were convicted of making illegal contributions.

December 31, 1985 – Junior transport minister Suzanne Blais-Grenier resigns after months of flak about squandering government money during two trips to Europe.

May 12, 1986 – After weeks of stonewalling and denials, Industry Minister Sinclair Stevens resigns as evidence poured out showing conflicts of interest between his role as a minister and his private business interests. After lengthy hearings by a royal commission, Chief Justice William Parker found Stevens guilty of fourteen counts of conflict of interest. The irrepressible Sinc was all set to run again in 1988, but Mulroney refused to sign his nomination papers.

January 18, 1987 – Mulroney fires junior transport minister André Bissonnette after the Montreal *Gazette* reported he was involved in $3 million worth of land flips in connection with Swiss arms manufacturer Oerlikon Aerospace's development in his Saint-Jean riding; Bissonnette was acquitted, but his agent and local Tory party president, Normand Ouellette, was found guilty of fraud. Bissonnette did not run again.

February 19, 1987 – Mulroney fires Roch LaSalle, who had been minister of public works from 1984 to 1986 and then minister without portfolio. LaSalle's indiscretions are almost too numerous to mention and almost all of them concern government leases and public works contracts given to friends, relatives and political supporters. What caused his sudden fall from grace was the revelation in *Maclean's* magazine that his right-hand aide, Frank Majeau, had a record for criminal assault and had been a partner of Montreal mob hitman Réal Simard in a Toronto nude dancer booking agency. Two weeks later the news came out that another aide, Gilles Ferland, had a record for insurance fraud. LaSalle always claimed that he had not known of the two men's records even though he had been close to Majeau for twenty-five years and to Ferland for seventeen. (Ferland was quietly rehired a few weeks after the public dismissal, but Majeau was not.) Majeau has always said LaSalle knew everything about him and sued LaSalle and the government for wrongful dismissal. LaSalle has had three farewell parties held for him in his old riding; LaSalle himself admitted to a reporter from the Joliette *Journal* in 1988 that $50,000 raised at one of these functions, which was supposed to plump up party coffers, has gone into an account over which he has sole control instead of into a riding trust account as election law requires. LaSalle told the paper he would use the money in conformity with riding association rules.

February 2, 1988 – Mulroney fires Supply and Services

Minister Michel Coté after the minister admitted failing to declare a $246,000 loan from a Quebec City businessman under the government's conflict-of-interest guidelines. Mulroney himself never declared the $324,000 loan he received from the PC Canada Fund for decorating his official residences, and at first Jean-Pierre Kingsley, the assistant deputy registrar general, said on February 5, 1987, that the PM's loan fell under the conflict guidelines and should have been declared. After a weekend of "consulting" with officials, Kingsley recanted. Mulroney stood in the House to read a letter from Kingsley saying his loan did not fall under the guidelines. Later, the government drafted conflict-of-interest legislation, nicknamed "the Gucci bill" by Opposition MPs, which included a clause to exempt party leaders from disclosing loans or gifts from their parties. (The legislation died because Parliament was dissolved before the bill went through final stages.)

There were many other scandals besides these ones involving Cabinet ministers. Others, just as bad, involved Tory MPs, senators, aides, political organizers, cronies and fundraisers. Here is just a sample:

April 20, 1985 – Canadian Press reporter Tim Naumetz breaks a story saying a Toronto advertising agency with close ties to Finance Minister Michael Wilson was awarded – without bidding – a $234,000 contract to advertise a bond sale for the Finance Department. Lawson Murray Ltd. received the contract in November 1984. Doug Robson, one of the company's two vice-presidents, had been Wilson's executive assistant when Wilson was trade minister in Joe Clark's 1979 government and was still president of Wilson's riding association. He had just returned to the company after setting up Wilson's new Finance Department office. But the firm's president, Douglas Lawson, was also connected to Wilson – he was his brother-in-law. Wilson's sister, Wendy Lawson, was a director of the company.

June 17, 1985 – The House of Commons discovers that Robert Byron, a public servant who heads the government agency awarding advertising contracts – and who was a vice-president of an advertising agency connected to the Conservative Party – had awarded five contracts to his old firm without competition. The contracts, worth $169,600, went to Case Associates Advertising of Toronto; Byron had been a Case vice-president until November 1984. He had also been a member of the 1984 Conservative campaign committee. Harvie Andre, then the supply and services minister, told the House that Byron was doing "an excellent job" and that a government department that had three of the Case contracts was "extremely pleased" with their work.

September 8, 1985 – The Ottawa *Citizen* reports that Mulroney crony Sam Wakim won $200,000 worth of Export Development Corporation legal business, which up till now had been with Ottawa's Gowling and Henderson. Because the firm's managing partner, Gordon Henderson, would not play ball on certain issues – especially refusing to make his executive committee hire Wakim and Bill Jarvis, a former MP and now the president of the PC Party – his firm lost the business along with the two lawyers who had been handling it. Wakim shopped the lucrative contract around to place himself in a good law firm; he and the Gowling lawyers were finally hired by Toronto's Weir and Foulds. Jim Kelleher, at that time the trade minister, had issued a directive ordering the EDC to consider hiring outside law firms to help its seven-member staff. For years Henderson was unpopular with Mulroney; perhaps the fact that his firm recently took on former Tory justice minister Ray Hnatyshyn (who was defeated in the November 1988 election) as a partner will mend those fences.

June 1986 – Montreal businessman Pierre Blouin, a PC organizer in Quebec, is fined $3,000 after pleading guilty to two charges of influence peddling. Blouin, who died shortly after his conviction, tried to extract $70,000 from Quebec businessman André Hamel for a $1-million government lease for a Canada Employment and Immigration Centre in Drummondville.

The Drummondville case was complicated by its ties to Mulroney's principal secretary, Bernard Roy. The lease had been held for years by Hamel, but he was a Liberal. Still, Hamel put in a lower bid for the contract than did his rivals, Les Immeubles Brodilaf, the winning firm. (Blouin had also tried to get kickbacks from one of Brodilaf's owners, Richard Dionne.) Roch LaSalle had also insisted the contract go to Brodilaf. Hamel sued the government for $1 million in damages, claiming that Roy had intervened against him. Public servants in DPW said on the record that their recommendations were over-ruled. Both Mulroney and Roy admitted that Roy had been heavily involved in the decision and had met with Drummondville Tories several times in 1985 and 1986 to talk about it. Later, the new minister of public works, Stewart McInnes, admitted the Brodilaf bid was $65,000 higher than Hamel's, that his department had changed the criteria for leasing contracts without telling all the bidders. Hamel, weary of fighting, finally settled out of court in September 1988.

September 5, 1986 – Bill Fox, Mulroney's press secretary, admits expense accounts claiming he had taken certain journalists out for drinks were not accurate. Under freedom of information law, Bob Fife and Tim Naumetz, reporters who were working for Canadian Press at the time, found Fox's 1985 expense accounts for the Commonwealth Conference in Nassau. Fox filed claims for $569.20, noting the money was to pay for drinks for seventeen journalists including the *Globe*'s Jeff Sallot, the *Star*'s Val Sears and Joe O'Donnell, and Wayne Brown, the chief of Standard Broadcast News. None of them remembered Fox paying for their drinks.

April 8, 1987 – Public Works Minister Stewart McInnes admits the RCMP are investigating a lease awarded to Jean Paul Tessier, an old friend and client of Bernard Roy. According to several former aides to Tory ministers, including one to former public works minister Roch LaSalle, the prime minister's principal secretary told LaSalle to break the lease on Place Vincent Massey in Hull, which housed Environment Canada, and renegotiate it at a much higher rent. By doing this,

Tessier's company, Les Entreprises Duroc, profited by $10 million. LaSalle overruled department officials twice, in December 1984 and again in January 1985, and forced them to make a new lease. Three days after the lease was rewritten Tessier slapped a $10-million mortgage on the building. Although the Opposition charged that the government's decision cost taxpayers $15 million, the RCMP investigation into the whole mess, including Roy's role, was closed in the winter of 1988 when the police concluded Roy had not used his influence to help his friend.

April 9, 1987 – Opposition MPs tell the House of Commons that Montreal ad man Jean Peloquin is in conflict of interest. Not only was he co-chairman (with Robert Byron, the former Case executive) of the committee that vetted government advertising contracts, he was a partner in a firm, Les Productions Indigo, with Mulroney crony Roger Nantel, that had received $300,000 worth of contracts in 1986 from three government departments. (Nantel was a partner in Media Canada, which received $125,000 a month to place all government ads in newspapers, magazines and on radio and television. He also received millions in government ad contracts in another company, but still declared bankruptcy in November 1987.) At first Supply and Services Minister Monique Vézina claimed that Peloquin was no longer a consultant with her department, but when told he was still in his office there, her response was succinct: "As the government, we have the privilege to choose the companies in whom we have confidence," she said. "If you had to hire a company to promote your programs, wouldn't you hire a friend you can trust? I know I would."

In fact, in the first two years of Tory rule, they gave $12.8 million worth of government ad contracts to ten firms run by Tories. It must be said that the Trudeau Liberals had done the same thing. Some things never change.

June 30, 1987 – External Relations Minister Monique Landry confirms the RCMP are looking into a $25,000 – or 5 per cent – kickback demanded from Wajax, a public company that makes heavy equipment. The story, originally broken by the CBC's Jason Moscovitz, was confirmed to the *Globe and Mail* by Wajax chairman Ronald Chorlton, who said that a Quebec Tory fundraiser, Guy Racine, had asked Wajax president Bernard Scobie for the money in connection with a federal $425,000 foreign aid contract for firefighting equipment. Scobie said Racine had told him many companies had paid the kickbacks, and most of the money would go into Tory party coffers. When the story broke, Quebec Tories denied Racine was involved with the party and his employers said he was no longer with them. After the RCMP investigation, charges were laid by Quebec's solicitor general's office.

December 4, 1987 – Mario Taddeo, forty-nine, a construction magnate and land developer worth at least $18 million, and a Tory fundraiser from the Montreal suburb of Laval, is murdered in his office at a gravel quarry at Mirabel Airport by a professional hitman who also kills one of Taddeo's employees. No one has ever been arrested for his murder.

With help from Roch LaSalle and other senior Tories, Taddeo was involved in Mirabel Airport landflips that enabled him to acquire the quarry from a local farmer. Taddeo was hoping to win the federal contract to build the new road between Dorval and Mirabel and needed the quarry, which was on the proposed route. (He was also bidding on a $4-million federal contract to build a landing apron and terminal building at Mirabel, but his closest competitor was Liberal Senator Pietro Rizzuto. When Rizzuto came in as low bidder, the government cancelled the bidding process and said they would renew it later.)

October 12, 1988 – Henri Paquin, fifty, another millionaire land developer and Tory fundraiser from Laval, is blown up in his Mercedes-Benz by a remote-control bomb. He was involved with Gervais Desrochers, another close friend of LaSalle, in more Mirabel projects such as the Hydroserre hydroponic greenhouse project for which they received $750,000 in government grants. From the mid-seventies, Paquin employed his childhood friend Michel Gravel in his denim-bleaching factory, Dentex, but on October 18, 1984, sued Gravel for a mysterious loss of $562,636 between 1982 and 1984. Paquin's statement of claim said he discovered the loss after Gravel had left for the House of Commons. However, the two men settled the matter secretly and out of court soon after the election.

September 19, 1988 – Police find the body of John Grant, a wealthy and well-known Halifax lawyer on the board of the PC Canada Fund, who cut his own throat in Dartmouth's Wandlyn Inn some time on September 18. Grant, who was also the president of the PC's 500 Club, an exclusive fund-raising association restricted to donors of $1,000 or more, was the national party's Nova Scotia vice-president. Mulroney had appointed him to the board of the Canada Development Investment Corporation in October 1984.

Grant's wife Deborah was about to run for mayor of Halifax, but in June 1988 he was fired from his law firm, Cox Downie and Goodfellow, under suspicion of fraud and immigration scams. Reprimanded by the Nova Scotia Barristers' Society on Friday, September 16, and threatened with proceedings which could have led to his disbarment, he decided to take his own life. Later, close friends disclosed that for years he had been subject to bouts of severe depression.

September 23, 1988 – The Montreal *Gazette* reports on irregularities concerning the sale of the Moisie radar base in Mulroney's riding to a well-connected Tory. Hugh Derby Hylands, former chief of property management for the federal Public Works Department in Montreal, claimed in an interview that his department was politically pressured to sell the land to Raymond Lefebvre et fils for $175,000, land he estimated was worth at least $6.5 million. Hylands said the bids were altered to favour the company and he had had to work with political staff over the sale. Although he wrote a personal letter to Public Works Minister Stewart McInnes about the deal, he received no answer and nothing was done until the news stories appeared. Perrin Beatty, then the defence minister, admitted to the House that a PMO official had made "routine inquiries" about the sale.

Former Tory environment minister Suzanne Blais-Grenier, who had openly alleged that the party had a systematic 5 per cent kickback scheme operating in Quebec and was tossed out of the Tory caucus, received documents about the sale from Moisie mayor Bernard St. Laurent, which she passed on to the police, telling them clearly it was only a fraction of the available documentation and that St. Laurent would give them the rest. The police, she said later, never bothered to talk to St. Laurent. On November 29, 1988, the PMO announced that an RCMP investigation into the deal had found no wrongdoing.

October 27, 1988 – The Montreal *Gazette* reports that Tory senator, co-chairman of the 1988 federal election campaign and Mulroney crony Michel Cogger was paid $225,000 by Guy Montpetit, a Montreal businessman, to lobby for him for government contracts from 1986 to 1988. The payments were disclosed in court files after a Japanese businessman, Takayuki Tsuru, sued Montpetit to recover $39 million in loans. Montpetit, the president of GigaMos Corporation (which had been looking for $45 million in federal money for a silicon smelter laboratory for computer components), paid Cogger to lobby for federal government contracts with his friends, including former Mulroney aide Charley McMillan, in the PMO, with senior ministerial aides including Tom Creary, chief of staff in Robert de Cotret's office, and Paul Brown, then chief of staff in Pierre Blais's office, and with civil servants. The money was paid into a personal account, not through Cogger's law firm.

On December 24, the *Gazette* reported that a helicopter firm, Les Hélicopteres Trans-Québec, paid $37,000 to a man who worked full-time on Cogger's farm in the Eastern Townships. This was the helicopter company that flew Mulroney around during the 1984 election campaign. The *Gazette* also noted that a Montreal real estate developer paid $5,000 for renovations on Cogger's Eastern Townships farmhouse and that Montpetit paid $2,416 to another hired hand on the property. Despite Opposition calls for an RCMP inquiry into the matter, nothing was done.

During Montpetit's trial in June 1989, he testified that he

also lent $100,000 to Cogger to help the senator's financially troubled company, Pleuri-Canaux.

November 5, 1988 – Jean Paul Tessier, Bernard Roy's old friend from the Place Vincent Massey leasing scandal, pops up again in another leasing scandal. This one, reported by the *Globe*'s Andrew McIntosh, reveals that Tessier is a partner with some other well-connected and prominent Tories in Le Bourg du Fleuve, a company that won a ten-year, $10.4-million leasing contract in Trois-Rivières in April 1988. As McIntosh reported, quoting letters from officials and Roch LaSalle, who was public works minister at the time, the company won the contract despite the fact that keeping existing leases would have saved the government $7 million. When Public Works officials recommended tenders, the bid was constructed in such a way as to ensure that Le Bourg du Fleuve was the only company that could meet the requirements. Despite objections from public servants, the contract went ahead with the blessing of Stewart McInnes, the new public works minister.

December 8, 1988 – Former Gamelin, Quebec, Tory MP Michel Gravel is sentenced to twelve months in jail and fined $50,000 after pleading guilty to fourteen counts of fraud and influence peddling in connection with at least $97,000 in kickbacks he demanded from Hull businessmen for contracts on the new Museum of Civilization in Hull. Gravel, originally charged in 1986 with fifty counts, stalled his case legally for two and a half years, proclaiming his innocence and taking his case to the Supreme Court of Canada.

For the Conservatives it was vital to delay his trial until after the November 1988 election, and no one was surprised when he pleaded guilty. By doing this, he prevented any of the seventeen prosecution witnesses from testifying against him. As early as September 1988, however, several sources were saying a deal had been cooked on Gravel: he would plead guilty just four or five days before his trial and in return he would be sentenced well after Christmas, when he would receive a light sentence of a year in jail and a fine of $50,000. But several sources said that an informal part of the deal – which had nothing to do with the police or the Crown attorney's office – was that he would also get a payment of $350,000 from unspecified sources. On December 7, 1988, five days before his scheduled trial, he pleaded guilty; on February 6, 1989, he received the sentence he was expecting. Later, when the police were asked about the $350,000 payment, a senior officer said it was not a police matter because it is not illegal to pay someone to plead guilty. Gravel spent two days in a detention centre in Hull, eight days in jail in Montreal and then six weeks in Waterloo, a "country club"-style prison in Quebec, before moving to a Montreal halfway house for a few weeks. Soon he was putting in his forty-hour work week of community service from his home.

January 13, 1989 – Edouard Desrosiers, Tory MP from Hochelaga-Maisonneuve from 1984 to 1988, a former convicted bank robber, is charged with three counts of uttering forged documents, one count of fraud and one count of breach of trust. The charges followed a three-month RCMP investigation into House of Commons research contracts he had given to his constituents since 1985. On June 9, Andrew McIntosh, now writing for the *Gazette*, reports that André Girard, Desrosiers' executive assistant from September 4, 1984, until June 7, 1985, told the RCMP in the fall of 1988 that he thought "it was current practice to do this kind of thing." On Tuesday, June 27, 1989, Desrosiers was charged with three more offences: corruption, breach of trust and theft.

February 21, 1989 – Tory Joseph Hamelin, the past president of the Saint-Hubert riding association and former president of the Chambly riding association, and three female associates are charged with fraud and bribery in connection with kickback schemes connected to Richard Grisé, Tory MP for Chambly. Hamelin's girlfriend, Danielle Hervieux, who was initially nominated as the Conservative candidate in Saint-Hubert, was quickly dumped a month before the election and replaced by another candidate; she was among those charged with Hamelin.

February 24, 1989 – Solicitor General Pierre Blais used his cabinet writing paper to try to sell office furniture manufactured by one of his constituents. The letter suggested new MPs might want to buy office furniture and equipment from the company. Later, Blais, responding to opposition charges of "tacky" behaviour, admitted he should not have used ministerial writing paper.

March 23, 1989 – Claude Levasseur, a former Tory organizer in the Trois-Rivières riding and campaign manager for his former business partner, MP Pierre Vincent, is fined $2,000 after pleading guilty to influence peddling. According to reporter Andrew McIntosh who broke the story, on October 5, 1985, Levasseur approached Cap-de-la-Madeleine land surveyor Jean-Marie Chastenay, who had been awarded a $50,000 government contract. Levasseur asked for a 5 per cent kickback on the contract, promising future contracts if Chastenay cooperated. Chastenay said the $2,500 price tag was too high, so the two men settled on $2,000. Chastenay, who had taped the entire conversation, turned the tape over to Tory MP Michel Champagne, who turned it over to the police.

April 14, 1989 – Richard Grisé, Tory MP from Chambly, Quebec, is charged with three counts of fraud and eight counts of breach of trust after a seven-month RCMP investigation into allegations of a kickback scheme involving short-term House of Commons contracts as well as Employment and Immigration grants. Although the PMO knew about the investigation well before the election, the police did not raid Grisé's office until November 21, the day of the election. Grisé left the PC caucus in mid-April 1989 to sit as an Independent.

A month later he pleaded guilty to all eleven charges. He was sentenced to one day in jail and fined $20,000. On May 30 he resigned his Commons seat and apologized to the House. NDP candidate Phil Edmonston, who came second to Grisé, later said he knew in June 1988 that Grisé was involved in illegal activities and that he had told the RCMP. Edmonston also accused Mulroney of covering up the Grisé affair before the election.

June 3, 1989 – Newspaper reports state that Ken Waschuk, a Regina pollster who was part of Mulroney's 1983 inner circle at the Ritz Hotel in Montreal during the long fight for the Tory leadership, is under RCMP investigation in an influence-peddling scheme. Saskatchewan Justice Minister Robert Andrew admitted to the legislature that Waschuk has received a $150,000 loan from Montreal businessman Guy Montpetit. Waschuk was Mulroney's 1983 leadership campaign chairman in the province and a senior organizer in the 1984 campaign. His 1985 appointment to the Air Canada board was renewed in 1987, but cancelled abruptly on April 26, 1989. Air Canada officials refused to comment.

Montpetit's company, GigaText Translations Systems, had received $5.25 million in Saskatchewan government money for a computerized translation system, which did not work. When the police were finally called in, it was revealed that Montpetit had put $150,000 into Waschuk's Bermuda company, Libra International, money that could be traced directly back to the Saskatchewan government's investment. And it was also revealed that Senator Michel Cogger asked Waschuk to help Montpetit get Saskatchewan government contracts.

Given this sad litany of scandal and illegalities, it is easy to understand Suzanne Blais-Grenier's allegation that a kickback network exists in Quebec. Other senior Quebec sources, however, sources that include former aides to some of these people, say the system is much wider and deeper than that; they say it exists across the country. We just haven't found it yet.

During this entire period not one deputy minister or associate deputy minister or assistant deputy minister or director general or any senior public servant in any capacity got into trouble with the police over misuse of public funds. But these are the people who had to process the contracts and leases for their political masters.

Is it any wonder Ottawa voted out its Tories?

4

•••••••••••••••••••••••••••••••••••••••

Command Centre

When Brian Mulroney walks out of the Green Chamber of the House of Commons, he usually takes a sharp right and mounts the staircase to his office just above the Commons lobby, facing the front lawns of Parliament Hill. Most Canadians think this office is the Prime Minister's Office, but it's only part of it; just a few of his staff work here and in other offices scattered along the hallway. In Ottawatalk, PMO (true Ottawa insiders eschew "the" when alluding to these lofty offices) is a powerful government department hunkered down in the Langevin Block across the street.

The Langevin Block is the command centre of political and bureaucratic Ottawa. This is where you find the Deputy Prime Minister's Office, where Don Mazankowski is actually running most of the government's day-to-day business, and the Privy Council Office, where Clerk Paul Tellier makes sure the public service carries out the government's orders.

In Trudeau's day, because of the influence of his Clerk, Michael Pitfield, PCO was far more powerful than it is now. Today, PMO and DPMO are the important offices in the

Langevin, while PCO has evolved into more of a "process shop," or administrative support system, and less the key policy and tactical player it was during the Trudeau years. Increasingly in the Mulroney government, critical power and influence are wielded from outside the Langevin Block by a coterie of businessmen and lobbyists whose advice PMO and the government value far more than that of its bureaucrats.

The Langevin Block sits right on the corner of Confederation Square and Wellington Street, facing the Parliament Buildings. Behind it, facing Sparks Street but connected by major arteries of heavily guarded tunnels and bridges, which are monitored by security cameras, are the Post Office Building, home of the Federal-Provincial Relations Office, and a couple of undistinguished office buildings, which house overflow staff from PMO, PCO and FPRO. Most of PCO is actually in the Blackburn Building.

There is always plenty of unseemly scrambling by political staff and bureaucrats to occupy an office in the Langevin itself; if you can't be in it, near it will do. That is why bureaucrats and politicians grind their teeth when they are banished across the river to Hull to toil in unglamorous departments like Secretary of State or Indian and Northern Affairs or Supply and Services. Once you've been transferred to Hull or Confederation Heights or Vanier and are forced into cheerful conversations at lunch about "quality of life" or "convenience," pity hangs heavy in the air. People who work in the Langevin walk with an extra little swagger; their presence at a dinner party almost always ensures a social success. Some of them even carry beepers.

Traditionally, the key organizations that assist the prime minister in the conduct of his responsibilities are PMO and PCO, but Mulroney has elevated the Deputy Prime Minister's Office, making it almost as powerful as PMO through the exercise of its tactical and administrative smarts. Deputy Prime Minister Don Mazankowski, who also holds the Agriculture portfolio and is sometimes called "the minister of everything," is a skilled politician and strong administrator who has taken over the routine running of PMO, leaving Mulroney to do what he does best, politicking, and what he loves best, foreign travel and building up his reputation as an international statesman. Mazankowski, once a Clark supporter, is utterly loyal to The Boss, and happily carries the can in much of the regular battering the government gets from the Opposition in Question Period.

The Federal-Provincial Relations Office, overseen by Senator Lowell Murray, coordinates the PM's constitutional work and acts as his overall liaison between the federal government and the provincial governments.

For budget purposes, PMO, DPMO, PCO and FPRO, four powerful offices all known by initials, fall under something formally called the Privy Council Program in budget estimates. The program also includes task forces and commissions of inquiry, such as the Dubin Inquiry into the use of drugs in sport, as well as the Office of the Senior Advisor to the Cabinet, which has meant Dalton Camp's little shop, now disbanded. Because Camp was a political appointee masquerading as a bureaucrat, the prime minister finally had to devise a separate bureaucratic structure for him. The Privy Council Program also includes something called Ministers' Offices, which means offices for Justice Minister Doug Lewis in his extra capacity as House Leader and for Lowell Murray as Government Leader in the Senate and minister responsible for FPRO.

For ambitious young political aides, the way to a big job is to do a stint in PMO or DPMO and with any luck someday go back as principal secretary. For bureaucrats, the ticket to power is a three- or four-year assignment in PCO or FPRO with their hopes fixed firmly on returning in twenty years as Clerk of the Privy Council. Jobs in any of these shops are not easy to come by. You need powerful mentors to get you in, street smarts to enable you to survive when you get there, the brains to stay ahead of everyone else and the constitution of an ox to withstand eighteen-hour working days.

PMO is the political office of the prime minister. As such it has responsibility for providing political and partisan advice to the PM about the conduct of national affairs and the establishment and execution of national policy. It is composed of people who share the partisan loyalties of the PM and whose interests and future prospects are radically dependent on the fortunes of the party of which the PM is the head. It is essential to the conduct of the PM's responsibilities that key decisions be tested against the partisan interests of the government, as expressed both in Parliament and in the country as a whole. The people in PMO polish his image, arrange his schedule, answer his mail, write his speeches. They advise him on the timing for everything from a national election to the introduction of a controversial bill in the legislature.

Tom Axworthy, Pierre Trudeau's principal secretary from 1981 to 1984 and now head of the Bronfman Foundation in Montreal, described PMO's responsibilities quite thoroughly in an intriguing but little-noticed 1988 paper entitled *Of Secretaries to Princes*. "The personal office of the leader should contribute four functions to the strategic Prime Ministership," he wrote. "Intelligence: knowing the trends; Partisanship: promoting the party perspective; Crisis management: keeping a grip; Co-ordination: knitting things together."

Of the four objectives, Axworthy stressed the importance of intelligence. As he noted wryly, "My foremost objective – often breached – was 'no surprises.'" Gathering intelligence, he explained, means knowing what the Opposition is up to, but it goes far beyond that. "Information is power. Personal networks are crucial for managing information flow" (in other words, a prime minister requires daily doses of reliable gossip from impeccable sources), "but polls provide the most reliable assessment of public opinion." From 1980 to 1984 the PMO ordered quarterly polls of public opinion and presented the results to Cabinet. Mulroney, of course, is well known for his reliance on polls, and most experts assume they are now ordered monthly or more often.

PCO is the bureaucratic department of the prime minister.

Many federal departments are vast and are responsible for the delivery of key federal programs. PCO is tiny by comparison but critical in its impact; it is responsible for the administrative oversight of the entire government on behalf of the prime minister and the Cabinet system over which he presides.

PCO is composed of professional, nonpartisan public servants whose fortunes are not, in principle, immediately dependent on the fortunes of the party in office or on the personal fortunes of the prime minister. Officials in the PCO feed and support the Cabinet system, structure the government's decision-making agenda, record Cabinet decisions, communicate them to the bureaucracy at large and attempt to ensure that the decisions so taken are conscientiously executed. Where problems emerge, PCO alerts the PM and his Cabinet colleagues. Most important, PCO provides advice directly to the prime minister on the conduct of the nation's business. It is organized into "secretariats" named after the particular Cabinet committee each supports. It also provides advice to the prime minister on organization of government, allocation of manpower to ministries and ministers, and advises on senior bureaucratic appointments.

Tom Axworthy summarized these distinct functions of PMO and PCO succinctly when he wrote, "Partisans bring creativity; public servants provide perspective. The political arm makes things move; bureaucratic routines prevent errors." This distinction is paralleled in each minister's office, where there is a political staff, headed by a politically appointed chief of staff, and the administrative organization of the department, headed by a deputy minister.

This, or something like this, is the theory. The reality, however, is far richer, more complex and more subject to change and adaptation than this simple outline would suggest. Obviously, there is blurring at the edges. The prime minister must have people around him whom he can trust and who are effective, and he will find them wherever he may. He must have an organization serving him that will keep him on track, keep him out of trouble and advance the fortunes of his government, and he can be expected to put in place whatever organization appears best fitted to achieve these ends. Political survival is no respecter of governmental theory or of the niceties of traditional administrative practices, and the current setup under Mulroney is not an aberration. Each administration and each PMO/PCO setup is unique and rightfully so.

When Mulroney took office in 1984 he made the mistake of staffing PMO with nothing but loyal cronies instead of with experienced people who could fill in the gaps in his own knowledge. (Mulroney had little choice, however; the only Tories who had any experience were Clark people who were, by definition, unacceptable. Later, a few "Clarkies," as they were known, were let into the tent.) Almost all the early appointments proved to be disasters. They were viscerally hostile to the bureaucracy, vengeful towards the Liberals, even suspicious of other Tories, especially Tories who had supported Joe Clark. They were rude to the press; once, press secretary Bill Fox got so angry at one reporter he told him he was going to tear his lungs out.

Peter White, who was in charge of patronage appointments, processed them with such indecent speed that his office often did not have time to notify the happy recipients before their good luck appeared in the press. Many had no idea why they were being appointed to certain boards and commissions, and White almost always failed to inform the chairman of the body receiving these new appointees. New members of the Parole Board were processed without consulting Parole Board Chairman William Outerbridge. William Taylor, who was then running the Social Sciences and Humanities Research Council, Timothy Porteous, then the director of the Canada Council, and the National Arts Centre's director general, Donald MacSween, rarely knew who was coming on their boards until they saw the appointments in the papers.

Not every senior person was a disaster. One good appointment was Geoff Norquay as senior advisor on social policy, but

Norquay was never in the inner circle because he was a "Clarkie," and he left in 1988 to become the Ottawa lobbyist for British Petroleum.

By January 1987 it was clear that many of the first Mulroney staff were on their way out. The prime minister brought in top public servant Derek Burney, an efficient deputy minister at External Affairs, to do the dirty work. Burney's first job was to make sure there was only one route to the prime minister, and that was through him. PMO was in shock. Up till this point top aides were able to see Mulroney just about whenever they liked and lobby him personally on issues dear to their hearts. One by one they quit or were fired.

"The only two major players left," wrote Michel Gratton, the press secretary who left in March 1987 and published a memoir of his years with Mulroney a few months later, "were Bonnie Brownlee, perhaps the toughest of the bunch, who would remain where she always was, at Mrs. Mulroney's side, and Keith Morgan, the Boss's riding liaison man, who would sadly witness the departure of my 'buddies,' knowing he had no choice but to stay on in a job nobody else could handle, as the PM's representative and unelected MP for Manicouagan." Today Keith Morgan, one of the few to survive the Burney purge, is still there, and his son, Richard, is Mulroney's executive assistant. His wife, Giselle, the former associate national director of the federal PC Party, is now the assistant deputy chairman for the Montreal region of the new Immigration and Refugee Board.

Gratton, then a columnist with Ottawa's *Le Droit*, joined as a press secretary in June 1984 before the election. He resigned in March 1987 amid a small scandal caused by his asking two women reporters for dates when they had requested interviews with Mulroney. Properly repentant, the irrepressible Gratton returned to his old love, newspaper work, and now is the Toronto *Sun*'s Ottawa columnist.

Six months after he resigned, he published a memoir of his years in PMO, *So, What Are the Boys Saying?*

In fact, his book was a good-natured insider's glimpse into

PMO and into the prime minister's life, and it did Mulroney no harm. But Mulroney was furious and people close to Gratton say the journalist has become upset with the abuse he has since taken from former friends in PMO and in the PC Party. Gratton says he is contemplating another book and this one will pull no punches.

Today Mulroney's early appointees are forgotten but not gone. Almost anywhere you see Brian Mulroney you will see remnants of this group, like Bill Fox or policy advisors Fred Doucet and Charley McMillan, hanging around, working as "consultants." In fact, it is interesting to note that of the sixteen original senior staff members who left the PMO with the Burney shake-up, nine are now Ottawa lobbyists.

When Brian Mulroney appointed Conservative strategist Dalton Camp to a deputy-minister-level job in the Privy Council Office in August 1986, Ottawa was aghast. The prime minister had thumbed his nose at the public service by giving one of its cherished deputy-level jobs to a political advisor. An advisor, moreover, who had founded Camp Associates, a Toronto-based advertising agency that was reaping the profits from winning the government's most prized advertising contracts worth millions of dollars. Camp Associates is now owned by Camp's brother-in-law, Tory campaign chairman and Senate appointee Norman Atkins, and run by another Tory strategist, Hugh Segal.

Scenarios flew around the city. One was that Camp, who was nearly at retirement age, wanted the higher pay and perks that went with the job. Political staff make considerably less than deputies. Other critics hinted darkly that Camp was part of a Tory fifth column, a mole in the public service system, one who would have access to highly confidential government documents not normally available to political aides. No one wondered why Camp was brought in; obviously he was there to help straighten out the mess PMO had created for itself during the first two years of the Mulroney government. It was making Camp a public servant, politicizing the job, blurring the lines, that offended so many.

Explanations from Mulroney's office were unconvincing, and the experiment failed. A year later, in 1987, Mulroney stopped pretending that Camp was an ordinary deputy minister and created a new and separate office under the Privy Council Program called Senior Advisor to the Cabinet. Camp, a Red Tory from the party's Ontario Big Blue Machine, was "marginalized," as Ottawa likes to put it, by the more powerful forces of the Quebec political machine run by Senate Speaker Guy Charbonneau and such Mulroney buddies as Principal Secretary Bernard Roy, and Michel Cogger and Jean Bazin, who were also appointed to the Senate.

PCO Clerk Paul Tellier also refused to play ball. Except for Camp, every deputy minister in Ottawa fell under his authority, so Tellier refused to sign Camp's expense claims and did not invite him to deputies' information-sharing breakfasts or to official meetings. With only a secretary, an executive assistant and a driver for staff, Camp was left to plot strategy in his office, strategy to which few paid any attention. In early June 1989, Dalton Camp left Ottawa for good, returning to his home in rural New Brunswick.

But back in 1987, as he frantically cast around for a smart manager to pull his office together, Mulroney realized that he needed Derek Burney as his principal secretary. Burney, whose Tory credentials went back to when he was president of the Conservative Club at Queen's University, had impressed the prime minister during the economic summits with his toughness and skill. Mulroney figured the appointment was worth risking flak about politicizing his office by appointing a career public servant to the most partisan job in government. In a way, the choice was a back-handed compliment to the public service; here was the PM tacitly admitting his old buddies couldn't rise to the occasion. Reviled mandarins smiled to themselves and chuckled over their gin and tonics on the battered dock of the Five Lakes Fishing Club.

Burney's housecleaning, establishment of severe and unwavering lines of authority and astute political judgement allowed the prime minister to survive far better than he had during his first three years in office. Since Burney's departure in 1988 to become the Canadian ambassador in Washington, the office has suffered again. Burney's successor, Stanley Hartt, does not have the administrative skills the job requires. Hartt has, however, kept the route into the prime minister's office as narrow as Burney did.

Hartt himself is an interesting example of blurring the edges. Although he was never a crony and was usually considered a Liberal, Hartt was a Montreal lawyer with Stikeman Elliott and an old friend of Mulroney's. Mulroney brought him to Ottawa in 1985 as deputy minister of finance. No one pretended he was a hotshot administrator: the department had plenty of good managers, especially Fred Gorbet, who eventually succeeded Hartt as deputy, to take care of that deficiency. He was there because he was imaginative, energetic and a charismatic leader and it was not long before he succeeded in winning over a department of suspicious senior technocrats. For bureaucratic high flyers, Finance continued as the place to be, just as it was when Mickey Cohen was running the department for Pierre Trudeau and Marc Lalonde. After two years Hartt went back to his law practice but before too long he resurfaced in the PMO.

Hartt has some strong allies who are helping him run PMO. One is Tom Trbovich, a new senior advisor who had been Michael Wilson's chief of staff. The reckoning at PMO was that Trbovich would bring to it some of the efficiency of Wilson's office. The press office is still not strong. Bruce Phillips, the former director of communications, was set aside in a senior advisor's job while he waited for a diplomatic appointment (he was offered the consul general's job in Atlanta but rejected it, hoping for Boston). To reporters viewed as critical of the government, the people in the press office now are still as hostile and unhelpful as the old team. Any reporter deemed to be "an enemy" does not get calls returned.

A curiosity of PMO today is its volunteer staff. One is Michael McNeil, head of government relations at the Canadian Automobile Association. A tireless party worker, he arrives at the Langevin every morning between 6 and 7 a.m. to work on tour plans for Mulroney's trips, both small domestic trips and major foreign ones. Former journalist Luc Lavoie is in charge of tours and McNeil reports to him. After two or three hours supervising the tour team, which includes a couple of other volunteers, McNeil goes to his paying job. At the end of a full working day, he's back at the Langevin until 9 or 10 or later every night.

Aside from Hartt, the main player today in PMO is Marjory LeBreton, the best-liked person there and one of the most efficient. (Her sister, Kay Stanley, is equally popular, despite being parachuted into a civil service job as head of the Status of Women office after she failed to win an Ottawa seat in the 1984 election.) LeBreton, also an ardent feminist, has always been unabashedly partisan. Hired as a secretary by Flora MacDonald in the 1950s, she has worked for every Conservative leader since John Diefenbaker. Despite her senior organizational role in the 1984 victory, she was left out of the action in the early days of the Mulroney prime ministership – partly because she was a woman, partly because Mulroney's cronies underestimated her influence with the party rank-and-file across the country, and partly because she was labelled a Red Tory who was close to Joe Clark. Following the election, she went to work in the Camp Associates Ottawa office.

The fiasco of all the patronage scandals brought her back into the fold in 1986. She took over the patronage appointments job from Peter White and started to clean up the mess. She insisted that more women and more ethnics be appointed and that the government be able to justify the appointments on the basis of competence. Political affiliation was no longer enough. She did not always win these battles, but she went a long way towards ensuring that people of dubious credentials did not slide in quite as easily as they had before.

PMO was invented by Pierre Trudeau in 1968. Before then, prime ministers used civil servants loaned from government departments. As Axworthy describes it, Trudeau "initiated one of the most significant structural changes in the history of the Canadian government. He made it clear that his personal staff would be openly partisan. A new category of official was created – the political advisor."

The document that best explains how PMO works is a 1971 paper given in Regina on September 8 by Trudeau's principal secretary, Marc Lalonde, to a meeting of the Institute of Public Administration of Canada. At the same IPAC conference, PCO Clerk Gordon Robertson delivered an equally important paper on his office, called "The Changing Role of the Privy Council Office." Both papers are still considered the classic explanations of the offices.

(Lalonde, who had been an advisor to Lester Pearson before he worked for Trudeau, gives credit to Thomas D'Aquino for help in preparing the paper; at that time D'Aquino was an ambitious young lawyer from British Columbia, anxious to make his way in Ottawa and working as an aide to Trudeau. Today, as head of the powerful business lobby group, the Business Council on National Issues, D'Aquino is considered a Tory.)

Lalonde pointed out that the PM's staff has grown substantially over the years. When R.B. Bennett was prime minister in 1935, he had a staff of twelve; Mackenzie King, Louis St. Laurent and John Diefenbaker made do with about thirty people. By 1968, at the end of Pearson's term, it had grown to forty. "These figures are somewhat misleading," Lalonde noted. "Up to 1968 it was the practice to have a number of officers and clerical staff seconded to the Prime Minister's Office from the administration, their salaries being paid for by the seconding department." So in 1968, Trudeau split PCO in two, creating a political office called PMO.

By 1971 Trudeau had 85 on his PMO staff; in 1984 there were 87 with 275 people working in the PCO and FPRO. Budget estimates gave PMO $4.2 million in 1983-84. In 1985-86, Mulroney's PMO had 117 staffers and a budget of $6.6 million.

Today Mulroney has about 90 on his staff, but his office has not really shrunk. A large chunk of PMO was carved away to form DPMO under Mazankowski and to serve the Ministers' Offices section of PCO, so the total PMO-DPMO staff adds up to 146. This total does not include the many people hired as consultants or on contract.

An analysis of the 1989-90 budget estimates (the famous Blue Books that are released after a budget and that provide such a goldmine of information for persistent diggers), as well as of figures released by PCO financial officers, tells an interesting story that contradicts the supposed savage restraint imposed by the 1989 Wilson budget and the government's policy of across-the-board staff cuts.

The figures show that Mulroney's PMO is now the largest and best-financed ever. In addition to the 90 in PMO, about 56 work in the Ministers' Offices, 174 in the PCO and 69 in FPRO. Three bodies still occupy space in the Dalton Camp shop even though he is gone. A further 189 people work in Administration.

A rough addition of political staff today is 148, excluding Administration, making it the largest PMO in history. Bureaucratic staff add up to 243; throw in Administration and you've got 432 – again, the largest bureaucratic staff in history. Add it all up and the total PCO program staff jumps to 591 for 1989-90, up from 579 in 1988-89.

And what is it all costing? The easiest way to estimate costs, advise PCO officials, is to subtract certain annual fixed costs as well as the costs of royal commissions and task forces. The annual fixed costs, which run at about $5 million, include such things as the value of the Langevin Block rental from Public Works and the costs of health plans. Because royal commissions and task forces chew up such a major part of the Privy Council Program budget, politicians like to blame rising costs on these, but they rarely are the real culprits. The last commission that was indeed breathtakingly expensive was the Macdonald commission on the economy, which between 1983 and 1986 gobbled up $26.2 million.

Here, minus the annual fixed costs for such things as rent and insurance, are the budgets for the PCO program for the past seven years. The costs of royal commissions have been deducted and appear in brackets beside each year.

YEAR	PCO PROGRAM BUDGET	ROYAL COMMISSIONS
1983-84	$31.1 million	($13.3 million)
1984-85	$37.6 million	($12.9 million)
1985-86	$40.7 million	($8.9 million)
1986-87	$40.5 million	($5.1 million)
1987-88	$43.2 million	($1.5 million)
1988-89	$43.9 million	($4.3 million)
1989-90	$48.3 million	($5 million)

The total estimated budget for the combined political and bureaucratic apparatus known as the Privy Council Program is $59,160,000, up from $51,209,000 in 1989-90, an increase of more than 17 per cent, but this amount will probably grow even more. Each year supplementary estimates are passed by the House to add money to departments that have used up their allotments before the fiscal year end. The PCO program is almost always one of the budgets that needs a financial booster.

It doesn't matter who the prime minister is, however, or how smart his advisors are, no one person can do as much as he and his party and his country expect.

"In a four-year term," writes Tom Axworthy, "a prime minister will have the time to work extensively on four or five issues at most. The Cabinet may be able to devote substantial effort to a further twenty-five or thirty problems. The impact of a government depends on which twenty-five issues receive the top priority out of the 1,000-plus Cabinet memoranda that will be produced by the bureaucracy in a four-year term."

Axworthy believes that the most valuable resource in Ottawa is the time of the prime minister. To work on the four or five issues that most concern him, he must say no to hundreds of other requests. As Axworthy put it ruefully, "It is the happy task of the PMO to deal with the disgruntled." Pierre Trudeau concentrated on four major issues between 1980 and 1984: constitutional reform, the national energy program, anti-inflation policy and the peace initiative. To help Trudeau concentrate on these four areas, said Axworthy, PMO "systematically reduced paper flow, spun out functions like Order-in-Council appointments to ministers, and took care that his luncheon guests included outsiders knowledgeable in his priority areas."

For Brian Mulroney, the important issues have been the free trade agreement with the United States and the Meech Lake Accord. In his second term, he has concentrated on deficit reduction and foreign affairs, but he has not yet established his agenda and Meech Lake is still important. Don Mazankowski has been delegated to worry about everything else.

Most Canadians know little about the powerful mandarins who work in PCO and FPRO. This suits the politicians and the mandarins very well. No one wants a situation like that of the Trudeau era when the Clerk, Michael Pitfield, was himself so controversial. Pitfield, a protégé of Trudeau's, had been climbing the bureaucratic ladder steadily – he joined PCO in 1965, became assistant secretary to the Cabinet in 1966, deputy secretary in 1969, deputy Clerk in 1971 and deputy minister of consumer and corporate affairs in 1973 – but few in Ottawa were prepared for his leap into the top job in 1975. He brought in his own protégés, bright young people like Bob Rabinovitch, who worked in the powerful little shop called P&P, the priorities and planning secretariat for the Cabinet.

In 1979 Joe Clark fired Pitfield but kept the staff and the structure intact. When Trudeau won the 1980 election, he brought Pitfield back. Two years later, in 1982, he appointed Pitfield to the Senate as an Independent, and replaced him with Gordon Osbaldeston, a far less controversial figure than the often emotional and difficult Pitfield.

Osbaldeston, a merry and outgoing man who now teaches at the University of Western Ontario's business school, became the perfect model of an invisible mandarin, never talking to the press, never upstaging his boss. He too brought in his protégés, notably Ian Clark, a brilliant young scientist and Rhodes scholar from Vancouver with a degree from Harvard's Kennedy School of Government. Clark became a powerful assistant secretary to the Cabinet and is now deputy minister of consumer and corporate affairs.

Other senior bureaucrats who worked in PCO during these early Mulroney years included Jack Manion, who was responsible for deputy minister and other top-level personnel decisions (below the DM level, appointments are handled by the Public Service Commission), and Blair Seaborn, the least known of all, who ran the highly secret and sensitive Security and Intelligence Committee, which is, in fact, a committee of Cabinet, chaired by the prime minister.

And of course there was Michael Kirby, a Liberal strategist and former academic who ran FPRO during the constitutional negotiations, was briefly deputy minister of Fisheries and appointed to the Senate in 1984. (Trudeau did not hesitate to use political talent when he needed it and he too was sometimes accused of politicizing the bureaucracy.) A gentle and courteous Quebecer, Gérard Veilleux, replaced Kirby. Today he is the secretary to the Treasury Board and much touted as a possible Clerk.

The current head of FPRO is a Mulroney recruit, Norman Spector, a Montrealer who had been working as the most senior public servant in the British Columbia government, and was a key player in the 1982 constitutional negotiations for Bill Bennett, then the premier. After William Vander Zalm took over in B.C. in 1986, there was no room for Spector, a soft-spoken but tough-minded Ph.D. who was fluent in French and Hebrew, so Mulroney grabbed him. The architect of the Meech Lake Accord, Spector is highly regarded by his peers across Canada and most mandarins believe he is the leading candidate to replace Paul Tellier as Clerk, despite his lack of Ottawa roots and his failure to join the Five Lakes Fishing Club.

When Paul Tellier replaced Osbaldeston in 1985, official Ottawa was at first delighted. Tellier, a handsome and charismatic Quebecer who drove a Jeep as his official car, had been Trudeau's point man on the referendum fight, leading a SWAT team of strategists known as the Tellier Group. His prestige during the Mulroney years has been diminished. That is partly because in 1984 the newcomers in PMO were determined to wrest power away from PCO and turn the Privy Council Office into a support system of paper pushers who would do as they were told and keep their opinions to themselves. The new government arrived with a different view of the political decision policy process, one in which the political level generates its options and the bureaucratic level develops the means of implementing them. What really hurt Tellier's reputation, however, was not his failure to keep power in PCO – everyone understood why he couldn't do that – it was his failure to stick up for the bureaucracy under incessant attacks from Tory ministers and backbenchers. Osbaldeston was also accused of failing to protect public servants from unfair bashing by politicians, but PCO insiders say this judgement is not fair. They say that Osbaldeston prevented many wholesale firings by pointing out, again and again, that acts of Parliament protected many of these office holders, like the CBC president, Pierre Juneau, and the National Arts Centre's Donald MacSween. Osbaldeston could not save Ed Clark at Treasury Board or the Canada Council's Tim Porteous, who were both fired.

In 1983, when the Opposition Tories knew they would probably win the next election, they sent their official "critics," the politicians assigned to shadow specific government departments, through each department to meet the senior officials and get a briefing on the department and its operations. This was done with Pierre Trudeau's acquiescence.

Senior Tories also asked friendly bureaucrats to make lists of suspected Liberals. One bureaucrat was promised a plum diplomatic posting if he would finger suspected Liberals and provide a list of lucrative government contracts that the Tories, before they were elected, could not get their hands on. He refused, but another bureaucrat agreed and the posting materialized soon after the election. Meanwhile, new ministers, their chiefs of staff and political aides met for hours to discuss the senior bureaucrats in their departments, trying to find out who were Liberals and who could be counted on to be on their side.

Using the results of this intelligence, and of thorough research into the background of each senior bureaucrat, the Tories put together a hit list of mandarins suspected of being too closely linked to the Liberals. Jamie Burns, a close associate of Mazankowski who was then running his own lobbying company, was in charge of the list. Once he rejoined Mazankowski as chief of staff in September 1984, he pursued the heathen with vigour.

As Parliament lurched into the summer of 1989, PMO was in a state of confusion. Once again, the detested Ontario Big Blue Machine was on the outs, to languish in Toronto until needed for another campaign. Except for Mazankowski's operation and Marjory LeBreton, PMO was again in the hands of Mulroney's Montreal mafia. Mazankowski's old informal "Ops" (Operations) Committee, the committee that had become as powerful as Pitfield's P&P in the late 1970s, had been formally structured and enlarged and the result was it lost its sex appeal, its insider cachet. ERC, the prime minister's powerful new Expenditure Review Committee, was still being tested. As chaos reigned, it was a golden opportunity for PCO to sneak out and quietly retrieve lines of power they'd lost.

5

·····································

Can You Forgive Them?

The boys in the Conservative alcove at the far end of the Parliamentary Dining Room were feeling no pain. The drinking was going on nice and steady and voices were growing just a little louder every hour. When nature called, an honourable Tory member from Saskatchewan figured it wasn't going to be easy, that walk to the men's room, so far down at the other end of the restaurant and out the door, up the stairs and around the corner. In fact, the call was pressing and sometimes a fellow just has to make do. He unzipped, then and there, and peed against a corner of the Tory alcove.

Well, Speaker James Jerome did not think this antic was funny and naturally he heard about it because the Speaker hears everything that goes on in the House, so he banished the honourable member from the Parliamentary Dining Room for life. No point in being Speaker if you can't throw your weight around from time to time. (In fact, the honourable member eventually started appearing again in the restaurant and the Speaker, upon reflection and after a quiet chat, agreed to look the other way.)

But that was not the first or last escapade to make this particular member famous. There was the fabled incident, now passed lovingly into Commons lore, when he was playing poker with the boys up in a third-floor office. These poker games were a legend on the Hill in the sixties and seventies. The boys – people like Jim Coutts, then Trudeau's principal secretary, and Denis Ethier, a Liberal MP from Eastern Ontario who was also an assistant deputy Speaker, and Liberal MP Bryce Mackasey, and occasionally Jack Horner, the Tory from Alberta – used to play for very high stakes. At some games, claim some reliable witnesses, stakes of $20,000 a night were not unknown.

And on some occasions and in some games (this is certainly not to malign the gentlemen named above because other poker games existed here and there along Commons corridors), there were whispers that the stakes were even higher: contracts and projects in the members' ridings. I'll raise you that wharf in the bay for that airplane hangar in your constituency.

Not surprisingly, the games themselves lent themselves to legends. One night, they say, tempers in one third-floor poker game got a little heated. Who knows who said what to whom? The story was that Jack Horner got raging mad at Tory MP Stan Korchinski. Like the rest of the Alberta Horners, Jack is a big man and the way the legend went, he got so mad that he picked up Korchinski and hauled him out to the hallway and hung him over a bannister so that he dangled three floors above a marble floor. Korchinski hung on for dear life. At one point his neck was stretched across the railing. Eventually someone pulled Horner off the poor wretch and grabbed Korchinski and maybe even saved his life. Korchinski stayed out of the House for the next six months or so, long enough to give the welts and bruises that decorated his neck from ear to ear time to fade. One problem with this story, says Horner today, roaring with laughter, is that it isn't true. While he concedes he's heard it many times, he swears it never happened. What is true, he says, is that because of his brawn he was asked on occasion to assist with unruly members; one time during Question Period his leader, Robert Stanfield, asked him to haul out a drunk and disorderly colleague who had just stumbled back from a noon-hour reception at the Russian Embassy.

But some of Korchinski's problems were all too true. In October 1983 an Ottawa judge fined him for being drunk and obstreperous in a cab; Korchinski pleaded guilty. The cabbie, one Marcel Aubut, was a stubborn fellow; later in November he brought a charge against Korchinski for failing to pay cab fares on two different occasions, fares that added up to $13.

MPs revel in their Hill lore. They love to tell about the night Greek actress Melina Mercouri danced in the Green Chamber. They love to reminisce about the wonderful poker parties in Jim Jerome's office. They hug themselves over the Assistant Deputy Streaker incident: an assistant deputy Speaker (not Denis Ethier), caught by a flustered cleaner *in flagrante delicto* with a sweet young thing in his office, chased away the cleaner in fury. When he returned to his office, he was horrified to find it locked. The girlfriend was so angry that she wanted to be alone for a while. The bare-assed MP was lucky to find a towel somewhere before he solicited a little assistance in getting his office opened and retrieving his clothes.

How the boys mourn the old days, the good old days before 1983 when the House still held night sittings. Night sittings meant coming back to the Hill in the evenings and long poker games and carousing and womanizing. Night sittings created the kind of all-party clubbiness and camaraderie that enforced the unwritten rule: You don't tell about me and I won't tell about you.

They mourn the good old days before 1984 when they could put their wives and kids on the payroll, eat a full-course dinner in the Parliamentary Dining Room for $2.75, pay a buck to get their hair cut and let their restaurant bill run on and on. They are nostalgic for the time when the caucus wasn't full of broads. (Today, 39 women among 295 MPs is, to the Old Guard, a House full of broads.)

Most of the men and women in the House work long, hard hours for their constituents, for their parties and for causes they believe in. "Most of the MPs on the Hill, in fact 90 per cent of them, are hard-working, honest, nice people," said one official who has worked with parliamentarians for many years. "But the other 10 per cent? Well, they're just a bunch of goddamned crooks. They're the ones who give the rest a bad name."

Anyone who has ever read Anthony Trollope's political novels, which start with *Can You Forgive Her?* and end with *The Duke's Children*, will feel at home in the political culture of Ottawa's Parliament Hill, a world of saints and scapegraces, of brilliant orators and drunken drones, of punctilious people who balance out their expense accounts to the nickel and those like Jean-Luc Joncas, the Quebec Tory MP who thought nothing of charging separate car mileage for his wife and himself on the drive home to the constituency, even when they were both in the same car. Between 1985 and 1988, he claimed $77,000 in mileage refunds, much of it for trips he said he took when parliamentary records show he was in Ottawa. Trollope saw the vanities and foibles of politicians, of their wives and families and their backers. He wrote about how they tangled themselves in financial webs of debts and obligations, how they messed up their lives with illicit love affairs, how their ambitions and hopes so often fell short of reality when a Cabinet post just slipped past them or a government fell. New MPs, just stepping through the members' entrance for the first time, would do well to read his cautionary tales. Ottawa in the 1980s is not so different from Westminster in the 1880s.

In 1985 former Speaker of the House Lloyd Francis blurted out some of the unsavoury side of Hill life during a few unguarded moments in a lengthy taped interview with journalist Thomas Earle on the eve of his departure for Portugal where he was taking up the ambassadorship. "The House was a den of sin in the 1970s," Francis told Earle, and then went on to spill out details of sexual harassment and sexual procurement, kickbacks, patronage, electronic eavesdropping and untendered contracts for millions of dollars. Poor Francis thought the tapes would be locked up in provincial archives for fifteen years, but because no written undertaking to that effect was attached to the material, they were released inadvertently in July 1985. While Francis was furious at the Public Archives for letting them out, he never denied the stories. How the House ever reached such a state of affairs, and how it cleaned up its act between 1980 and 1985, is one of the most fascinating stories in recent Canadian political history.

Since Ottawa was chosen as our national capital in 1857, Parliament Hill has operated like a self-contained city-state. To understand the story, you have to understand something of the history and culture of Parliament Hill. You have to know that this state, with nearly 3,500 citizens, is at once the most public of our political institutions and yet the most secretive. Exempt from freedom of information law, it goes its own way, reined in only when a shocked auditor general or audacious journalist makes the shenanigans public. The parliamentarians who rule this city-state are the first to bellow when a government department runs its business badly and wastes taxpayers' money, but many never believed their own affairs on the Hill, which are also paid for with taxpayers' money, should be open to public scrutiny and reform.

Goldwin Smith, a nineteenth-century Oxford don, called the town "a sub-arctic lumber-village converted by royal mandate into a political cockpit," and there are many who would argue that it hasn't changed much over the years. The streets back then were just dirt roads. Thick forests pressed in close to the town. In winter the snow and bitter cold made it almost impossible to get around; in summer the heat was terrible and the mosquitoes intolerable. Coming to Ottawa was not an easy or short journey for most early members of Parliament, and when they arrived they found few amenities. Unlike the city, though, the Hill was an oasis of comfort and convenience.

Construction of the Parliament Buildings began in 1860. By

the time it was finished the Hill had its own liquor store, barbershop, restaurant, post office and library. It had its own furniture shops and its own upholstery and curtain workshops. It was easier, determined early administrations, to make their own chairs and tables and desks than to try to find them in Ottawa or even in Montreal or Toronto.

To this day MPs enjoy these services – and more. There is a steam room and a masseuse. There's a beauty parlour, an acknowledgement that women MPs are here to stay. Members may order room service from the Parliamentary Dining Room. There's a shoeshine service, a tailor shop, a picture framing service (up to $400 of framing a year is free) and a fully equipped gym. There's even a daycare service, initiated during Jeanne Sauvé's term as Speaker. While the Senate treasures its independence, it cheerfully piggybacks on these services.

The ruler of this city-state, which ran on a budget of nearly $190 million in 1988, is not the prime minister but John Fraser, the Speaker of the House of Commons. As if to underline that fact, the Speaker's Centre Block quarters are actually larger and more beautiful than the prime minister's. Almost unknown outside Ottawa, except as a ceremonial figure who wears a black three-cornered hat and long gown and who sits at the head of the Chamber and looks irritated during Question Period, the Speaker on the Hill is God. And is treated as such.

You can divide the people working on the Hill into two groups: the political group, which includes 295 members of Parliament and about 1,100 political staff (each Cabinet minister and MP is allotted a budget for a certain number of people known as exempt staff), and the Commons employees, a bureaucracy of about 1,700 people. So in all, aside from MPs, there are about 2,800 people working on the Hill, from the Clerk of the House to cooks and messengers, all of them reporting to Speaker John Fraser. (Quite separate, but also reporting to the Speakers of the House and the Senate is the parliamentary librarian, with a staff of about 240.)

The three top bosses under Fraser, all with deputy minister rank, are Robert Marleau, the Clerk of the House, Ed Riedel, the Administrator, and Major-General Gus Cloutier, the Sergeant-at-Arms. It is the ancient struggle for power between the Administrator and the Sergeant-at-Arms that in past years provided much of the drama in the history of the House. That struggle was finally resolved in the Great War of 1980 - 85.

Luckily for him, the Clerk was always more or less nicely out of it because his responsibilities were, in a sense, intellectual. The responsibilities of the other two senior bureaucrats, on the other hand, involved spending money and doling out perquisites, and it's when you've got that volatile mix of money, perks and MPs that you've got trouble.

The Clerk, the man in the black robes who sits at the head of the Table in front of the Speaker's chair, runs the legislative and procedural side of House business with a staff of about 170 people. They include clerk assistants, clerks at the Table, the law clerk and parliamentary counsel, staff working for the committees, for Table research, for the journals branch, for the parliamentary relations office and for the private members' business office.

Until modern times, most clerks were political hacks, with the exception of Sir John George Bourinot, who joined the Commons staff in 1868, rose to become Clerk and wrote *Bourinot's Rules*, the chief guide to parliamentary procedure. C.B. (Bev) Koester, an academic and the former Clerk of the Saskatchewan legislature, was appointed Clerk of the House in 1979, and he developed clerkdom as a profession in the House; during his time, he worked closely with the British Clerk at Westminster to train and develop promising Canadian talent. Before Koester, most clerks in his branch were high-school graduates; now the Clerk's office recruits only bilingual university graduates with high academic achievement to their credit. Last year, when the House advertised for two clerks, more than four hundred highly qualified university graduates applied.

Koester's two protégés were Mary Anne Griffith and Robert Marleau, who both joined the House in the early 1970s. Marleau's expertise lay in running the members' international travel services, organizing international delegations, while Griffith was a procedural expert and advised the Speaker on rules. A crisis developed in 1987 when Koester had a heart attack. Marleau was chosen as acting Clerk because it was the sober judgement of all concerned that the House was not yet ready to accept a woman Clerk. When Koester was named Clerk Emeritus in 1988, Marleau was appointed permanent Clerk despite the fact that Griffith was deemed just as capable. House insiders said she accepted the decision with great dignity because she believed it was more important to appoint someone trained in House procedure than to risk having the government choose a political hack.

The word around the Hill was that the elderly Toronto *Sun* columnist Doug Fisher, an ex-CCF member of Parliament (he beat C.D. Howe) who became a right-wing journalist, wanted the job. Observers thought he might have the inside track because of his flattering interviews with Brian Mulroney. A more plausible candidate would have been Bill Clarke, the former Tory MP from Vancouver Quadra who was defeated by Liberal Leader John Turner in 1984 and again in 1988. Bilingual and a procedural buff, Clarke was a "House man," as the men's club likes to call people steeped in House lore, and if he had won in 1984 he would have been the strongest candidate for Speaker.

To outsiders, the most visible part of the Clerk's job is to sit at the table in front of the Speaker, and they wonder what he does there. Does he listen to the speeches? Not exactly, smiles the courteous and scholarly Bev Koester, who now lives in Kingston, Ontario. "Being Clerk meant you didn't listen to speeches, you listened for crises. Things like unparliamentary language, or words that were a tip-off that something was about to happen."

The Administrator's position was established in 1968 as a

rather junior job, and the first to fill it was Jean-Marc Hamel, now better known to Canadians as the chief electoral officer. The Administrator's clout equals that of the Clerk and Sergeant-at-Arms, and his staff, at 830, makes up the largest empire in the House. It includes the office of the comptroller, human resources, reporting and distribution services, support and information services, internal audit, purchasing and matériel management and restaurants and cafeterias. The Administrator is the only senior House official who does not wear a uniform of some sort and who does not have some kind of ceremonial role in the Chamber. Until the late 1970s this was a sore point with some administrators, particularly Georges St. Jacques, the Administrator in the early 1970s, who craved a fancy-dress uniform.

Ed Riedel, the former House comptroller, is the Administrator today. He presides from the great corner office in the South Block. This is the administrative heart of the Hill, where the soft hum of word processors and the chipper little blips of electronic mail combine in harmony. This is where, with enormous tact and discretion, Riedel has to inform defeated MPs what their severance and pensions will be, or where he occasionally may have to read the riot act to surly MPs who would prefer not to pay a catering bill for a reception they almost forgot they had.

The man you see on television wearing a funny three-cornered hat, a black swallow-tailed coat and a sword, and carrying the mace at the front of the Speaker's Parade as it proceeds into the House each day is the Sergeant-at-Arms. The present Sergeant-at-Arms, Gus Cloutier, oversees a blue-collar staff of about 675, composed of security guards, messengers, furniture makers and cleaning and maintenance staff. Cloutier served in the RCAF from 1952 until 1978, then became executive assistant to a succession of mostly Liberal defence ministers. Although he was made Sergeant-at-Arms in 1978, just as Auditor General James MacDonnell was beginning his historic audit of the House, Cloutier threw in his lot with the old regime – with old friends like Mulroney crony Patrick MacAdam – not with the new.

Anyone wanting to catch a glimpse of this legendary figure from the Great War can pop into Hy's Steakhouse on Queen Street at noon and often find him, usually with his subordinate, Peter Fleming, at a centre table where they have a commanding view of all those who enter. (Otherwise, you'll find them lunching in the Parliamentary Dining Room; again, always at the same table.) There has been much private merriment in the House the last few months over a secretary who was recently hired. Because rules about job competitions are fairly strict these days, no one is sure how she made it, but it seems she was a hostess at Hy's and noted this fact on her application form. After leaving Hy's, she worked briefly at Defence, where she was "laundered" with public service experience and distanced from Hy's, and then went on to the House.

Responsibilities among the three officials were not always divided as they are now. Before 1979, the administration of the House was chaotic, often corrupt and riddled with patronage and nepotism. That state of affairs suited many people very well. The person who lost the most in the reform period was Gus Cloutier, but he did not give it up without bloody pitched battles and endless corridor skirmishes.

House administration had been a problem for more than a century. In 1880 the Speaker complained of pressure from both sides of the House to provide patronage appointments, and Prime Minister Sir John A. Macdonald described the system of recruitment as "vicious," resulting in the employment of many who "were quite ignorant and untrained and unfit for their work." For over a century the Sergeant-at-Arms, for example, was free to hire just about anyone he liked for the hundreds of blue-collar jobs on the Hill. It was a wonderful source of patronage for the party in power and gave the Sergeant-at-Arms enormous personal power.

The effort to reform the House started in 1979 after then

auditor general, James MacDonnell, at the request of the House, had studied the administration and reeled back in shock at what he found. He issued a draft report in 1979 and loaned Réal Chatelain, his deputy auditor general and now auditor general of Quebec, to the House as interim Administrator to start the reform process. But as the CBC's Jason Moscovitz reported in a 1983 two-part television series on the reform process, Chatelain "didn't last a year. He was lied to, lied about, made to look bad at every opportunity. He was perceived as a threat and he was a threat. The old ways of patronage and uncontrolled spending were gone." Chatelain's job was complicated by three events – the serious illness that year of Clerk Bev Koester, the defeat of the Clark government and the retirement of Speaker James Jerome, who was appointed to a federal court judgeship.

The next year MacDonnell issued two final reports, which were received by the new Speaker, Jeanne Sauvé. One report, according to her successor, Lloyd Francis, was private and listed the kickback schemes and other illegal activities he had uncovered. The second was public and simply rapped House administration over the knuckles for its sloppy and wasteful spending and for its personnel practices. Sauvé was lobbied by many MPs to fire Chatelain (who quit soon anyway, warning his replacement not to take the job because of all the problems and backstabbing), but she refused. In the public report, MacDonnell listed some of the following horror stories:

No government questioned spending requests from the House; they were passed automatically. The personnel department was a joke. Jobs did not go to those who were qualified, they went to someone's buddy or someone's relative or to someone recommended by an MP, senator or Hill employee doing a friend a favour. No tenders were called for food for the restaurants and cafeterias, nor for office equipment. Financial controls were chaotic and fraud was common. No one signed for the food deliveries and no one weighed or measured them. Restaurant employees routinely carted out hams, turkeys, beef roasts and liquor in green garbage bags and took them home, so it was no surprise that the Parliamentary Dining Room and cafeterias were losing $3.5 million a year.

There were people on the payroll no one knew were there. Several cleaning women and other blue-collar workers, well beyond retirement age, were on the payroll, including one woman who was eighty-three. The army of 450 cleaners cost $32 million a year, earning "two to three times the norm for commercial cleaning of government office buildings," wrote the auditor general, but each worked only four and a half hours a day, spending the rest of the time on coffee breaks and lunch hours.

The auditor general's summary was devastating: "The quality of general and financial administration is significantly below a minimum acceptable standard," he reported. "We found serious deficiencies in the House administrative organization and in budgeting, operational planning, human resource management, performance and management reporting. As a result of these deficiencies, management control over provision of services is inadequate. The efforts of House staff to meet demands for more and better services have not been balanced with adequate concern for the economy and efficiency of spending and the prevention of irregularities."

On top of this stinging report were the problems he outlined privately to Sauvé, problems discussed years later by Lloyd Francis on the CBC tapes. There he said that drunken parties were held in the House, where women were expected to undress. "I had a very attractive young girl about thirty who came to see me and she said, 'Mr. Francis, I haven't got a job. I was invited to a party and a senior personnel officer told me I was to take my clothes off and I refused. He took me aside and said, if you don't take your clothes off, you're not going to have a job.'"

Two senior House employees ran a kickback scheme that involved secretarial employees. "The two officials had an arrangement with employment agencies that made secretaries give back up to 40 per cent of their salaries for as long as three or four years," Francis said in a phone interview from Portugal in 1985 when the taped story broke. When one of the secretaries complained to the Speaker, the officials involved threatened to fire her and only Sauvé's personal intervention stopped it and ended the practice.

Francis also said that two senior House employees planted sophisticated bugging devices to eavesdrop on committee hearings and other House activities, and that although most of the offenders were fired, at least one was convicted of embezzlement of funds from extra-parliamentary organizations.

One astonishing reaction to Francis' revelations came from former Speaker James Jerome, the man who asked the auditor general in 1978 to study the House administration. In an interview in early July 1985 with Barbara Yaffe, then a Hill reporter with the *Globe and Mail*, Jerome said he was "very surprised" by the revelations. "There was no indication of transgressions or wrongdoing when I was there," he told her. "I am very surprised by Mr. Francis' remarks. It certainly was never prevalent as a concern during my thirteen years as a member of the House of Commons. Never."

Sauvé asked Art Silverman, an accomplished accountant and administrator whom she had met when she was minister of communications and who was then working as comptroller at the Department of Communications for deputy minister Bernard Ostry, if he would be willing to replace Chatelain as the new Administrator. Silverman agreed to try to clean up the Augean stables on the Hill, and only because Sauvé backed him up with her own iron will and determination did he succeed. It was an effort that cost both dearly. They made enemies of MPs from all parties who resented losing some of their privileges. Furious at losing their patronage perks and being asked to pay their restaurant bills, these members never credited Sauvé and Silverman for introducing new services they now take completely for granted.

This enmity is one reason Sauvé is often still dismissed as a poor Speaker who could not control the House. She was bitterly resented both as an efficient manager and as a woman. Part of her problem was that she had never wanted the job, was never a "House" person, the kind of MP who steeps himself or herself in procedural lore. She would have much preferred a straight Cabinet job.

Sauvé's worst problems came with the two parliamentary committees responsible for overseeing the running of the House, the Board of Internal Economy (known as the BOIE) and the Management and Members' Services Committee, the MMSC. The BOIE consisted, in those days, of senior government ministers who drew up the budget and organized the administration of Parliament (today it is an all-party group). The MMSC was an all-party group of MPs. The MMSC's core members during those years were Tories Robert Coates and Marcel Lambert (for a few months between 1962 and 1963, a Speaker himself) and Liberals Gérard Duquet, Roland Comptois and Marcel Roy. A few committee members, however, did support the reforms, which put them at odds with some of their own party. Leading this group was Tory MP Jack Ellis; others included the Tory Whip Bill Kempling and the NDP's Mark Rose.

"People have their own fiefdoms to preserve," Ellis told Jason Moscovitz during his television feature on the House, "and she was upsetting these fiefdoms, left, right and centre."

Bob Coates and Gérard Duquet were more to the point. "Mr. Silverman is a very bright fellow," Duquet told Moscovitz icily. "He might be the right man for the job if he was doing it the proper way and not thinking that he runs the House of Commons and he's the boss." And Coates, the chairman of the MMSC, objected to Silverman's thrift. "The Administrator has been very cost-conscious, and to too significant a degree, is trying to run this place almost as a profit-making institution. Well, it isn't."

The criticisms of Silverman were really veiled attacks on Sauvé, but because in the parliamentary tradition you can't publicly criticize the Speaker, Silverman became the lightning rod for much of the abuse. Coates, however, did not hesitate to be especially patronizing about Sauvé. "A new Speaker has to get used to her job," he told Moscovitz, "and naturally it is not the same as an old pro sitting in the Chair. You see that in the daily proceedings in the House. She has to understand how the House of Commons functions in a different way than she did as a minister of the Crown."

Marcel Lambert was particularly outraged by the attempt to clean the place up. In November 1980 Canadian Press reported him as saying that some of the new managers "will have to be taken on a shakedown cruise."

One of the things Sauvé did that drove many MPs wild was try to reduce the House's travel budget. She made arrangements with Air Canada and Canadian Pacific Airlines to register each MP on the airlines' frequent flyer programs. The House paid for the memberships and the deal was that all the bonus points would come back to the House to help reduce travel costs. This move was in line with an almost unenforceable government directive that prohibits any government employee from collecting frequent flyer points. But the MPs were angry at losing what they regarded as a legitimate perk for all the flying they did back and forth between Ottawa and their constituencies. They ignored the fact that it was Sauvé who made arrangements for their trips to be first-class and who also saw to it that the number of trips allowed to them and to their spouses or families was increased.

In June 1989 Toronto *Sun* reporter Tim Naumetz must have given Canada's senators a shiver of anxiety with a story saying senators had cost taxpayers hundreds of thousands of dollars by keeping their bonus points. In contrast, MPs had saved taxpayers up to $1.25 million by turning their points back to the House. "If a senator used all the free passes to fly return from Ottawa to Vancouver on the Air Canada travel plan," wrote Naumetz, "they would get a free trip for two around the world with two tickets to Europe thrown in." The best senate spokesman Gord Lovelace could come up with when he was asked about the issue was that the senators had dismissed the idea because it would take one full-time person to administer the plan.

The anti-Sauvé, anti-Silverman group in the MMSC, and many other MPs like them, were deliberately rude and vicious in the House at a time when Bev Koester was seriously ill and Sauvé had only old, weary, fussy men helping her with procedural rulings; instead of being handed neat and professional rulings each day on difficult issues, she was up night after night researching precedents herself. And when she wasn't doing this, she was dealing with the endless fights and wars between her new management team and those like Gus Cloutier who bitterly resented the reforms.

Sauvé's most public battle with the Sergeant-at-Arms concerned a luxurious restaurant he set up in the early autumn of 1980 on the sixth floor of the South Block. This elegant establishment was reserved exclusively for senior Parliament Hill employees. The menu and prices – $2.75 for a full dinner – were similar to those in the Parliamentary Dining Room, but this eatery was even more exclusive. MPs were not welcome; nor were the Press Gallery or senior bureaucrats from other government departments.

Cloutier did not tell Sauvé about the new facility until it opened. After visiting it once she expressed her anger publicly: "I was surprised that it was opened in the first place and I have grave doubts about its usefulness. It's not my style to make snap decisions. Opening that restaurant was a snap decision by somebody other than me." Realizing the restaurant was a *fait accompli*, she left it open for a few months to see whether it would pay for itself. By July 1981 it was clear it wouldn't. On July 23, 1981, she closed it, revealing that a study had shown it was losing $12 on every meal it served and had run up a deficit of $85,156 in eight months. Closing the restaurant was a slap in the face for Cloutier and Sauvé's clear signal to everyone on the Hill that she was the boss.

Another complicating factor that made her work during this reform period difficult was the introduction of television in the House in 1978. Sauvé was the first Speaker who had her on-the-job training on national television. Other Speakers had bumbled their way through the first months in merciful obscurity. Her gaffes, indecisions and problems as she learned her job were all too obvious to the rest of Canada.

The auditor general, however, was pleased with her work. In a letter dated May 25, 1983, Kenneth Dye, who had replaced MacDonnell and had completed a follow-up audit of the House, wrote in words very few auditors general have ever used: "It is gratifying to note the significant improvements that have occurred since our 1980 comprehensive audit."

Still, Dye was obviously astonished by the rancour still beating in the hearts of some MPs. In carefully worded language, because this letter after all was a public document, he added: "As we have previously expressed to you, the results of the audit reflect favourably on the significant efforts that have been made in the past three years by your management team under your leadership. In the light of this situation, I find it indeed unfortunate that the relationship between House management and the Management and Members' Services Committee is such that there continues to be unresolved frustrations, differences of view and communications problems expressed by some members of the Committee."

Today Dye is itching to let his auditors roam through the Senate's books, but the chamber of sober second thought has no intention of undergoing the reforms the Commons went through, nor of letting the auditor general near its records. The Senate has never been audited.

Dye told reporters in June 1989 that he had advised Senate Speaker Guy Charbonneau a year earlier that he wanted to conduct a full audit of Senate operations but the only response had been a vague mention of an independent audit by a private-sector firm. Dye was angry. "They might exclude a lot of things like senators' travel. They'll be told to look at the safe areas."

Before it was over, the struggle to bring sound management to the Commons destroyed Jeanne Sauvé's health. She was appointed governor general in December 1983, but a serious illness, widely rumoured to be Hodgkin's Disease, nearly killed her. She was not sworn in until May 1984, and even then she was still puffy and frail from intensive cortisone treatment.

Silverman also suffered, especially from the dirty corridor campaign of anti-Semitism that accompanied his efforts to clean up the mess. In a 1980 *Globe and Mail* story, a reporter wrote, "The latest weapon is fairly low-level but persistent anti-Semitism that has been directed in the general direction of Mr. Silverman. The evidence of the campaign is found in corridor gossip that has surfaced from a number of different sources in recent weeks, as well as in anonymous letters that appear to be part of a carefully orchestrated campaign."

Certainly Silverman was never known for his patience, and his rebuilding of the administration from the ground up was often, out of necessity, severe and fast. But he and Sauvé did have their allies. Bev Koester was on their side. Many MPs actively supported their work, including Tories Jack Ellis, Bill Kempling, Scott Fennell, Gus Mitges, Joe Clark and Ray Hnatyshyn. The NDP's Mark Rose was another ally; so was the Liberals' Bob Kaplan. By Christmas 1983, when Sauvé left the House, close to death, her place was taken by her trusted ally Lloyd Francis, deputy Speaker since 1980. He remained Speaker until the fall of 1984, when Mulroney appointed him ambassador to Portugal and he was replaced by Toronto Conservative John Bosley.

Bosley, one of the few experienced Tory parliamentarians to speak French well enough to be a candidate for the job, arrived in the Speaker's office knowing the whole history of the administrative reform and committed to continuing it. This was bad news for the coterie of rabble-rousers who had made life miserable for his predecessors. Bosley, an Upper Canada College and Trinity College graduate from a Toronto Establishment family, was no more a good old boy than Sauvé and Francis, so he too was an unpopular Speaker.

Just a few weeks after taking office, Bosley again raised the price of parliamentary restaurant meals, a move that was like a red flag to the bulls. It didn't matter to them that the posh dining room had lost $5.4 million in 1983 - 84, up $300,000 from the year before. And this after tough economy measures from Sauvé, including replacing the green garbage bags with clear plastic ones, stamped "Property of the House of Commons" to discourage thefts of food and liquor. Most journalists who enjoyed the cheap meals at the restaurant were also hostile to Bosley.

A five-course dinner went up from $4.40 to $8.00, still half the cost of a similar meal off the Hill. Bosley also introduced a "light lunch" for $5.00. As one official said wryly, "This meant it only required one waitress to carry it." Heavily subsidized food made sense, Bosley said, when being an MP was a part-time job and members were paid accordingly. In 1985 they were making $70,000 a year, of which $18,000 was tax-free, and they could afford more realistic prices. It is still shocking to see how so many patrons of the Parliamentary Dining Room tip. Conveniently forgetting that the food is subsidized, they look at their bill of five bucks for a four-course lunch of fresh poached salmon, fresh shrimp, rare roast beef, fresh fruits, fine cheeses and French pastries and coffee, and figure that they can leave a chintzy 10 per cent tip, or 50 cents. Only the women MPs and senators, many of whom have once done their own share of waitressing, can be counted on to tip a decent amount.

To add insult to injury, the price of a haircut rose as well, from $1 to $6. Steve Paproski, the Tory MP from Edmonton North, still gets a discount, however; he pays the Commons barber a dollar a day to fluff up his hair.

Bosley's strike was seen as a declaration of war to the old gang who had hoped to slide happily back into yesteryear when an invitation from the Speaker to drop by his office meant a chance to play a little poker, not to endure a scolding about an unpaid restaurant bill. Bosley made matters worse in May 1985, when he supported the decision to cut off credit to all MPs who ate in the restaurant because several had refused for months to pay thousands of dollars' worth of food bills. He even took away control of the restaurants and cafeterias, Cloutier's last major empire, and turned them over to Silverman to run.

Like Jeanne Sauvé, John Bosley paid dearly for his support of Commons administrative reforms. He was trying to cope with his new job and also with a lopsided House, the likes of which no one had ever seen before. Mulroney's Tories had swept in with 211 seats and took up one whole side of the Chamber as well as each end of the Opposition side. The Liberals were reduced to a demoralized rump of 43 MPs ineptly led by John Turner. While the experienced Liberals who survived the election, including many former Cabinet ministers such as Donald Johnston, Lloyd Axworthy, André Ouellet, Bill Rompkey and even Jean Chrétien, slumped for months – even years – in their front-bench seats almost cata-tonic with shock, it was left to a small informal group of energetic young MPs to spearhead Opposition attacks. They included Sheila Copps, Don Boudria, John Nunziata, all elected in 1984, and Brian Tobin and Jean-Claude Malepart. Vociferous, offensive and unyielding, they soon became known as the Rat Pack.

They delighted in unnerving Bosley and claimed he was giving preference to Tory MPs during Question Period and House debate; at the same time, disgruntled Tories thought Bosley was far too tough on them, too nice to the Grits and all in all far too grand a personage in his style. They liked the idea of taking him down a peg or two.

These MPs scented Bosley's weakness: he enjoyed being Speaker. He worked hard at it. He loved the pomp and circumstance. He and his lively wife, Nicole, thrived on the entertaining that comes with the job and they did it well, trying out new chefs and new menus for special events in the Speaker's private dining room or in his office. But perhaps they did it too well; they grew too grand for the rest of their party, and this was to prove part of their undoing.

It is a long parliamentary tradition that a prime minister

"does something" for an ex-Speaker. Old Speakers are an embarrassment to have hanging around the House. Roland Michener, Speaker from 1957 to 1962, went to Government House. Marcel Lambert had to wait years for his reward, but eventually Brian Mulroney put him in the Canadian Transport Commission. Alan Macnaughton, Speaker from 1963 to 1966, went to the Senate; his successor, Lucien Lamoureux, Speaker from 1966 to 1974, went to Brussels as Canadian ambassador to Belgium. James Jerome, Speaker from 1974 to 1979, went to the Federal Court of Canada as associate chief justice. Jeanne Sauvé went to Government House. Lloyd Francis went to Portugal. So far, John Bosley has gone nowhere. He maintains his seat, as member for Don Valley West, with dignity and cheerfulness, but those who are close to him know that his heart was broken. Brian Mulroney will never forget that Bosley supported Joe Clark right to the end.

Art Silverman left his job as Administrator nearly a year before Bosley did, content that the House he loved as much as any member was finally running smoothly. Under Sauvé, Francis and Bosley he had installed and trained a professional management team. He had masterminded the creation of OASIS, the high-tech communications system that gave each MP and House official access to eighty-four television channels with all regular programming as well as channels devoted to everything from airline schedules to committee meetings. MPs now had an electronic library through OASIS; if they wanted to study their performance on "The Journal," or "Canada AM" the day before, all they had to do was dial it up.

Silverman left for an assistant deputy minister's job at Indian Affairs and Northern Development and later moved to head up the Ottawa office for the Western Diversification Program. At his farewell dinner in the Speaker's private dining room, a splendid affair for about forty people hosted by Bosley, Jeanne Sauvé, Bev Koester and Jack Ellis offered heartfelt tributes to this fearless administrator. Ellis, a big, rawboned man usually lumped with the party's dinosaurs, was moved to tears with remembrances of past kindnesses on Silverman's part. And Koester, with one of the city's toughest and most cynical audiences listening intently, read a passage from the Bible describing a man of integrity. Silverman, he said, was such a man.

When Vancouver South Tory John Fraser was elected to succeed Bosley at 1:48 a.m. on October 1, 1986, it was the first time the House had ever elected their own choice by secret ballot. Fraser inherited a very different House from the one John Bosley had tried to rule in 1984. This time members were chagrined, perhaps even slightly ashamed of their treatment of Bosley. Most felt John Fraser had been given a raw deal on the tuna affair and had taken a lot of blame that rightfully belonged on the shoulders of PMO staff. They knew Fraser had always been a Clark supporter and that Mulroney had left him to twist in the wind with the tuna scandal, denying that his office had ever been told about it as Fraser had claimed. The House was delighted to make up for Mulroney's abandonment of his minister. (Afterwards, PMO whisperers told everyone that the election of Fraser was in fact Mulroney's idea and he had done plenty of arm-twisting to make sure it happened.)

And finally, John Turner told the Rat Pack to cool it. They realized that their efforts to cheer on their side and undermine the government benches were backfiring. The public was fed up with their high jinks.

The House had also been sobered by the series of scandals that had permanently stained the record of the new Mulroney government. From September 4, 1984, to the day Fraser won his election just two years later, five Cabinet ministers, including Bob Coates, Fraser himself, Marcel Masse (who was soon reinstated), Suzanne Blais-Grenier and Sinclair Stevens resigned in major scandals. As these scandals erupted one after another, the Chamber had turned into a snakepit during Question Period. MPs now tried harder to be more civil.

The 1980s have been a turbulent decade for the Commons. It has been ruled by four very different Speakers. It has been hauled out of an administrative sewer into modern and efficient and honest management. It has seen members' services grow and become far more sophisticated. The House has also seen important reform of a different kind, reform of House rules and procedures, most of which were proposed in June 1985 by former Tory MP James McGrath, chairman of the Special Committee on Reform of the House of Commons. The purpose of this committee was to look at ways of giving the ordinary MP more power. As *Globe and Mail* reporter Susan Delacourt summed it up in December 1987, "The idea was to make Pierre Trudeau's nobodies into Brian Mulroney's somebodies."

In a submission to McGrath's committee, Calgary South Conservative MP Barbara Sparrow, who was first elected in 1984, described the plight of the new backbencher: "As a new Member of Parliament, I do not know the mechanics of this institution as well as some of my colleagues. I am absolutely amazed at how little input private members have into the formulation of legislation, policies and/or regulations. It appears to me that most of the time we are told what a minister will be announcing in 48 hours and we do not have access, any means to study or contribute or change the finished product. But members must go to their constituencies to explain and support the decision of the government. Sometimes this is extremely difficult."

The report recommended a new vehicle for delivering power to ordinary MPs, a streamlined permanent standing committee system, much like the powerful ones that exist in the United States Congress. Each of the twenty-nine newly structured standing committees and the ten special and legislative committees would be autonomous and operate with its own staff and budget. Mulroney and his Cabinet were pleased. Plenty of committees would keep his overflowing backbenches busy and, at the same time, there would be far too many committees for the tiny Opposition rumps to monitor.

The problem with this proposal, as keen observers saw

instantly, was that it created a new layer of bureaucracy in Ottawa, one sandwiched between the public service mandarins and the senior political staff in PMO and in Cabinet offices. The struggles to assert power would be tremendous, and committee chairmen, seeing their role as comparable to that of a U.S. Senate committee chairman, would soon be pushing Cabinet colleagues for power, staff and money. The other interesting question this proposal raised was financial: would Parliament grant funds to each of these committees? If funds were limited to a general overall budget, the scenario was clear: powerful committee chairmen would try to grab the lion's share of the money, leaving other committees, led by weaker, or at least less pushy, chairmen without the resources to do the job.

The results were a kind of typical Canadian compromise. The committees are independent and they do occasionally bare their fangs and snap and roar. But McGrath's group had hoped, for example, that the new committees would be granted the power, in the way U.S. Senate committees can, to reject senior appointments to Crown corporations, boards and agencies, and senior deputy ministerial appointments as well. So far, the committees have looked at only a handful of patronage appointments; few backbench Tories are going to incur Prime Minister Mulroney's legendary wrath by questioning his judgement. Certainly not if they ever want an appointment of their own.

No one can say committee members haven't been busy. Figures from the Speaker's office show a 59 per cent increase in the average number of hours committees meet. Recorded committee hours have doubled since 1985 and now run at about 2,400 hours a year. Before 1985, about 72 reports a year were submitted; now they are averaging 108.

Ultimately the committees do not have the power they sought. A good example of their impotence was the extensive report with 100 recommendations on new broadcast legislation submitted by the Committee on Culture and Communications. During its hearings, the committee had listened to 334 witnesses and spent $482,100, the second highest budget of any House committee in 1987. Not happy with the results, Communications Minister Flora MacDonald spent four months mulling over the report in 1987 before she told the committee to start all over again and deal with policy, not legislation. The report was mothballed indefinitely. Similarly, two years ago, Justice Committee members made 108 recommendations to expand access-to-information and privacy legislation; the government rejected 98 of them.

The only committee that seems to have been successful in establishing itself as a powerhouse is the House Finance Committee, run by Tory maverick Don Blenkarn. Blenkarn and his colleagues have not hesitated to thump the government over credit card interest rates, tax reform and rules governing financial institutions. But look at their budget. This committee has more money than any other; in 1987 it spent $720,000, and that was without any travelling costs. Just to give you an idea, the Committee on Elections, Privileges and Procedure, which does such things as grill the government about lobbyists and patronage appointments, spent $58,100. And the Public Accounts Committee, chaired by the former Liberal MP Aideen Nicholson (considered one of the best-briefed and hardest-working MPs in the House), spent $47,800 "to review the Public Accounts of Canada and the reports of the Auditor-General."

One committee that disgraced itself owing to the sheer ignorance and inexperience of its members was the Labour, Employment and Immigration Committee, chaired by Tory Fern Jourdenais. Jourdenais was later removed as chairman and replaced by Claude Lanthier, but he made the mistake of thinking a deputy minister was accountable to committees. Deputy ministers speak before committees to offer background information and to represent their ministers, but only ministers are accountable to parliamentary committees. Deputies merely carry out the will of their ministers, and if the committees don't like that will, they should take it up with the minister.

Not understanding this fundamental rule of parliamentary government, in June 1987 Jourdenais's committee displayed great hostility to Gaetan Lussier, the deputy minister of employment and immigration, accusing him of arrogance in the way he ran his department. They said he was lying, they told him he was uncooperative. On one occasion they even went so far as to demand he swear an oath confirming that he was telling the truth.

As the *Globe*'s Jeffrey Simpson pointed out in a column, the prime minister and Benoit Bouchard, the minister of employment and immigration at that time, should have defended Lussier. "If the MPs don't like the letters their constituents are receiving from the department, if they dislike the immigration and refugee policies of the government, if they think the government is costing the Conservatives political points, they're pointing fingers at the wrong guy."

Jim McGrath's report was a step backward with regard to administrative reform. The good old boys won. He recommended that new powers be given to an enlarged Board of Internal Economy; the Speaker was now to do, in many instances, what the board told him or her to do. The BOIE is now at the top of the House's organization chart with the Speaker just below. Nor would McGrath recommend that the Administrator be given independent power and report to the Speaker. His answer to that thorny question was that the Clerk should always retain ultimate authority. This means that a party hack could be appointed as Clerk and overrule the Administrator as he or she pleased. Today, canny observers of the House have said that slowly and surely the place is slipping back into its bad old ways, ways that suit the old boys' club very well.

After the Tories came back to Parliament in November 1988 with a smaller majority – from 211 seats to 168 – there was less need for committees to keep their backbenchers busy. The government also was trying to reduce the deficit and saw committee costs as one place that could use a little trimming, so they boiled down the number of permanent standing committees to fourteen. But the committees eliminated should make anyone stop and think: Communications and Culture, Consumer and Corporate Affairs, Human Rights, Environment and Forestry, Aboriginal Affairs and Multiculturalism. All touchy areas, all areas of great interest to many Canadians and therefore of great interest to the press. All areas that cause the government acute discomfort from time to time. But the Opposition hasn't squawked because they want the extra research money the government has promised them in exchange for the committee cutbacks.

This, then, is the world John Fraser runs. A complicated, expensive world. From all accounts he is having a good time. But some of the bitter legacy of the reform days still lingers. Last year, when Bev Koester took early retirement on the basis of ill health, no one at the House thought to honour him. Koester had been one of the most important forces in House reform and had turned the Clerk's empire into a professional legislative service, admired and copied throughout much of the democratic world. Jeanne Sauvé, however, did not forget her old comrade-in-arms. She invited Koester to put together a list of people she might invite to a farewell dinner in his honour at Government House. "How many should I ask?" he inquired of her office. They suggested a dozen. So Koester made up a list of five or six close friends from The Wars, who, with their spouses, would make up the party.

The next query from Rideau Hall was typical of Jeanne Sauvé. "Where are the names of your family?" she asked. Koester's startled response was that if he included his four children and their spouses he would not have any room for the Ottawa colleagues he wanted to have and, furthermore, he doubted that his children could attend given that they were scattered across the country.

"Give us their names and addresses," was the next response. So all the Koester kids were invited with their spouses and all of them came at their own expense, and it was a helluva party.

6

· ·

What's in It for Me?

In Toronto Terry Litt, who runs a company called Executive Accord, spends his days sitting at a computer terminal stuffed with a program of one thousand variables and juggling employment contract possibilities for powerful people. When a big corporation is romancing a new chief executive officer, Litt works out the CEO's pay, pension and perquisites, marrying this golf club with that private school, balancing this interest-free housing loan with that executive jet. He fine tunes the whole business right down to what happens to little Susie's Branksome Hall school fees if Daddy has a stroke or how long the Palm Beach condo will be available if Daddy gets bounced in a hostile takeover. Litt's vocabulary is salted with such phrases as "golden handshakes" and "golden handcuffs" and "golden parachutes." Come the merger or the bad biopsy, Litt's clients are prepared in signed triplicate.

But that's Toronto and we're talking about Ottawa. In Ottawa, except for a very few elected politicians and the governor general, there are not a lot of perks in any job and almost no push and shove in negotiations. Ottawa's perquisites are almost all intangible. There's the knowledge that you played a part in a major government decision. That you work daily with the most powerful people in the country. That you have access to insider information, such as when the government will shuffle some deputy ministers or when they'll call an election. That you're on a precedence list that guarantees you an automatic invitation to take part in state occasions like openings of Parliament, economic summits, Order of Canada ceremonies or royal visits.

Still, the powerful in Ottawa do have some perquisites to make life a little sweeter, and if a few quietly pad in a few extra items, who's to know?

The most blatant perk is the "$2,000 car allowance," listed primly every year in the public accounts books as part of the budget for the prime minister and every Cabinet minister as well as for the Opposition leader, the Commons Speaker and the Speaker of the Senate. The two grand has nothing to do with cars; it's a straight cash handout. It's nonaccountable (don't bother us with tacky receipts, please) and nontaxable (hardly worth the effort, don't you know). Not one politician would dare risk the wrath of his or her colleagues by campaigning to eliminate it.

On top of the car allowance come a car, a driver, a gas credit card, car phone and all maintenance, repairs and insurance free, courtesy of the Canadian taxpayer. When it's more convenient, these VIPs may use special extra allowances for taxis and car rentals. The $2,000 allowance is a holdover from the days when ministers did not have official limousines. Ever since, they have pretended not to notice that the allowance has not been abolished. One insider says that a parliamentary reform committee tried to get rid of the benefit a few years ago and was told to mind its own business.

People throw the word "limousine" around too casually in Ottawa. Limousines, especially stretch limousines, are generally considered vulgar, "very Toronto," and few people in the capital use them. Most, including Cabinet ministers, just make do with big cars, Oldsmobiles and Chryslers and Buicks.

Deputy ministers drive smaller versions from the same manu-facturers. The only people in Ottawa who may be said to cruise around in limos are the prime minister, and the governor general, who hates to fly and, in 1985 amid some criticism, equipped hers with a compact disc stereo for long journeys. The stretch white limos tourists see parked in front of hotels are usually there to ferry drunken teens home from grade twelve graduation parties.

If we begin our examination of Ottawa perks at the top of the table of precedence, we'll see that the governor general's job is almost all perks and very little pay. Originally, the pay was fabulous; the 1867 British North America Act set it at £10,000 a year, a fortune at that time, which is why so many titled Englishmen wanted the posting. But it never occurred to anyone that inflation might be a problem and the pay stayed the same until 1949, when the British devalued the pound. To protect the salary, the Canadian government set it at the value of the pound in 1949, which meant a salary of $48,666. Again, for the next thirty-seven years, no one thought to raise it. Most governors general had to dig grudgingly into their own pockets to do the job gracefully. Finally, in 1986, the salary went up to $70,000. It comes tax-free; the governor general is the only Canadian constitutionally exempt from income tax.

While $70,000 tax-free may seem munificent to most Canadians, it would barely cover the cost of Madame Sauvé's outfits from the Montreal couturiers Réal et Réal. Hers is a job that requires a lot of clothes, including many formal evening dresses, cocktail outfits, suits, hats and coats, and there is no clothing allowance. Mind you, her husband, Maurice, himself a former politician, is prosperous. A story surfaced in January 1989 that he made a great deal of money helping Paul Desmarais's Power Corporation find a buyer, Stone Container Corp. of Chicago, for its majority shares in Consolidated Bathurst. Sauvé had worked as executive vice-president of administration and public affairs at Consolidated Bathurst from 1968 to 1981.

The governor general has two impressive and splendidly furnished official residences, one surrounded by eighty-eight acres of landscaped gardens and lawns at Rideau Hall in Ottawa and the other in historic quarters at the Citadel in Quebec City. The vice-regal food, prepared by celebrated chef Michel Pourbaix, is delectable and it's free – not that Madame Sauvé eats much of it; her trim figure is no accident. Ed Lawrence, the greenhouse gardener at Rideau Hall, fills the rooms daily with luscious bouquets of fresh roses and lilies and freesias. An outdoor gardening staff keeps the grounds mani- cured to a fare-thee-well and the rosebeds groomed and blooming. The governor general is waited on hand and foot by devoted maids and butlers and footmen; uniformed aides- de-camp are always hovering nearby to help her greet people, escort her to her limousine, do little errands. Two heavily epauletted aides-de-camp, for example, escort her to the annual Press Gallery Dinner every year and have added to the hilarity of the evening by holding up sign boards instructing the audience to "groan" or "applaud."

Former governors general receive pensions of about $65,000 a year, help from experts at the National Archives for their papers and up to $75,000 to $80,000 annually for an office and staff to assist them in answering mail and writing their memoirs.

Madame Sauvé's top administrator, Léopold Amyot, ranks as a deputy minister and is the only senior public servant in Ottawa to rate what is, informally, an official residence. Aside from Rideau Hall, there are eleven grace-and-favour houses on the property, and they include everything from a pair of pretty brick semi-detached houses to flats over the garages. Rideau Hall staff – gardeners, chefs and other workers – live in most of them and pay nominal rents; some whispers are that these are as low as $50 a month. Two of the best houses are the enchanting little turreted gatehouse used for years by the governor general's personal secretary, and a rambling white cottage near the front of the property, used for many years by Donald McKinnon, the comptroller. Amyot enjoys the best accommodation, a spacious Georgian brick house, known modestly as The Cottage and tucked discreetly in a back corner of the property.

Esmond Butler, Amyot's predecessor who served a succession of six governors general, lived in The Cottage with his wife, Georgiana, paying very little for thirty-one years, making him, in effect, the highest-paid public servant in Ottawa. (Reliable sources say Butler was paying between $100 and $200 a month when he left in 1985.) After he left, the Sauvés tried to move into the house themselves because they craved the privacy it offered, but the effort was sandbagged in an interesting power play between Sauvé and Jean Pigott. Sauvé presented a well-argued case for moving to The Cottage and turning over all of Government House for state functions. Her officials pointed out that Sauvé was the Queen's representative in Canada and that she had vice-regal authority over the little kingdom. Not so, retorted Pigott. As chairman of the National Capital Commission, *she* was in charge of the residences on the property and the move was simply not on. The Sauvés stayed where they were.

Chef Pourbaix and his cooks feed an army of people every day, everyone from the Sauvés and senior administrators to the gardeners and security officers. What the staff pay for noshing is another secret; we know only that they buy tickets for the meals. Catty types around Ottawa used to say that some senior pennypinching staff members simply never ate at home; they even came to Rideau Hall for breakfast.

At the next rung down on the protocol ladder, Prime Minister Brian Mulroney enjoys the perks of his job perhaps more than any PM in recent history. His relish of all the little extras is amusingly portrayed in late Tory member Sean O'Sullivan's marvellous 1986 autobiography, *Both My Houses*.

"On August 31, 1978, I was on vacation from my studies at the seminary in Rome and was invited to lunch with Mulroney at the Mount Royal Club in Montreal," wrote O'Sullivan. "Brian was at his charming best; there was a staff of four looking after three of us in a private upstairs room. The table was so broad that when I asked for the salt, it couldn't be passed from one diner to another across the table but had to be carried around. Good wine flowed freely and at the end of the meal, I pulled out some Robert Burns cigars I'd bought in the States. When Mulroney saw them, he said, 'Get rid of those goddamned Presbyterian cigars,' and buzzed for the house cigars, explaining that they were Fidel Castro's special selection. Amazed by all this splendour around me, I finally said, 'Brian, I can't get over all this.' He turned to me and said, 'Sean, can you imagine if we'd won?' "

Well, he did win, and his $153,400 annual pay, more than double that of the governor general, is only the beginning of his perks. He has the use of two residences, 24 Sussex Drive and a large white clapboard country house with a guest cottage at Harrington Lake. Both come complete with maids, butlers, nannies, chefs, gardeners and go-fers galore. The National Gallery loans the residence and the Mulroneys' offices pictures and sculptures, while the government pays for art rentals from the Canada Council's Art Bank.

In 1984 Mulroney piously told Canadians that he would pay for his family's own food. After being hassled by the press about his boast during his first year in office, he announced that he had written a cheque to Revenue Canada for $4,000, the amount he calculated owing the government for six months of food. He gave the cheque to Revenue Canada because, his office explained, it was too difficult to sort out the private family groceries from food for entertaining purposes. The Mulroneys based the amount on Statistics Canada's assessment of $200 a week to feed a family of five. This worked out to about $3,000, and Mulroney's press office said he'd added another $1,000 of his own volition. That was back in 1985, and we haven't heard any more about his groceries since then.

Although Mulroney's predecessor, Pierre Trudeau, was notoriously cheap – his bodyguards stopped carrying cash because he was always borrowing from them – he was punctilious about distinguishing between private and public food and wine. If a personal friend was visiting, Trudeau would take wine out of his own wine cellar. If the visitor was on government business, the wine came from a government cellar.

Along with the free room and board, the prime minister gets free first-class air passes on all Canadian airlines, but since he usually flies in a Defence Department Challenger jet, he rarely uses them. This is one gift that goes on giving: the passes are good for a lifetime. Airline officials are loath to comment on whether spouses of prime ministers also have free passes, but according to reliable airline sources, if the wife of a former prime minister wants to fly with him, two first-class tickets are quietly issued.

Another perk for which the average Canadian traveller would be grateful is VIP courtesy service from Customs officials whenever the prime minister's family returns from trips. This means that no piece of luggage in the prime ministerial entourage, including the bags of aides, is ever searched, nor are any Customs declarations ever questioned.

The residents of 24 Sussex Drive enjoy all the same domestic services as the governor general. Ed Lawrence, the Government House gardener, provides flowers, and National Capital Commission gardeners keep the grounds spiffy. But even the NCC, with its staff landscape architects and its heritage gardening specialists who work on historic sites right across Canada, were not able to come up with a satisfactory plan for the prime minister's garden. In March 1989 the NCC admitted it had given a $27,000 contract to Toronto landscape architect Janet Rosenberg to count his shrubs and study his rose bushes.

The culinary talent of Kurt Waldele, the long-time chef at the National Arts Centre, is one of the more appealing perks *chez* Mulroney. Waldele is one of the two or three most gifted chefs in the city. When the Mulroneys moved to Ottawa in 1983, a friend, Pierrette Lucas, recommended they hire his services through the NAC catering arm. Originally, the Mulroneys had hoped to hire him as their personal chef at

24 Sussex. Mulroney's former heavy-handed aide Fred Doucet had the gall to ask NAC director general Donald MacSween to let 24 Sussex have Waldele on permanent loan, all the while keeping the chef on the NAC payroll. The intention was to reduce payroll costs at PMO, which are always scrutinized eagerly by the press. Sources close to MacSween say he bravely refused, but mindful of his own skin, looked the other way every time his chef's services were required.

While Waldele eventually found the Mulroneys a talented young chef, François Martin, from his own staff, he steps in himself as executive chef on great occasions, whether they are in Ottawa or in other Canadian cities. Waldele pretests most meals for Mila Mulroney in his own private dining room at the National Arts Centre. Before a royal visit to, say, Halifax, Waldele will fly in well ahead of time, loaded with meticulously packed cartons of silver and china reserved specially for these occasions. He'll import little luxuries local grocery stores might not carry – rare mushrooms or wine vinegars or fresh herbs. Understanding how easy it is to bruise another chef's ego, Waldele always has a tactful preliminary discussion with the resident executive chef to work out the menu and the responsibilities. He also looks after smaller private celebrations; the christening of baby Nicholas, for example, or a prime ministerial birthday.

But his protégé, François Martin, quit in June 1989, telling Le Devoir's Michel Vastel that since the 1988 election, 24 Sussex had become "bigger, fatter, more chic."

A new major domo arrived to oversee household operations, he disclosed, as well as a new maître d'hotel whose job was simply to do the flowers. Once proud of being part of their team, and happy to work the fifteen-hour days the job demanded, Martin quit in disgust and became the first staff member to talk publicly about life at 24 Sussex Drive.

When the prime minister steps down, his indexed pension, like any MP's, will be based on his best-earning six years in the House, and he will be able to start collecting it immediately, because as long as they have served at least six years there is no minimum age for MPs to start collecting their pensions.

It is a sweet deal, one designed by a committee of MPs for themselves. It means that a politician can retire at forty or forty-five and start collecting pension benefits right away instead of waiting, as most plans require, until he or she is sixty or sixty-five. This is a particularly sweet deal for former MPs who go on to federal patronage appointments like judgeships. For instance, when Trudeau appointed former justice minister Mark McGuigan to the federal court, McGuigan had served sixteen years in Parliament, so he immediately started getting his full pension of 75 per cent of his best six years' earnings. He also started receiving his judge's salary and building up new pension credits on that. His total pay package today is more than $200,000.

MPs who have served less than fifteen years have their pensions adjusted according to the years they've been in the House, and those who have been there fewer than six years receive no pension but do get six months' severance pay. That's one reason, it is widely believed, that Richard Grisé, former Tory MP for Chambly, was hanging on to his parliamentary seat even after pleading guilty to fraud in 1989 – he wanted his pension. He was persuaded to resign and apologize instead.

When Pierre Trudeau left office in 1984, he received a $67,000 annual indexed pension. He also collects the old age pension plus a hefty salary estimated to be in the $300,000-range from Heenan Blaikie, his Montreal law firm. Like Trudeau, when Mulroney leaves office he will receive archival and office help, as well as security services, as long as he needs or wants them.

Guy Charbonneau, currently Speaker of the Senate, is entitled to a senator's basic salary of $67,600, including a tax-free allowance of $9,300. His Speaker's pay adds another $28,100 for a total pay package of $95,700. Unlike the House Speaker, Mr. Charbonneau, a powerful Quebec businessman who was appointed by Joe Clark in 1979 as a concession to Brian Mulroney, is allowed to work outside Parliament and he sits on many boards.

Like all other senators, the Speaker receives free first-class air travel passes for up to sixty-four trips a year, and a rail pass for unlimited travel. His offices are among the most sumptuous on Parliament Hill, and Senate staff serve him royally.

John Fraser, Speaker of the House, does considerably better than Charbonneau in the perks sweepstakes. Along with his job come two residences. One, next to his offices in the House, is a tiny but charming apartment with a bathroom, sitting room and bedroom. The only drawback is the lack of a kitchen; his food has to come from the Parliamentary Dining Room. The second residence is at Kingsmere, Mackenzie King's summer home in the Gatineau Hills. Kingsmere was allowed to deteriorate badly over the years until John Bosley moved in and the Official Residences Council decided it needed a major renovation. Before Bosley, most Speakers used it as a rough-and-ready weekend place. The caretakers were always in despair because valuable or historic pieces of furniture routinely went missing, often when the Speaker's teenage children needed to furnish a college apartment. Now the house is beautifully renovated. Enlarged and decorated with antiques, Kingsmere was a job society decorator Giovanni Mowinckel did not quite finish before he fled to Italy in the winter of 1987.

The House Speaker's salary is $126,500, made up of his MP's salary of $80,000 in pay and tax-free allowances and the Speaker's additional stipend of $46,500. The Speaker's role has a strongly ceremonial aspect, with a uniformed parade each day into the House, and Fraser is treated accordingly. A maître d'hôtel and two personal valets wait on him. The Speaker does so much entertaining that he receives extremely generous entertainment allowances. A Speaker's spouse may also entertain in the House, using the Speaker's private dining room and the chef and staff from the parliamentary restaurant. The reason all this entertaining goes on in the Speaker's large and luxurious office quarters goes back to the parliamentary tradition of the Speaker's impartiality. It would be unseemly to be seen in the restaurant noshing with partisan members.

Anyone who has ever lost his or her perks suddenly, someone like a fired Cabinet minister or a minister who takes a drubbing in an election, admits the shock is dreadful. Each little thing underlines the ignominy of defeat. Having to carry your own bags at the airport. Driving your own car. Arriving at a hotel and not only getting no view and no terrycloth robe but wondering where the basket of fruit and the bottle of wine went. Researching your own questions for Question Period. Writing your own speeches.

While no one else in Cabinet gets the perks of the prime minister or Speaker, ministers don't fare badly. The pay package is $126,500, which includes a tax-free allowance of $20,000. Most prized by ministers and their spouses is the driver who appears almost instantly at a new Cabinet minister's front door. No more hunting for parking spots, no more waiting for taxis. "Best of all," one minister's wife says, "these guys have the best gossip in town." What else do they have to do as their big cars idle hour after hour in front of the West Door of the Commons? No minister in Ottawa can keep an affair with his stunning press assistant a secret, or a drunken toot in Hull quiet. These drivers know when a shuffle is coming, when a minister is in trouble, when a new star is on the rise. They know when the boss is mad and why. They know if he or she is spending too much money, has trouble at home, is worried about a delinquent child, or is waiting for the results of hospital tests.

They know everything but they are infuriatingly discreet except with each other. Still, every once in a while a story slips out. Everyone in Ottawa knew, for example, when one of Monique Bégin's drivers quit. One day the former Liberal health minister was abandoned by her driver halfway between Ottawa and Montreal. Completely fed up with her continual complaining and abuse, he suddenly snapped, stopped the car, got out and crossed the highway to hitchhike home to Ottawa.

As a sign that they've arrived in the big time, new Cabinet ministers first buy a new car, usually from a favourite car dealer in their riding, then decorate their offices. They can spend as much as they like on decor because few people ever question their bills. They can buy furniture from any store they like and hire any decorator they please. When the new Tory ministers came in in 1984, they couldn't wait to scrub away the spoor of the hated Grits, and their decorators had a field day. Some of the biggest spenders included Robert Coates, who blew $143,000 on his National Defence offices; Communications Minister Marcel Masse, who spent $106,000; Treasury Board President Robert de Cotret, who spent $59,000; Finance Minister Michael Wilson, who spent $46,000; and Barbara McDougall, who was then minister of state for finance, who spent $40,000.

Gordon Osbaldeston wrings his hands over the cars and the decorating because he knows reporters love to get their hands on such bills. In the June 1988 issue of *Policy Options*, the former Clerk of the Privy Council published a wise and witty piece called "Dear Minister: An open letter to an old friend who has just been appointed to the federal cabinet," and among his nuggets of good advice are the following:

> I hope there is no need to tell you to make certain that your personal affairs are in order, and that you are clear of all real/perceived conflicts of interest. And for heaven's sake, don't redecorate your office or order a new car – you will read about the cost in tomorrow's newspaper! By the way, never authorize a purchase unless you know the cost. Otherwise you may find some admiring aide has ordered you a $5,000 desk – try explaining that to your constituents! Just remember, people believe that if you show common sense in small matters, you will probably act sensibly when it comes to big issues.

This sage advice obviously did not reach four ministers who

decided they needed to redecorate after the 1988 election. One was Environment Minister Lucien Bouchard, whose plans included an $8,000 custom-made bookcase. After his office was called by a reporter about the expenses, Bouchard cancelled the order and equipped himself with cheap bookcases from the Swedish furniture store IKEA instead. The publicity about his frugality was positive and IKEA was delighted – until the timing of the order was revealed.

Ministers travel in style, although over the last five years journalists have developed a way of souring this pleasure too, as they rake through old hotel bills and Visa receipts, obtained under access to information law. Frequently ministers fly on government Challenger jets, but when they travel on commercial airlines, it's always first class.

One senior official in Ottawa who routinely refuses to fly first class is auditor general Ken Dye, who makes a great point, as he puts it, of "flying in the back of the bus." He makes sure his officials do too. One way canny bureaucrats wiggle around this kind of stricture from a boss like Dye is to delay booking their flights until the last minute; that way, surprise surprise, the only seats left are first-class.

Unlike MPs or bureaucrats who have to stay at hotels that offer government rates, ministers may stay in any hotel they choose. According to one former Liberal minister, ministerial aides usually get large cash advances before any major trip that are used to pay expenses not covered by credit cards or billing. In his government an advance of $10,000 before a major trip overseas was not uncommon. This money was always nonaccountable; in other words, the minister did not have to send in receipts for it. A crooked minister could use it for anything he or she liked – a mortgage payment, a fling at a slot machine, a little jewellery for the wife. Eventually, the advance would show up in the minister's overall accounts, but no one would ever ask for receipts or a break-down of expenses.

While ordinary MPs get a limited number of first-class trips to their ridings and to other parts of Canada for themselves and members of their families, Cabinet ministers enjoy first-class air passes for unlimited travel. If they want to take their spouses along, no one bats an eye. About six weeks after the 1984 election, Air Canada cancelled the ministerial passes for the defeated Liberals, but Canadian Pacific Airlines allowed them to go on using their passes until the new year. This enabled one enterprising Grit, former secretary of state John Roberts, to travel most of the way to China and the Soviet Union and back again before his pass ran out.

According to former senior pilots with the government's executive flight service, the Prime Minister's Office has found a way to get staff on desirable trips, especially overseas; they simply let them travel on the backup aircraft that always follows the prime minister's plane. Journalists never look at the passenger flight manifests filed with the backup plane because they were led to believe that the prime minister cancelled his backup plane after its existence was discovered in June 1985. Not at all. The day after Mulroney's press secretary, Bill Fox, announced that the practice of having a jet follow the PM around in case his plane was held up for any reason was "crazy" and would be discontinued, a backup plane was ordered as usual but this time the transport document shows the following instructions: "Do *not*, *not* tell the press." These backup planes are never more than a few minutes away from the prime minister's plane, although they often take off and land from different airports. The Defence Department admits they exist all right, but it calls them "training flights."

Government politicians who do not make it to Cabinet fight hard for the posts that bring added pay and perks. The deputy Speaker, for example, gets an extra $23,300. The government whip will find an extra $12,100 in his or her salary each year, while parliamentary secretaries and deputy chairmen of the Committee of the Whole each get an extra $9,700 and the assistant government whip can add an extra $6,900 to his or her pay.

The salary of the Leader of Her Majesty's Loyal Opposition went up to $126,000 in 1989, and he too gets an official residence. The House of Commons pays for Stornoway's chef and other servants including maids, a gardener and a driver for Turner's government car. A 1981 act of Parliament also allows the Opposition leader to have a summer residence, but so far no one has ever asked for it. Given the mood of Canadian taxpayers these days, no one would dare.

Some of Turner's perks have come, albeit unwillingly, from his party. The Liberals subsidized his office by $1 million a year, an amount needed to cover the costs of image consultants like Gabor Apor and Henry Comor, and to boost the salaries of the revolving door of staffers. Most of Turner's staff earn higher salaries than the political aides working in Mulroney's office. The extra $1 million also covered the $3,000 monthly rent on Geills Turner's Toronto apartment; preferring to live in Toronto, she comes to Stornoway only for family holidays like Christmas or Easter or for occasional party functions held at the house. Simple arithmetic shows that the $1 million poured into the leader's office each year since 1984, which is over and above the amount allocated by the House, roughly adds up to the Liberal party's debt, which, at the beginning of 1989, stands at about $5 million. "If we weren't subsidizing Turner's office, we wouldn't be in debt," groaned one party fundraiser who quit in disgust.

Some Opposition MPs have a chance to make a supplementary income from the House; the leader of the NDP, for example, earns $106,000 and gets a driver and car plus the $2,000 car allowance, but he does not get a house. Herb Gray, the Liberal house leader, makes an extra $22,400, while the NDP house leader, Nelson Riis, earns an extra $9,600 a year.

Ordinary MPs have to content themselves with the subsidized food, the messengers who bring bottles from the House liquor store and pick up dry cleaning from the House cleaners, the gym and masseur, the tailor shop, the free picture framing. "I learned to tip the guy in the print shop with a bottle every December so he'd do my 'Householder' [the MP's quarterly newsletter to constituents] before anyone else's; that way I'd be sure to have it out before Christmas," said one canny former MP who estimates this little trick cost him a case of sherry over his parliamentary career.

After every election, new MPs receive the Manual of Allowances and Services from House Administrator Ed Riedel, which outlines in meticulous detail every service and perquisite to which they are entitled. MPs have come a long way since the 1960s, when two members shared an office and a secretary. Today, while they bellyache about the "services" they lost in the reform, they're looked after like little potentates. Here is just a partial list:

- The richest government pensions available, fully indexed to the cost of living.

- The ability to give short-term contracts from his or her office budget to researchers and other people outside House or constituency staff, "to make studies or otherwise advise the Member with respect to the Member's official duties." This is the privilege that led to RCMP charges in late 1988 against two Quebec Tories, Richard Grisé and Edouard Desrosiers, who were convicted of giving out fraudulent House of Commons contracts to people in their ridings who endorsed the Commons cheques and gave the cash back to the MPs for a consideration of $100 or so per cheque.

- Generous allowances for staff both in the House and back in the riding, enough to give each MP a legislative assistant, another junior assistant and two secretaries in Ottawa as well as a constituency assistant and secretary in the riding. Each MP has an annual budget of about $130,000 for running his or her offices (at least $26,000 of which must be applied to riding office salaries), with an extra $12,000 to rent an office and cover some expenses in the riding. MPs also receive travel allowances for getting around in their constituencies, and those with very large rural ridings get up to $20,600 a year to help them cover their territory.

- Well-equipped offices, both in Ottawa and in the riding. In Ottawa, each MP gets two colour television sets, each with a converter; one video cassette recorder; a personal computer and laser printer; a word processor; three electric typewriters (two with memory, one without); a fax machine; a photocopier; two calculators; four full-service telephone sets as well as a cellular phone and telephone answering equipment; ten thousand sheets of thermo-engraved writing paper a year, not to mention engraved cards, pads and other stationery items. Riding offices are similarly equipped and new MPs may spend up to $5,000 for new furniture; re-elected members may spend $3,000.

- Free parking on the Hill.

- Free long-distance telephone privileges, with a coded government card.

- Free French lessons in Ottawa and free French immersion courses in Saint-Jean, Quebec, for members and their spouses with all expenses paid.

- Free VIA Rail passes for each member of their families. Each MP's child gets his or her personal VIA card.

The Commons itself offers all kinds of support for members, especially for research. It was not until 1969 that the government decided to pay for House research staff for Opposition parties; a year later it decided that it too, as the governing party, deserved a research budget. Today the budget is worked out on a proportional basis decided by the number of elected members per party. In the 1988-89 fiscal year the Tories' research budget in the House was $1,008,600, while the Liberals received $674,200 and the NDP made do with $461,400.

These researchers are in addition to an army of professional economists, political scientists, statisticians and other professionals provided by the research branch of the Library of Parliament for MPs and senators. The library researchers are occasionally grossly misused by parliamentarians. Take the MP whose staff put in a "most urgent" request for any and all information available anywhere on "nail care." Library staff scrambled, poring through every possible book and periodical index, borrowing obscure pamphlets through interlibrary loan. Hardened as they are to misbehaving members, even they were shocked to discover the research was for an MP's wife, who was writing a paper for her cosmetics course at a local community college. Other researchers have slaved over papers on obscure subjects only to realize that they were doing high school and university term papers for members' and senators' kids. Cabinet ministers have been known to pull the same stunt with bureaucratic staff.

Few can surpass the gall of former Winnipeg New Democrat David Orlikow for abusing the perquisites of office. The Parliamentary Library is required to obtain any book requested by an MP or senator; if it doesn't have the book somewhere in its stacks, staff either borrow it through interlibrary loan or, failing that, buy it. Every week, year after year after year, Orlikow appeared in the library with a list of books he wanted to read immediately, and almost all these books were crime fiction. Often his lists were simply scissored out of the weekly *New York Times* Book Review section or out of Canadian newspaper lists, with little pencilled ticks beside the ones he wanted. Not surprisingly, the library did not have these new books, so the librarians gritted their teeth and ordered them. Their estimate of the cost of providing Orlikow with bedtime reading? Between $500 and $800 a month. Although Orlikow returned the forty or so books he borrowed each month, the library does not have the room to store commercial fiction, so it would have to turn the books over to a private company that gets rid of surplus books.

Some perks and privileges don't appear in Ed Riedel's thick book of services; among them are the junkets, the understood rewards of the gentlemen's club on the Hill. Kosher trips are organized and *paid for* by the House's Parliamentary Relations Secretariat, run by Ian Imrie. Only certain approved associations fall into his orbit and they include interparliamentary associations between Canada and Japan, France and the

United States as well as the Inter-Parliamentary Union (known as the IPU), a Canadian NATO group, the Commonwealth Parliamentary Association, the International Association of French-Speaking Parliamentarians, and the Canada-Europe Parliamentary Association. Finally, there are three officially sanctioned friendship groups: Canada-Italy, Canada-Germany and Canada-Israel. Party whips are the officials responsible for doling out legitimate junkets; rebel MPs who have somehow displeased their leaders will freeze in hell before they get one.

Trips that are paid for by their sponsors instead of by the secretariat are usually questionable. One has to think only of outfits like the Canada-Korea Friendship Society, which has encouraged trips back and forth between Canada and South Korea for years. The keenest spark behind this group was always its founder, Robert Coates, who was also a powerful mover behind Canada-Taiwan trips and Canada-South Africa trips and Canada-Argentina trips. Anywhere you could find a friendly right-wing government anxious for a little credibility by rubbing up against Canadian parliamentarians, there you'd find Bob Coates.

He was not the only one. With him on junkets to Taiwan would be Otto Jelinek. Coates and Jelinek were wild when the federal government issued a deportation order in February 1986 against one Patrick Chang, Taiwan's top trade representative in Canada. CSIS had had its beady eye on Chang for some time and the deportation order came directly from Cabinet and the prime minister, who ordered Walter McLean, then the junior immigration minister, to administer it.

According to immigration sources, the deportation order was linked to a junket Chang had arranged for a group of MPs and senators to Taiwan in late 1985. Mr. McLean's action did not sit well with Chang's friends, Bob Coates and Otto Jelinek, who led a delegation of furious Tory MPs to protest the decision, a delegation that lobbied hard for better trade relations with Taiwan.

A good example of why junketing gets a bad name turned

up in the fall of 1985, when two pro-Korean Cabinet ministers, Sinclair Stevens and James Kelleher, offended senior
Japanese auto executives and trade negotiators who were
complaining that Korea was getting preferential tariff treatment for its automobiles. Japanese negotiators felt, and justifiably so, that Korean junket diplomacy had given Korean
automaker Hyundai an unfair advantage, but when they complained to Stevens and Kelleher they were rudely rebuffed.

Coates' free trips to Korea over several years were no secret,
nor was his love of the good life in Seoul with the first-class
treatment he received at the Shilla Hotel, and at various *kesing*
parties, complete with singsongs, lengthy Johnny Walker
toasts and beautiful girls who fed him with chopsticks.

Unquestionably, Bob Coates was the junket king of Parliament. Here is just a partial list of free trips he took during his
time in the House:

1966 – trips to the United Nations in New York.

1971 – Commonwealth Parliamentary Conference in Kuala
Lumpur, Malaysia.

1974 – European Parliamentary Group Conference in
France and Brussels.

1975 – Taiwan, as a guest of the Taiwan government.

1976 – NATO meetings in Brussels and in Williamsburg,
Virginia.

1978 – South Africa, as a guest of the South African government.

1979 – Romania with Brian Mulroney, president of Iron
Ore of Canada, and Mulroney crony Patrick MacAdam, as a
guest of the Romanian government.

1979 – Korea, representing Canada at the funeral of slain
president Park Chung-hee. (Coates founded the Canada-
Korea Friendship Society this year.)

1980 – Bermuda.

1980 – Iraq, with his executive assistant, Rick Logan, as
guests of the Iraqi government.

1981 – West Germany, a twelve-day trip for Tory MPs, paid

for by the West German government. Patrick MacAdam also went along.

1981 – Korea, leading a group of parliamentarians who belonged to the Canada-Korea Friendship Society.

1982 – Argentina, with three other parliamentarians, as guests of the Argentine government.

1982 – Korea, with a group of MPs as guests of the Korean government.

1983 – Korea, to attend the opening of the new Candu reactor, as a guest of the Korean government.

1983 – Taiwan, along with Otto Jelinek and six other parliamentarians who belonged to the Canada-Taiwan friendship association, as guests of the Taiwan government.

Two-week junkets to South Africa paid for by interests in that country, which often included wives, have been taken over the years by several Tory parliamentarians. They included Lloyd Crouse (now lieutenant governor of Nova Scotia), Heath Macquarrie, Dan McKenzie, Jake Epp (who went with a Prayer Breakfast Group paid for by the South African government), John Crosbie (who went as a guest of the South African Foundation, a business group closely connected to the South African government), Robert Wenman, Ronald Stewart, John Gamble and William Vankoughnet.

Winnipeg MP Dan McKenzie came back from a 1982 junket to enrage the Canadian black community with his observation that the blacks in South Africa could not keep up intellectually with whites but that they made "great mechanics."

It would be wrong to suggest that the only parliamentarians who take freebies are Tories. The Liberals' Marcel Prud'homme, a strong supporter of Arab causes and the PLO (he took Yasser Arafat's brother to the 1986 Liberal leadership review convention), never turns down an Arab-sponsored trip to the Middle East, and many Liberal MPs have visited Israel as guests of the Canada-Israel Committee.

Ottawa mandarins enjoy a few perquisites of power too, but none that can compare with those of top parliamentarians.

Deputy ministers get cars worth up to $20,000 (a size or two down from ministers' cars), drivers and car phones. They are permitted first-class travel and accommodation. They rate big corner offices with private bathrooms; they also may rent, at government expense, pictures and sculptures from the Art Bank. Workaholic executive assistants, dressed for success in Harry Rosen's finest, run around behind them, carrying their briefing books. Their rank entitles them to invitations to important government functions and celebrations where they can be sure of good tables, and they may also use the Parliamentary Dining Room.

The deputy minister of transport and the deputy minister of employment and immigration run vast bureaucracies that stretch across the country. Each department is enormously complicated, each has immense discretionary spending powers. Each must function in both official languages; in fact, employment and immigration must also serve client groups in a wide array of languages.

Compare the DM's pay and perks to that of Brian King, the CEO of Connaught BioSciences, a federal Crown corporation until the Tories privatized it. In 1989 Connaught was worth about $700 million, and it earned revenues of $200 million in 1987-88. King's salary in 1987-88 was a not ungenerous $468,000. His severance deal put this amount in the shade. Estimates of King's golden parachute, which included getting three years' salary on top of his stock options, were in the area of $5 million.

But deputies don't complain about their pay because they know that most of them make more money than their bosses, the Cabinet ministers. Today, a DM 3, the top rank of deputy, earns about $150,000 a year, almost as much as the prime minister. A DM 2 makes up to $135,000, and a DM 1 makes up to $125,000. Cabinet ministers tend to forget their own perks when they regard with envy the size of their deputies' pay cheques.

Deputies are allowed to go on paying into their pensions if they leave the public service early. Under Section 12.1 of the

Public Service Act, deputies with at least ten years' public service – and it doesn't have to be all at the deputy level – may go on kicking in pension money after they leave government until they turn sixty. Treasury Board figures out how much of their phantom salary they would be paying into a pension fund if they had stayed, and the deputy contributes this amount from his salary in his new private sector perch.

Public servants are not overpaid and neither are politicians. Many years ago, politics was the preserve of wealthy men who could afford to leave their businesses to go to Ottawa part of the year. Today, politics is regarded as a profession open to any capable Canadian, rich or poor. But it is no longer, in any sense, a part-time job, and today's MPs have a tough time of it. Their ridings expect them to maintain homes there, preferably to live there, certainly to support local causes and charities. But to maintain any kind of normal family life, politicians need their families with them in Ottawa. Few can afford to maintain two homes, so keep tiny apartments either in Ottawa or in their constituencies or board with relatives. The only ones who do it gracefully are those who have independent incomes.

Before we feel too sorry for public servants and politicians, we should remember that the biggest perk they enjoy is the sense of mattering, of making a difference for other Canadians. Few of us can say that. One former deputy who hied himself off to a richly paid job in the private sector a few years ago said it was just this privilege he would miss more than anything. "Yes, I'll be making a lot of money. But I still have to look at myself in the mirror every morning and I have to like the person I see. I'm not sure I will." Last we heard, he was hankering for Ottawa, having found among his new colleagues little sense that they mattered, or that they could make a difference.

PART THREE

POWER BROKERS

7

....

Men in Navy Blue Coats

They are the princes of the city, these mandarins. Quiet, self-effacing, soberly dressed men in navy single-breasted suits, white shirts and gleaming black Oxfords, they run this odd little town. "If I might suggest, Minister . . . ," they murmur gently in the ear of the flushed politician, about to lose his temper at a committee hearing. And under their breaths, their bland faces betraying nothing, they are muttering to themselves, "Must get this idiot under control, get him out of here, get someone to take him back to his office while I clear up this mess."

You see them flashing through the city in their discreet navy or black cars with the telltale reading lamps winking in the back window so they can scan their briefing books, their poker-faced drivers parking insolently on sidewalks or blocking entrances to let their bosses out.

Despite a much-touted and half-hearted effort to include women, most of them are men. They are at work by 7, most of them, and stay there until 9 or 10 or midnight and they do this, most of them, seven days a week. They run vast government departments but their main job is not to watch the bottom line but to keep their ministers out of trouble. To appreciate the difficulty of the job, one has only to think of disgraced ministers such as Bob Coates, Michel Coté, André Bissonnette and Sinclair Stevens. It's even harder when, as sometimes happens, a minister and a deputy hate each other's guts.

What exactly is a mandarin? Usually someone ranked at the assistant deputy minister level and up, although more finicky types would insist one should start no lower than associate deputy minister. The 1989 *Parliamentary Guide* lists 203 men and women ranked at the associate deputy minister level and up but, strictly speaking, many of these do not count.

You have to set aside the patronage appointees who head porkbarrel outfits like regional development giveaway programs. One example is former provincial Tory minister Leo Bernier, put in charge of the Northern Ontario Development Advisory Board, a group of former Tory politicians. Or John Van Zutphen, the Cape Breton contractor who recently stepped down as chairman of Enterprise Cape Breton, another giveaway program, which last year threw money at Vancouver stock promoters and ship wreckers who had never wrecked a ship. Van Zutphen courted successful grant winners in Cape Breton to build their new facilities for them.

Nor do you count a different kind of patronage appointee, former politicians and bagmen named to head important federal agencies. Erik Neilsen, the former Yukon MP and deputy prime minister who now runs the National Transportation Agency, and former Tory MP Jean Pigott, chairman of the National Capital Commission, have the rank and the perks of deputies, but they are not considered part of the mandarinate.

There are two circles in Ottawa's mandarinate, a broad outer ring that includes the bureaucrats who run cultural, scientific or education agencies, people like the National Gallery's Shirley Thomson or Geraldine Kenney-Wallace, head of the Science Council of Canada, or Paule Leduc, who is in charge of the Social Sciences and Humanities Research Council. Added to these are other distinguished Canadians, many of them public servants who have worked their way up through the ranks of government departments, who now run boards and commissions. A few examples include Judith Maxwell, the head of the Economic Council of Canada, John Grace, the Privacy Commissioner, Max Yalden, the Human Rights Commissioner, Auditor General Kenneth Dye, CBC President Pierre Juneau, and Inger Hansen, the Freedom of Information Commissioner. Another group that belongs in this circle are senior House of Commons and Senate officials and top ambassadorial appointments like Derek Burney in Washington or Donald Macdonald in London.

None of these players is part of the tight inner circle of "real" deputy ministers. That circle is made up of about thirty-five people who run government departments. Even here there is a pecking order. The handful of men who run PCO, FPRO, Finance, External Affairs, Treasury Board and Justice matter most. Although technically only PCO, FPRO and Treasury Board are powerful "central agencies," the others are considered kissing cousins. External is thought of as a central agency because of its clout; in truth, it is very much a department and in fact is known around Ottawa simply as The Department. If you have to ask "What department?" you're immediately filed away as an outsider. Technically, the Public Service Commission is a central agency, but everyone forgets about it because it has lost so much of its power to Treasury Board and PCO. Bank of Canada Governor John Crow is also considered, by tradition, to belong to the inner circle.

Central agencies like PCO and Treasury Board are important because they make the rules for all the other departments. These are the places where the action is, where major policy is formulated, where the money gets allocated, where the high flyers work. "Line departments," on the other hand, are the drudge departments, slaveships like Indian Affairs and Northern Development, Energy, Mines and Resources, Employment and Immigration, Statistics Canada or Public Works, usually very large ministries with hundreds of programs. They are administratively a challenge, and they are a necessary part of any mandarin's training on the way up, but they're not places he'll stay if he can help it. Unless they're in trouble, line departments do not usually operate close to PMO and PCO.

York University history professor Jack Granatstein is the reigning Canadian expert on the deputy ministers of the so-called golden age of public service, a period he dates between 1935 and 1957, when men like the legendary O.D. Skelton, Clifford Clark and Graham Towers founded a small, efficient and brilliant senior mandarinate. During those years, the white, Anglo-Saxon males who ran the public service tended to come from Queen's University, with a few from the University of Toronto and McGill and the odd upstart from the University of Manitoba or the University of British Columbia. Many went to Oxford as Rhodes Scholars; they tended to start their careers at External Affairs or Finance or the Bank of Canada. Even the rare French-Canadian who made it in those golden days often polished his resumé with a term at Oxford. The only woman who rose to senior rank during that period was Phyllis Turner, mother of Liberal Leader John Turner. Only one Jew, the Bank of Canada's Louis Rasminsky, and one Catholic, John Deutsch, were in the charmed circle.

"They were," writes Granatstein, "a remarkable group, a collection of friends and colleagues who looked, sounded, and spoke alike; lived close together; and to a surprising extent, socialized with each other during the work week and on vacations. Their backgrounds were more disparate than many believe, though their education and training were noticeably similar. They were all generalists recruited into the public service because of their brains and their non-specialized approach, rather than for their skills in particular disciplines."

Although there have been many changes in today's mandarinate, if you look at the backgrounds of some of the most powerful mandarins you will find they share a surprising number of the same credentials that distinguished previous generations. PCO Clerk Paul Tellier, a lawyer, went to Oxford. Among his possible successors, so did deputy minister of justice John Tait, a lawyer and a Rhodes Scholar, as did Bank of Canada Governor John Crow, and deputy minister of consumer and corporate affairs Ian Clark, a Rhodes Scholar who added a Master's degree from Harvard to his Oxford Ph.D.

In the last generation of mandarins, an Oxford degree is no longer the sole imprimatur. Ottawa has grudgingly accepted the fact that American and French degrees, so long as they are from the best schools, will do; the important thing is to get a little out-of-Canada academic polish. Fred Gorbet has a Ph.D. from Duke University and Norman Spector has one from Columbia. A few success stories have no degrees at all.

The handful of women at the top today all have outstanding educational backgrounds. There are twenty-two women in Ottawa at associate deputy level or above; only eight are in that inner circle of deputy ministers. Of these eight, four – External Affairs' Sylvia Ostry, PCO's Geneviève Sainte-Marie, Huguette Labelle, the chairman of the Public Service Commission, and Janet Smith, the deputy at Privatization – have doctorates and another, Maureen Law, the deputy at Health and Welfare, is a physician. The other three all have graduate degrees. Outside the deputy circle, Geraldine Kenney-Wallace and Shirley Thomson both have Ph.D.s and most of the other women are lawyers or have graduate degrees.

Getting to the top is tough and there is no one rule about how to do it. Some top mandarins enter public service late in their careers, recruited because of their success in another field.

But the more traditional way is simply to work your way up; in Ottawa, they call it playing the game. For bureaucrats and political staff alike this means being well plugged in, knowing what's going on, knowing the right people, working for the right ministers who are on the most powerful committees. It means being part of an interesting social network, going to the right dinner parties, getting invited to the right diplomatic functions, and it means living well – not necessarily lavishly. It requires careful career planning with plenty of powerful mentors to guide you and promote your interests. It means getting recognition for your work but only inside the system. Clever bureaucrats keep their names out of the papers, understanding that their political masters need the publicity. Nothing makes a minister more furious than seeing public servants getting ink.

You have first to keep your minister out of trouble and second to make him or her a star. You must offer the best briefings and the best intelligence and know how to manoeuvre the system with sophisticated lobbying and deal-making with your colleagues in other departments to give your minister the best shot at budget fights for pet projects.

Gordon Osbaldeston was the Clerk of the Privy Council from 1983 to 1986, and his study in London, Ontario, where he is now teaching at Western, is covered with framed Orders-in-Council, the documents appointing him to five deputy minister assignments. He's an expert on how to succeed and fail in the city, but he didn't always play by the traditional rules.

"There are two ways to live and work in Ottawa, and two kinds of people," he says. "One way to survive and prosper works for the kind of people who have a wide range of interests, who build enviable networks, who maintain busy social lives.

"Ottawa, contrary to myth, provides an entrée to all sorts of interesting areas of life, in the arts, in the media. The city offers lots of opportunities for people to engage in these different areas and offers lots of opportunities to socialize. These are people who are well informed, well travelled, cultured, who live a very balanced life. But then there is another, smaller group and clearly I am of this group. They're driven workaholics with narrower interests. All of their waking time is very much concentrated on work. I make no value judgements about either way. The first group is more fun and I was often envious of them, but I think the second group has more staying power."

With a University of Toronto bachelor of commerce and an MBA from the University of Western Ontario in his pocket, but no Oxbridge polish, Osbaldeston joined the Department of Trade and Commerce as a foreign service officer in 1953 and was posted to different jobs in the trade commissioner's service in Sao Paulo, Chicago and Los Angeles. By 1968 he was an assistant deputy minister at Consumer and Corporate Affairs; by 1970 he was deputy secretary of the Treasury Board. In 1972, nineteen years after he joined the public service, he was made deputy minister at Consumer and Corporate Affairs. Over the next ten years, he was deputy at Treasury Board, Industry, Trade and Commerce, Economic Development and External Affairs. Most of these ministries, take note, are key central agencies.

By 1982, twenty-nine years after Osbaldeston entered government as an embryonic trade commissioner, Pierre Trudeau appointed him to Clerk of the Privy Council. It was a long slog. During his years in Ottawa Osbaldeston worked seventy to ninety hours a week. He never got home before 7 or 8 and was out at least two to three nights a week at official functions. He and his wife, Gerry, tried to accept only one social function a week and usually that meant something at Government House, at 24 Sussex Drive or at an important embassy. Both the Osbaldestons hated cocktail parties ("No one says anything intelligent at cocktail parties"), but dinner parties, their favourite way of spending an evening, were almost impossible because he so often had to cancel at the last minute. "I was reluctant to commit to a dinner when the risk of offending some hostess was relatively high. If we were booked, however, Gerry would come and sit in my outer office to get me out on time."

He was also famous for his holidays. Instead of spending

long weekends hanging around and swapping gossip at the exclusive mandarin hangout, the Five Lakes Fishing Club in the Gatineau Hills (although he belonged, he's been there only twice), or skiing in a Laurentian resort, he and Gerry would pack their four kids into a motor home and go camping.

One of the distinctions of Ottawa, Osbaldeston believes, is that some people really enjoy power and thrive on its use, while others find it a burden and an obligation. Both types of people, he believes, can be responsible. "Some people go to Ottawa looking for power; some go and it almost descends on them. They acquire it because of a sense of mission."

An example of a couple who played the game as the Osbaldestons did not is that of David and Diana Kirkwood. Their history is almost a textbook case of how a talented, ambitious pair rose to power.

The best-known real estate agent in Ottawa for years has been the glamorous Diana Kirkwood, who works for Sherwood Real Estate, the old Ottawa firm that handles most of the city's exclusive house sales. Sherwood's is so exclusive that their newspaper advertisements never list prices – too vulgar – and their houses often do not sport For Sale signs on the lawns. Mrs. Kirkwood, a friend of the arts and a patron of the ballet, was quite properly anointed by *Chatelaine* magazine in the early 1980s as the city's premier hostess, with the best food, the best mix of people, the prettiest Rockcliffe house with a charming conservatory and a glorious garden. For years, Mrs. Kirkwood's husband, David, was a senior mandarin; he retired as deputy minister of health and welfare just a couple of years ago.

David, who had worked as a nuclear physicist at Chalk River from 1945 to 1948, had been enviously watching many of his friends join the foreign service, all inspired by the example of Lester Pearson, who was made secretary of state for external affairs in 1948. "Historians have never given adequate credit to the influence Pearson had on a whole generation of bright young people who admired him for the role he played on the public stage," Kirkwood mused one night in Ottawa, over a long dinner in the magnificent apartment he and his wife own in an old building in downtown Ottawa. (Weekends they spend at their new country house in the Gatineau Hills.) Diana had grilled a salmon her husband caught on one of his regular fishing trips to Labrador; the gravlax they make from his catch is justly celebrated in Ottawa.

As Kirkwood thought back to his early years in government, he said he could only think of them in the context of Pearson's role. "In 1945 Canada started playing a major role on the world stage. The UN was drawing up documents trying to plan the world of the future. Canada was one of the few countries not exhausted by war, and people like Hume Wrong, Escott Reid, Clifford Clark, O.D. Skelton, Arnold Heeney and Norman Robertson were the leading public servants of the day."

Kirkwood's background for the public service was conventional except for one thing – his training in nuclear physics. As a result, six months after he joined External Affairs, he was seconded to work as the secretary of a new advisory panel on atomic energy, a panel made up of senior deputy ministers who were determining what Canada's nuclear policy would be. "It was largely political policy, looking at things like weapons," Kirkwood said, "but I was lucky as a junior public servant to be in this very top group. These were the guys who ran the government and there I was taking notes." Ottawa then was very different from Ottawa today. "At that time the press didn't probe such groups; there was a policy, if you like, of 'decent restraint,' and any suggestion of leakages in Ottawa would have cut off our access to U.S. information."

When Kirkwood moved back to External and was sent to the NATO desk, his secretary was Diana Gill, a young woman from an established Ottawa family who was part of a fashionable crowd of young people in the city. Her uncle, Evan Gill, was a senior official in the Privy Council Office, and one of the young people working for him was a bright Montreal lawyer called Pierre Trudeau. Soon Trudeau was part of Diana Gill's crowd, a group who took Russian language lessons together. Diana Gill also studied ballet, an interest shared by Trudeau. "Pierre had a flat in Sandy Hill he shared with Clément Bouchard, who is now an entertainment lawyer," remembers Diana Kirkwood. "Pierre was part of a French milieu I was trying to work my way into. We all yearned to be part of the French-Canadian crowd.

"Once he asked me to come and show them some ballet movements, so I went over and showed them what a *plié* was and so on. He always supported dance. When I asked him, many years later, to come to an opening of Theatre Ballet, he came."

When, in 1952, Kirkwood was posted to Paris to work for Arnold Heeney, Canada's first ambassador to NATO, Diana was there working as Heeney's secretary. The two were soon married and the Heeneys hosted the wedding reception in their residence. As the young couple settled into diplomatic life, their apartment became a meeting place for other young Canadians in Europe. It wasn't long before Pierre Trudeau showed up again in their lives.

"He was a perpetual student, it seemed, and at that time he was there with D'Iberville Fortier [now Canada's Commissioner of Official Languages]. In Ottawa we thought Pierre was very poor because he went everywhere on the streetcar, but in Paris he showed up in a white Jaguar. It was a stunning change from the Pierre we knew! Later, we introduced him to a girl we knew and he took her to Sicily."

Later, when the Kirkwoods were back living in Ottawa, they joined the Five Lakes Fishing Club, of which Arnold Heeney was one of the founders. Kirkwood's rise was steady. He did his PCO stint after leaving External; by 1978 he was chairman of the Anti-Dumping Tribunal and deputy of Supply and Services in 1980. In 1983 he was appointed deputy at Health and Welfare. Throughout those years, as they raised four children and Diana Kirkwood supported cultural groups and went into real estate, they threw large parties that vied with those given by the Ostrys, the Gotliebs, the Gwyns and the Enderses for the most interesting guests.

Now retired, David Kirkwood runs the Canadian Mediterranean Institute, an organization dedicated to scholarly work in the Mediterranean countries – set up initially by Hamilton Southam and society decorator Giovanni Mowinckel.

However it's played, the Ottawa game can be a dangerous one. At first, all ministers are suspicious of deputies. Each knows that while someday every politician will be forced out by defeat, disgrace or pure exhaustion, the deputy will linger on, serving first this minister and then that, this government and then that. "One persistent notion about deputy ministers is that they are like the old bass lurking at the bottom of a fishing hole," Osbaldeston wrote in his book, *Keeping Deputy Ministers Accountable.* "They remain in departments for years, even decades, ruling their domain as they wish and using their vast and detailed knowledge of the department to control the endless parade of ministers."

Osbaldeston disagrees with this point of view; in his book he scolded the Mulroney government for mindlessly shuffling the deputies far too often, with disastrous results. To prove his thesis, Osbaldeston offers the following statistics:

Cabinet ministers stay an average of one and a half years in their departments and deputies stay an average of only two. Compare this to the average chief executive officer, who has been in his or her private sector post for nine years. In 1987, 50 per cent of the deputies had been in their jobs for less than one and a half years. The average duration of a minister-deputy team between 1984 and 1987 was less than a year. Most deputies spend less than three hours a week with their ministers.

Osbaldeston tacitly acknowledges the rotten relationships between some deputies and their political masters, stating that improving the statistics above would improve the relationships, but he also thinks mandarins need to teach their ministers a few tricks of the trade. "If the PM would put his new ministers on course for just three days and bring in experienced deputies to talk to them, it would help." The catastrophes Mulroney has had with rogue ministers free-wheeling their way through the system need not have happened. "For every five Cabinet ministers who are lost," he claims, "I could save at least three."

Today, Ottawa has lost some of its savour for would-be mandarins. Many dislike the political climate created by the Tories and are looking for work in the private sector. Many have left to join provincial governments, especially David Peterson's in Ontario. Others, who have run out of challenges in Ottawa, have opted for early retirement in their mid-fifties, to pursue new careers. Allan Gotlieb, for example, left the public service when he finished his term as ambassador to the United States to move to Toronto as a senior partner at Stikeman Elliott, chairman of the Canada Council, publisher of *Saturday Night* magazine and member of several corporate boards. Robert Johnstone, former consul general in Washington and one of the most respected Ottawa deputies, moved to Toronto to run a new international business centre based at York University.

The sour mood in Ottawa today has several causes. Bureaucrat-bashing by the Tories during their first term is one. But a more serious cause has been the phenomenon of "plateauing," first described nearly ten years ago by demographer Nicole Morgan in her book, *Nowhere to Go*. She outlined how the senior levels of the bureaucracy were filled with young, ambitious overachievers who had been promoted too quickly. The result was inevitable: too many young people at the top who were not budging once they got there. Nowhere for the ambitious overachievers coming in after them to go. And at a time when the government is cutting back on the public service, slashing positions across Canada, bureaucrats see themselves as unable even to move sideways.

David Zussman, the dean of public administration at the

University of Ottawa, and Jak Jabes, a professor in his department, have proved Morgan's predictions in two studies, one done in 1986, the other in 1988. The first study showed that 20 per cent of the mandarinate believed morale was low across the public service; the second study showed that 40 per cent now believed there was a serious morale problem. Osbaldeston found a similar pessimism when he interviewed deputy ministers for his book. In the 1988 annual report of the Public Service Commission, even the government officially acknowledged these problems.

The commission also admitted that the public service is aging. Not only is the government not bringing in younger people, it is not attracting the best and the brightest university graduates. Today, the best and the brightest are moving into business and law, not public service.

Not surprisingly, stalled male managers are beginning to blame affirmative action programs for women as the reason for their own failure to get to the top. Many believe incompetent women are being pushed up too quickly. "I'd have to have a sex change operation to get a promotion," grumbled several in interviews to Jak Jabes. Previous affirmative action programs have not been as unpopular as this one has been. No one objected after the Second World War, when veterans were brought in to displace women across the whole spectrum of the public service. Today, former military officers still have priority for hiring in government jobs. When the Trudeau government instituted an unofficial affirmative action program for Francophones, there was some mild whining from unilingual Anglophones, but on the whole the public service accepted it. The difference was that in those years the public service was growing, so there was room for everyone.

Today, the public service is shrinking, so affirmative action for women threatens some male bureaucrats. But the facts do not bear out their complaints. Yes, there are more women in the public service, but they are at the bottom levels. From 1976 to 1986 the population of female public servants went up 10 per cent, while the population of males went down by 14 per cent, but this all happened at the bottom of the pyramid, in blue-collar jobs. And though the 1988 Public Service Commission trumpets gains for women, their own figures make you wonder who it is that needs the sex change.

In 1988, 1,476 male public servants made more than $80,000 as opposed to 119 women. In other words, 92.5 per cent of those making more than $80,000 were men. In 1988 there were 3,978 men in the management category and 559 women, only 12.3 per cent of the total. Given that there are only 203 positions in Ottawa at associate-deputy level or above, and only 35 or so "real" deputy jobs, the percentages become much more dramàtic. Only 10.4 per cent, or 270, of the top EX (executive) positions have gone to women, while there are 2,336 men in that category, or 89.6 per cent.

EX categories divide into five groups. At the very top there are 82 men and 2 women or 97.6 per cent male and 2.4 per cent female. At the next level down, there are 201 men (91.8 per cent) and 18 women (8.2 per cent). It's also revealing to look at the appointments to management jobs to see how affirmative action is working. Here the statistics are only slightly better. In 1988 the government brought in 48 male mandarins and 16 female. Within the management group, they promoted 952 men (82.9 per cent) to management jobs and 197 women (17.1 per cent). And so the trend goes, winding its weary way through the statistics to prove that, baby, you've still got a long way to go.

Even among the first group of mandarins, the ones who ran the capital for so many years, there is evidence that life was not perfect and that the much-vaunted golden age was tarnished at the edges. Those men would have understood the frustration of Clerk Paul Tellier, who has seen power shift away from his office into the hands of politicians and cronies. When Norman Robertson, one of the greatest of the Ottawa Men, joined Prime Minister Louis St. Laurent's office replacing the first Clerk, Arnold Heeney, he complained to his wife, Jetty, "The new job is a mistake. There is nothing for me to do." Part of his problem was Jack Pickersgill, then St. Laurent's principal secretary. While Pickersgill liked Robertson and had suggested his name to St. Laurent, the prime minister preferred to get his advice from his peppery little political advisor instead.

It wouldn't hurt disheartened bureaucrats in Ottawa today to read the lessons of history outlined in Jack Granatstein's books. Here they will learn that bickering, jealousy, disappointment, frustration and thwarted ambition are all desperately old hat. The greatest key to survival in Ottawa's mandarinate is simple: just outlast the other guy.

8

•••

The New Carpetbaggers

The invitation sent out in late March 1989 was a classic, just what we have come to expect from the lads at Government Consultants International.

Join us for "Ramsay's coming out party," it trumpeted. "For the last 365 days Ramsay has purged his system of the government and the Sir Humphrey mindset, mindful of the auditor general's warning that contacting government could be harmful to a former deputy minister's health. For a year we have not allowed him to think about 'A-based' budgets, he has not been permitted to read the *Globe and Mail*, nor eat at Hy's. Ah, but now to celebrate his new-found purity of spirit, we are celebrating."

Who else but Government Consultants International could, or would, have sent out an invitation like this? General Ramsay Withers, the chief of defence staff from 1980 to 1983 who moved to the Department of Transport in 1983 as deputy minister, just days after quitting his job at Transport hops over to the city's most notorious lobbying firm as president and chief operating officer. They expect us to applaud.

Until recently GCI was owned by three Mulroney cronies, Frank Moores, Gerry Doucet and Gary Ouellet, who arrived in Ottawa in 1984 like carpetbaggers invading Atlanta, planning to cash in on their access to the PM and to Don Mazankowski. The links between these three and the government have been traced many times and are briefly as follows: Frank Moores, Tory premier of Newfoundland from 1972 to 1979, has been a close Mulroney friend since the mid-1970s; he nominated Mulroney for the leadership in 1976 and, fuelled by anonymous donations (some from mysterious financier Walter Wolf), he led the Dump Joe Clark forces after his resignation as premier. For a while he worked in Montreal, financed, according to John Sawatsky in his study of Ottawa's lobbyists, *The Insiders,* by three wealthy businessmen who told him they would back him until he hit on just the right business. He started a small investment company called Torngat Investments with fellow Newfoundlanders John Lundrigan and Senator William Doody. But he spent most of his time on the Mulroney leadership campaign.

In 1983, after Mulroney wrested the leadership away from Clark, Moores, who has always been close to Mazankowski as well, bought a small lobbying firm called Alta Nova from Jamie Burns, Pat Walsh and Fred von Veh, all aides to Mazankowski when he was transport minister in the 1979 Clark government. After the government fell, Burns, Walsh and von Veh set up Alta Nova as a consulting firm specializing in transportation issues. When they went back into Mazankowski's office after the 1984 election (Mazankowski returned to Transport with Burns as chief of staff, Walsh as marine advisor and von Veh as special legal advisor), Moores took over their company and continued to specialize in transportation lobbying. Walsh comes from Saint John, New Brunswick, home of the Irving firm, Saint John Shipbuilding. Former Alta Nova sources say the company had hired him to lobby for them to get contracts to build naval frigates.

Gary Ouellet, a Quebec City lawyer and a key organizer in the 1983 leadership and 1984 election, is close enough to

Mulroney to be included in private family celebrations at 24 Sussex Drive. Like Moores, he is close to Don Mazankowski and came to Ottawa in 1984 to head up then-junior transport minister Benoit Bouchard's staff. He was also involved with Michel Coté's 1984 campaign to win a seat in Quebec City. Later, when Coté was minister of consumer and corporate affairs, and GCI was lobbying for the Pharmaceutical Manufacturers Association of Canada, it was a useful connection because this was the ministry responsible for drafting Bill C-22, the legislation toughening up the patent act to give pharmaceutical manufacturers more protection from cheaper generic copies.

Gerry Doucet is another member of the St. Francis Xavier University mafia who became close to Mulroney during the prime minister's years at university. Doucet is also the brother of Fred Doucet, for years Mulroney's closest aide and still one of his closest friends. A Cape Bretoner, Gerry Doucet was a provincial Cabinet minister in Robert Stanfield's government from 1963 to 1970. After running unsuccessfully against John Buchanan for the leadership, he opened a government relations firm in Halifax, which now splits its work half and half between law and lobbying. Both Doucet brothers have been involved in business deals with Mulroney, who invested $15,000 in their now-defunct company, East Coast Energy. East Coast, a company designed to cash in on ocean oil drilling in the Maritimes, crashed into bankruptcy in 1985, owing $3.74 million to seven creditors and leaving more than a thousand shareholders with losses of $9.4 million. A welter of messy lawsuits followed, including one from Walter Wolf to recover his investment of $300,000.

GCI has made its three partners wealthy men without their even bothering to live in Ottawa. Moores keeps an Ottawa apartment but lives in Montreal (he has now withdrawn from daily activity in GCI). Ouellet commutes to his home in Quebec City, where he serves as secretary to the Old Port Corporation. His law firm there, Levasseur Ouellet, gets a neat share of federal government business. Although Ouellet claims he has nothing to do with the law firm, receptionists answering the phone tell callers that "Mr. Ouellet isn't in today."

Doucet spends most of his time in his Halifax law office, where he and his partners process a fair degree of government legal work and where he carries on with his own private lobbying business, which has been neatly linked to GCI. For example, when a Nova Scotia fisherman is looking for a fishing licence, especially for a lobster licence, he is very likely to go to GCI. Doucet does legal work for him in Halifax, charging a stiff fee for his trouble, and GCI lobbies Fisheries officials for the licence. Ouellet once confirmed rumours that the fees for such work would be $10,000 to open the file at GCI and $25,000 a year after that, for three years, if the application were success-ful. He shrugged off the suggestion that Doucet's billing on top of all this was double-dipping. Gerry brings us business, was his response, and he's entitled to a little extra. Gerry Doucet left GCI in the spring of 1989 to go into a new lobbying firm with his brother, Fred, and another well-connected former Tory aide, Pierre Claude Nolin.

By 1984, when Moores and his friends were opening GCI, lobbying in Ottawa had become an acceptable profession thanks to the popularity and straightforward style of long-time Ottawa residents and political insiders like Bill Neville and Bill Lee, the first men to start a lobbying company back in 1968. Today their old firm is called Executive Consultants Limited, or ECL.

It wasn't long before the swaggering newcomers were up to their ears in little scandals; Moores, for example, was appointed to the board of Air Canada in 1985 along with some other "Ritz Hotel gang" members. This was the group who had plotted Clark's downfall and Mulroney's victory from plush secret quarters in Montreal's Ritz Hotel, still the spiritual home-away-from-home of Brian and Mila Mulroney, who stay there frequently. Ritz manager Fernand Roberge was a key member of the group and won a coveted appointment to the Air Canada board, as did Ritz member and senior party bagman David Angus, chairman of the Progressive Conservative Canada Fund. Gary Ouellet was another Ritz gang member.

Moores had to resign from the Air Canada board when two situations were made public: that he was lobbying for Wardair and Nordair against Air Canada's interests and that he was lobbying for a European consortium, Messerschmitt-Bolkow-Blohm, which was trying to sell its Airbus to Air Canada.

Another storm erupted when it was revealed that Petro-Canada had hired GCI for advice on energy issues in Atlantic Canada because Gerry Doucet had clients in his Halifax practice who were potential competitors. After another swirl of unpleasant stories about the Canadian National Railways hiring GCI, the government ruled that Crown corporations should not be hiring lobbyists.

And there was the famous Ulf Snarby incident. Snarby was a Nova Scotia fisherman who wanted to overturn a federal Fisheries Department decision not to grant him a certain kind of fishing licence. Told that GCI had good connections, he paid the company $2,000 plus a $500 monthly retainer to meet Fisheries Minister John Fraser, whose help he needed to get a special dispensation on the licence. (Fraser was later dismayed to find out Snarby had paid to see him.)

The story doesn't end there. In 1986 new Fisheries Minister Tom Siddon was under attack in the House for granting $1 million in cod fishing rights to the Harbour Grace Fishing Company, whose shareholders included Brian Babb, Moores' son-in-law; Joe George, Moores' former special assistant; and the Nordic Fishing Company of Dartmouth, Nova Scotia, whose president was – you guessed it – Ulf Snarby.

Again in 1986 GCI's involvement in lobbying for the Pharmaceutical Manufacturers Association of Canada became controversial partly because of the $5-million contingency fees rumoured to be coming their way. (GCI has always denied they ever made this much from PMAC.) But more serious was

Fred Doucet's role in PMO in steering the patent legislation through. Although he has denied it, there is widespread belief in Ottawa that he handled the PMAC file in the Prime Minister's Office; a top official at Consumer and Corporate Affairs, however, has stated that Doucet regularly met with then-minister Michel Coté to discuss how to get the legislation through. As David Bercuson, Jack Granatstein and William Young pointed out in their book, *Sacred Trust*, Doucet "was seen as a man who made commitments without understanding much about the intricacies of a subject. In the first months of 1986, his involvement in the abolition of generic drugs in Canada was often cited as an example of this, in that his position did not take into account the provinces' responsibilities in the area of health, nor did he reckon the ultimate cost to the provinces and to consumers." Ottawans were shocked by the links between PMO and GCI on the drug issue, as his brother Gerry Doucet was the GCI partner responsible for the file.

Another new wrinkle the firm brought to Ottawa was contingency fees. Until 1984, lobbyists had all worked on a retainer basis, charging clients up to a rare high of $10,000 a month to represent their interests in Ottawa. The average fee for a large lobbying firm with a major client runs between $4,000 and $7,000 a month, and some fees, of course, are much lower. Much of the "lobbying" or "government relations work" that goes on is simply providing clients with insider gossip.

But that was not the way GCI wanted to bill its clients. Yes, they put clients on retainer, big retainers. Yet they also worked out contingency fees if they won whatever it was the client was after. To put it less elegantly, they wanted a piece of the action, and the phrase they use is "incentive fees." As Ouellet puts it, "It's an incentive for us to service our clients better." He defends this practice by saying everyone does it, something other Ottawa lobbyists vehemently deny. As Bill Lee, who was still running Executive Consultants Limited in 1987, put it at that time, "We have never accepted contingency fees and we never will. If our livelihood depends on getting the contract there is a terrible temptation to do whatever is necessary to get it, like cashing in some political chips. We're in for the long haul and we can't do it."

Mark Daniels, who until recently was president of the city's largest lobbying firm, Public Affairs International, Hill and Knowlton-PARG), also condemns the practice. "We are not in the contingency fee business," he said, adding that two-thirds of PAI's income comes from monthly retainers paid by clients while the other third comes from special one-time projects. A client will come in, ask them to help with a project, agree on a fee and pay it. There is never a question of taking a percentage of the win if the client gets a contract from the government.

"Contingencies," as the rest of Ottawa calls GCI's fees, have pushed the company ahead of PAI in total earnings according to one industry insider, but GCI still is second in number of clients and in retainer fees. Naturally, speculation is rampant on the amount of CGI's "contingencies" as people call them; one knowledgeable rival lobbyist said his estimate was that they took between 3 and 5 per cent of the total contracts. If true, that means contingency fees of between $3 million and $5 million on a contract worth $100 million. GCI will never discuss the percentages.

Senator Michael Pitfield was particularly critical of deputies who become lobbyists at an April 13, 1989, seminar on the relationship between Parliament and special interest groups. According to Pitfield, former MPs, Cabinet ministers and mandarins who become "information peddlers for a fee" are damaging the image of government and the quality of the public service. Pitfield warned that this trend had moved the role of interest groups "to a new and dangerous phase." One of the reasons for the trend, he told the seminar, was that the government had become increasingly secretive about its decisions, and this had created a situation in which the lobbying business "is allowed to camp in the fields of the mighty.

Access, which was once the right of a citizen and the obligation of a minister, is now being peddled for a fee."

Pitfield told the group that the trend had started back in the 1970s, "when former deputy minister of finance (and free trade negotiator) Simon Reisman and the former deputy minister of industry, James Grandy, took early retirement from the civil service and set up a consulting firm." Old-time Ottawa insiders say that the real reason the two deputies left to start their own firm was that Michael Pitfield, a Trudeau favourite, had been promoted to Privy Council Clerk over their more senior heads.

General Ramsay Withers had enjoyed a reputation as a straight-shooter, a distinguished bureaucrat, an upright man dedicated to public service. GCI openly specialized in two areas of government procurement, transport and defence, the two ministries in which Withers worked. A year later, GCI could sing out all it liked about his initial "laundering" period at GCI, during which they said he did not touch transport or defence contracts. Still, the odour rising from the appointment was pretty fishy. A partial list of GCI's clients shows you where they think the big money in government is:

Mercedes-Benz came their way thanks to Rick Logan. When Logan was moving into Defence in 1984 as Bob Coates' senior aide, he turned over his Mercedes-Benz account – and the car that came with it – to Moores, who was soon on the company's board. Mercedes-Benz is not interested in selling the government expensive cars, but it is keen to provide the Canadian military and Department of Transport with their trucks.

Saint John Shipbuilding was helped by GCI to win contracts to build six more naval frigates to add to the six they won in a 1983 contract. The company leads all other Canadian companies in total government procurement since 1980, with more than $6.5 billion in shipbuilding contracts.

Bombardier used to use Ottawa lobbyist Don Mitchell, a Liberal. But in 1985 Mitchell claimed that Bombardier officials told him he was losing the $128,000-a-year assignment to GCI because they had been advised by officials in the Prime Minister's Office to make the switch. Bombardier had a lot at stake; they were successful in taking over government-owned aircraft-maker Canadair for $205 million and won a $100-million contract to maintain the CF-18 fighter planes. (In 1987 Canadair, the former Crown corporation, gave the PC Canada Fund $25,750 and the Liberals nothing; that same year Canadair received Regional Industrial Expansion grants of $3 million.)

Messerschmitt-Bolkow-Blohm, a German company and part of a European consortium, hired GCI to help it sell its Airbus planes to Air Canada. They were successful, and the contract was worth $1.8 billion. Some speculate that the contingency fees earned by Moores may have been many millions of dollars.

Microtel, a subsidiary of British Columbia Telephone, is part of a joint venture with CANAC, a subsidiary of Canadian National Railways. The partnership won a $255-million federal contract to build a low-level air defence system.

Iron Ore Company of Canada, Brian Mulroney's old firm, provides GCI with a good way for the company to keep in touch with its former president.

Other firms that hired GCI include Toronto development company Huang and Danczkay, which wanted the contract to build Terminal 3 at Toronto's Pearson Airport (they got it); Gulf and Western, which wanted permission to take over publishers Prentice-Hall Canada (they got it); and American Express Canada, which wanted permission to open banking services in Canada (they got it).

Nabisco Brands Canada came on board GCI when its former U.S. president, Ross Johnson, was calling the shots. Moores and Johnson, a Canadian, were friends; Moores was influential in seeing to it that Johnson and Mulroney both received honorary degrees from Memorial University in Newfoundland on the same day in 1980. In 1983 Johnson helped raise a great deal of money in the United States for Mulroney's leadership campaign especially in the last-ditch battles at the Winnipeg leadership convention. After the 1984 election Johnson was at Mulroney's side for every White House dinner or gala event honouring Mulroney in the United States. In 1987 Johnson was appointed an officer of the Order of Canada, an honour awarded, an admirer on his nomination papers stated, because he "was largely responsible" for the success of Memorial University's 1980 fundraising drive. In fact, in 1980 all he did was get Nabisco to donate $100,000 to the university's $15-million campaign, and university officials, who gave him the honorary degree at Moores' urging, say they never saw him again. (For the past few years Johnson has been involved in the University of Manitoba's business school, his alma mater, where Nabisco also donated money for a chair in his name.) In 1987 Nabisco gave the Tory party $51,825 and in 1988 the company was one of the leading players in the campaign to support the free trade deal. Nabisco also topped the list of Tory contributors in 1988 with donations of over $100,000.

Ramsay Withers was not alone in jumping ship from government to lobbying. Over the last five years there has been a flood of bureaucrats, politicians, political aides and military officers who have decided life is short and lobbying, or "consulting" as they prefer to call it, is their chance to grab a piece of the action. At least nine former Mulroney aides who were fired or quit during the period when his office was being reorganized by Derek Burney, aides like Bill Fox, are now running consulting or government relations businesses.

One of the most recently opened is the Doucet-Nolin firm. After being elbowed out of PMO by new broom Derek Burney, Fred Doucet became ambassador for international summits. He insisted on being called "Ambassador" despite the fact that External Affairs protocol states that Canadians with ambassadorial rank who work in Canada do not use the title. Pierre Claude Nolin, a Laval lawyer and former chief of staff to Roch LaSalle when LaSalle was minister of public works, also worked for Mulroney in PMO before moving to Montreal to run the party organization in Quebec. A chubby-faced lawyer who is married to Camille Desjardins, the daughter of big-time Quebec contractor Pierre Desjardins, Nolin is one of the party's top lieutenants in Quebec, where he has been responsible, among other things, for fundraising and making sure grateful businesses pay their fair share to party coffers. In this activity he has always taken his direction from Mulroney, Bernard Roy and Senate Speaker Guy Charbonneau. His name surfaced frequently during the Gravel affair, always as a key player in Quebec's patronage networks.

How Nolin and Doucet will earn their bread and butter as lobbyists is still unknown, but a good guess would be that they will be signing up hungry Quebec contracting and engineering firms wanting to ensure their bids to Public Works are given every consideration. They will be helped by Gerry Doucet, who now knows the business inside out.

Some other senior political staff and bureaucrats who have been moving into lobbying firms and playing their role in turning Ottawa into Washington-on-the-Rideau include:

James MacEachern. A lawyer and former Tory aide in Mulroney's office in 1986, MacEachern also served as chief of staff to the minister of supply and services, Stewart McInnes. MacEachern joined GCI in late 1986.

Elizabeth Roscoe. Considered one of the most effective chiefs of staff since the Tories came into power in 1984, Roscoe left her job with Barbara McDougall in 1988 to run Camp Associates Advertising's Ottawa office; Camp Associates, owned by Senator Norman Atkins, the Tories' election organizer, but run by Toronto Tory Hugh Segal, not only sells its expertise in government and public relations but also has won millions of dollars' worth of federal advertising contracts. Camp has one of its own former vice-presidents, Bill Colvin, buried in the bowels of Supply and Services vetting millions of dollars' worth of federal polling contracts on a government-business executive interchange program.

Harry Near. Near, the Conservatives' campaign manager in

1988, had been an aide to Energy Minister Ray Hnatyshyn in the 1979 Clark government and returned to the private sector as an energy consultant in 1980. After the 1984 victory, he went to work for Energy Minister Pat Carney on a special contract of $150,000 – much more than other chiefs of staff were allowed to make – to set up her office and to brief her on her portfolio. Less than a year later he left to set up his own energy consulting firm, Near Consultants and Associates, in a loose arrangement with Camp Associates.

Bill Fox. Mulroney's former press secretary now runs Fox Communications Consultants, a one-man lobbying and communications consulting firm. His office, like Harry Near's, is in the complex set up by Camp Associates. Like so many former Mulroney aides (including Charley McMillan and Fred Doucet), Fox is rarely missing from Mulroney's side at major events like fundraising dinners or summit gatherings. In June 1989, Roscoe, Segal, Near and Fox brought their loose association together under the formal name, the Earnscliffe Strategy Group.

David Crapper. Elizabeth Roscoe's husband, Crapper was a Mazankowski aide who spent eighteen months in the Deputy Prime Minister's Office helping sell the free trade deal before joining PAI. He also worked for former health minister Jake Epp.

Doug Frith. When Frith, Liberal MP for Sudbury, and former House Leader, left politics in 1988, he also joined PAI.

Daniel Despins. John Turner's former press secretary is another PAI recruit.

Herb Metcalfe. A senior aide to former Liberal finance minister Marc Lalonde, and a strong Chrétien supporter in the 1984 leadership, Metcalfe opened his own lobbying firm, Capital Hill Group, soon after the 1984 election, and it has done well.

Jodi White. In 1988 White, Joe Clark's well-liked and well-respected chief of staff from 1984 to 1988, opened Sydney

House, a consulting business associated with Bill Neville's new company.

Mark Resnick. Joining the loose association with Neville and White's firms, Resnick set up Parallax Public Affairs. Resnick is a former Liberal aide who worked at the Canada-Israel Committee and at Liberal Party headquarters.

Daniel Tessier. Before joining ECL, Tessier worked as a Tory aide and party organizer in the 1984 election. He also worked in the office of the minister of state for finance, Tom Hockin.

Jon Johnson. Johnson, a former Mulroney aide, is the son of Manitoba's lieutenant governor, Dr. George Johnson. He is also Frank Moores' ex-brother-in-law. Johnson, who has a Ph.D. from the London School of Economics, worked for PAI as a vice-president before starting his own company, Government Policy Consultants.

James Crossland. Now a senior consultant in Jon Johnson's firm, Crossland worked for Mulroney in Opposition and served as secretary to the policy advisory group in Mulroney's office during the 1984 election. He also worked as a policy advisor to former industry minister Sinclair Stevens.

William Kennett. Kennett, a former Inspector General of Banks for Canada, is another GPC recruit who joined after taking a considerable amount of heat over his role in failing to anticipate the collapse of the Alberta banks.

Doug Arthur. Another former public servant at GPC, Arthur did studies for the federal government on the auto pact, and in January 1989 he was appointed a member on free trade dispute panels.

James McIlroy. Once a commercial litigation lawyer, Jim McIlroy worked as a senior policy advisor to former international trade minister James Kelleher. After his defeat in November 1988 (by then he was solicitor general), Kelleher and McIlroy both joined the Toronto law firm Aird and Berlis. Mulroney has appointed both to trade dispute panels. McIlroy is also a GPC associate.

Peter Burn. Another former Mulroney aide in 1983, Peter Burn is a lawyer who has also worked as an aide to John

Crosbie and Michael Wilson. He left Wilson's office in 1986 to join Grey, Clark, Shih and Associates, a trade consulting firm associated with Jon Johnson's company, GPC. His company is headed by Peter Clark, a former senior public servant in Finance. Like Clark, Arthur, Kelleher and McIlroy, Burn has received a Mulroney appointment to the U.S.-Canada trade dispute panel.

Mark Daniels. Daniels had spent fifteen years as a public servant, ending his career with a two-year stint as deputy minister of consumer and corporate affairs before joining PAI as president in 1987. Today he is vice-chairman of Hill and Knowlton-PARG, the British-controlled holding company that now owns PAI.

Alec MacPherson. Another public service recruit to PAI, MacPherson spent thirty-five years in government and left his job as a special advisor on trade and finance in the Finance Department to come to PAI.

Michael Cassidy. There are not many socialists in the lobbying game, but in April 1989 Cassidy, the NDP MP for Ottawa Centre defeated by Liberal Mac Harb in the November 1988 election, set up shop as a government relations consultant.

Why do so many former aides and bureaucrats and politicians join these firms? Because there is so much money to be made in the business and they are tired of making do on public service salaries. Lobbying turns them into entrepreneurs.

Many Canadians wonder what lobbyists actually *do* all day long. There they are showered and shaved and out the front door . . . what then? Okay, after breakfast at the Four Seasons, what *then*? Even lobbyists shift from one foot to another as they struggle to explain their role. Some are there simply to sell their access to the mighty, and everyone knows it but no one will admit it. What they will tell you is that making a decision on a licence or a contract or a piece of legislation is a complicated, multistage process and might be considered by the following authorities:

a) a government department
b) a politician or two
c) public servants in Treasury Board or PCO
d) at least one parliamentary committee
e) an interest group such as the Canadian Medical Association or the Consumers Association of Canada, themselves powerful lobby groups.

Arming the client with names, background information on programs, responsibilities, terms of reference, budgets and a list of phone numbers, the lobbyist used to say, "There you are, friend. This is where you go and this is who you see. Best of luck." They called themselves consultants and prided themselves on their refusal to lobby directly. "We don't 'do' advocacy," they would sniff.

Jon Johnson, the president of Government Policy Consultants, wrote an unpublished letter to the *Globe and Mail* in November 1988 objecting to being labelled a lobbyist in a column. "We specialize in policy analysis and strategic advice," he wrote, "and rarely act as advocates or 'lobbyists' for anyone. The academic training and career experience of our principals reflects our orientation as substantive public policy professionals – indeed most people who know our firm regard us as the most expert and substantive group of policy professionals in Ottawa. Unlike the other two or three big and alleged public policy consulting firms, we sell substance, not style; we don't open doors or act as an escort service." (This was a not-so-veiled reference to GCI, his ex-brother-in-law Frank Moores' firm.)

It's not easy for the unwashed public to understand the difference between "public policy" work and "government relations" work, and Johnson tried to explain how each works. Public policy work, he said, was analyzing government policies and devising strategic reactions to it. "We identify issues that can impact our client's bottom line or our client's reputation." (Translation: His company watches the government's spending plans with an eagle eye, looking for opportunities for its clients.) "Then we provide analysis and recommend strate-gies." (Translation: They then figure out how to bid on the contracts.) "Government relations" work means identify-ing the right contacts among politicians and bureaucrats, preparing briefs for the clients and often lobbying for them (making the calls, taking the clients to meetings, hassling the decision-makers).

Here's a simple example, a true one as it happens, of how the system works. Suppose a foreign food processor wants to find out why the Canadian government will not permit his apple juice into the country, and whether anything can be done about it. The lobbyist, who may have worked in Consumer and Corporate Affairs or in a trade office, calls up bureaucrats he has cultivated at Consumer and Corporate Affairs or at Health and Welfare, or both, and maybe puts some calls in to the trade offices at External. A few days later, he reports back to the foreign juice company that if they change the labelling on their cans they'd go a long way to solving the problem.

Occasionally, if the client is important enough or pays enough, the lobbyist will take the process a step further; he will make the calls himself. Often the problem is just a low-level affair, and a middle-ranking bureaucrat is perfectly happy to meet for a drink after work some day and explain the government's policy on the issue and even offer to pass letters on or to arrange another meeting. On other occasions, lobbyists fill a quasi-public relations function. Someone new comes to town and the lobbyist hosts a discreet lunch at Le Cercle Universitaire or the Rideau Club to introduce the client to the Right People.

Pre-Mulroney, and given that there were always exceptions to this rule, lobbyists tended to give advice and background and phone numbers and leave the client to take it from there. Today, advocacy is very much in style, forced on other firms by GCI's unabashed hustling: "We pride ourselves on results," GCI's chairman Gary Ouellet once said. "The other firms just push a lot of paper at clients, tell them to go away and read it and make their own decisions and appointments. Other firms specialize in policy analysis. They tell their clients, 'Here is what you should do.' Our culture is that we are results-oriented. Here we have dress rehearsals. We also pick up the phone and call bureaucrats ourselves."

There is a dark side to this kind of lobbying. Everyone in Ottawa knows that Ouellet is a close friend of both Brian Mulroney and Don Mazankowski. Suppose a bureaucrat were brave enough to tell Ouellet that his questions or pressure or "suggestions" were simply out of line. What guarantee does that hapless bureaucrat have that Ouellet won't badmouth him first chance he gets over a cosy supper *chez* Mulroney?

Clients of lobbyists usually want one of three things:

1) They want government contracts: for low-level air defence systems, for nuclear submarines, for passenger aircraft. They want contracts for building roads, cleaning offices, offering advice on management. Lawyers scramble for contracts to prosecute drug dealers or process native land claims. Translators want contracts to translate. Salesmen want to sell the government photocopiers, tractors, canned peas and toilet paper. They want contracts from Public Works, from Supply and Services, from Indian Affairs, from CIDA, and they want contracts ranging from a few thousand dollars to hundreds of millions of dollars. The federal government's Department of Supply and Services spends $10 billion annually just buying things from manufacturers, a system known as procurement.

Up until a few months ago, Supply and Services kept lists of approved suppliers and invited them to bid when contracts were available. The Free Trade Agreement has changed this system because now Canada and the U.S. are obliged to let each other tender for contracts of more than $31,000 in Canada and more than $25,000 in the U.S.

The government does try to spread its buying power out across the country, but there is no question that a vastly disproportionate share – 76 per cent – goes to Ontario and

Quebec, which have the largest manufacturing bases in Canada. Federal Crown corporations like the CNR spend an annual $14 billion; add that to provincial Crowns and you get a total of $34 billion. Everyone wants a share of this pie.

With an increasing trend towards privatization, many people expect the government will continue to cut back on hiring civil servants and trim department services, and hire consultants instead. Rather than have your own cleaning staff, why not use private cleaning services? Why not hire lawyers from friendly firms to prosecute drug cases instead of using Justice Department lawyers? Why not turn government scientific research over to private labs? This trend means more contracts.

The biggest contracts come, not surprisingly, from the Departments of Defence and Transport. In fact, most of the top ten contractors since 1980 have been defence contractors. Military contracting accounts for a staggering 60 per cent of the Tory government's total procurement budget. (It wasn't any different under the Liberals; between 1980 and 1984, military contracts accounted for 63 per cent of government procurement.) Transport comes second with 6 to 7 per cent.

2) They want legislation. For example, the Canadian tobacco manufacturers hired Bill Neville to lobby against the Tobacco Products Control Act, which, since January 1, 1989, has forbidden advertising of tobacco products.

3) They want regulatory approval or a licence. French pharmaceutical giant Institut Merieux SA, for example, wanted Investment Canada to approve its takeover of Connaught BioSciences and hired Ottawa lobbyists Herb Metcalfe and his Capital Hill Group to help push it through while Connaught hired Tory advertising and public relations executive Hugh Segal.

The best example of how a company used lobbyists to win regulatory approval or a licence was American Express's campaign to win a Schedule B Banking licence to operate as a bank in Canada. Banking regulations did not allow Amex to do this, but thanks to their connections and clever lobbying, they won. In the last five years Amex has gone through at least four or five lobbying companies. In 1984 Amex went after the federal government's credit card account; with help from Executive Consultants Limited, they were successful. After a brief relationship with a smaller firm, they switched to PAI to help them win the B Banking licence.

In 1987 the story gets more interesting. The following scenario has been confirmed by industry insiders (although not by anyone at GCI). GCI was hungry for the Amex business and they had the connections to get it. Gerry Doucet, the story goes, talked to his brother, Fred. Someone approached Mulroney's close friend, Nabisco president Ross Johnson, in New York. Johnson was on the board of Amex in the United States. He had a word with the president of Amex who, in turn, spoke to the president of Amex in Canada. Amex in Canada dropped PAI and took on GCI.

Eventually the American giant got what it wanted by supporting Mulroney's free trade initiative. Amex and its American chairman, James Robinson – aided by Nabisco's Ross Johnson – led a powerful group of American politicians and businessmen in an organization called the Coalition for Free Trade to help push the free trade deal through the U.S. Congress. As Amex vice-president Harry Freeman told a free trade symposium in Washington in 1987, "The ultimate goal would be a convergence of our two nations' domestic financial regulations." When the deal went through Congress in 1988, Freeman told reporters, "We beat them. We formed the largest business coalition in U.S. history to back the deal and we won."

During the 1988 federal election, Amex threw massive support behind the Tories' campaign. When the campaign stalled at midpoint because of John Turner's surprisingly strong performance in the leaders' debate, which led many Canadians to question the merits of the trade deal, the business lobby redoubled its efforts. They helped pay for lavish newspaper supplements and advertisements to encourage people to vote Conservative so that the free trade legislation would go through.

Amex got its reward on election day, November 21, 1988, when an Order-in-Council was passed that effectively allowed Amex to operate as a bank in Canada. The Canadian banking community went wild. As loyal Tory supporters, they felt betrayed by Mulroney and Finance Minister Michael Wilson. In an unprecedented display of anger, Toronto-Dominion Bank chairman Richard Thomson accused Mulroney of making a deal with Amex: Support our campaign and you get your licence. "This was done because Robinson supported free trade," said Thomson. "This was the deal that I guess the prime minister made with him." A phone call from Wilson forced Thomson to recant immediately, but many Canadians felt that Thomson was right.

Once other Amex deals started to become known, the suspicions grew. The company won a $50-million Treasury Board contract to have its travellers' cheques used by all public servants, including those working at Crown corporations and government agencies, a contract awarded in June 1988, said Amex vice-president Harry Freeman. Then it was also discovered that Amex had won a pilot project with the Finance Department and Treasury Board to pay all bills under $500 with the company's credit card. Federal officials and Amex executives have continued to declare, of course, that no deals were made, but try telling that to the executives behind VISA and En Route cards.

A lot has been written about lobbyists in the last few years; the best guide is John Sawatsky's 1987 book, *The Insiders: Government, Business and the Lobbyists.* For a few months Sawatsky wrote a newsy monthly guide to the lobbying industry in *Vista*, Magna International's new business magazine. As Sawatsky has always pointed out, lobbying has been going on in Ottawa for decades, but until recently it has always been by organizations whose interests were quite clear: the Grocery Products Manufacturers' Association, the Chamber of Com-

merce, the Canadian Manufacturing Association, the Canadian Medical Association, the Pharmaceutical Manufacturers
Association. Lawyers have always done a little discreet lobbying and lobbying is what the Senate has always been about.

The main lobbying firms today, ranked in order of size, are
Public Affairs International, Government Consultants International, Executive Consultants, Government Policy Consultants, William Neville and Associates, Corporation House (run
by the well-liked and respected former Chamber of Commerce president Sam Hughes), and S.A. Murray and Associates, a growing Toronto-based firm run by Tory Susan
Murray, who also maintains an Ottawa office.

Until recently, Public Affairs International, or PAI, was run
by Mark Daniels, a bureaucratic lifer who was deputy minister
of consumer and corporate affairs from 1985 to 1987. Because
PAI is a discreet and highly respected firm set up and run by
long-time Ottawa hands, no one murmured a word about
Daniels and possible conflict of interest, much to GCI's
annoyance. Why go after us and not mention Daniels and PAI?
they'd whine. Good question. And they knew the answer as
well as anyone. GCI had quickly developed a reputation as a
firm in for the short haul, using their access to Mulroney and
his buddies.

Other firms did not allow GCI to waltz in and take over
without a fight. PAI, which was considered a Liberal firm in the
1970s and early 1980s, had covered its rear end by hiring
several Conservatives after the Mulroney victory, including
Bill Neville, who had left the lobbying business to run as a
Tory candidate against John Turner in 1974. He'd spent the
intervening years working as a senior aide to Robert Stanfield
and Joe Clark, as well as a senior executive with the Canadian
Imperial Bank of Commerce. Then PAI brought in Pierre
Fortier, a popular Ottawa lawyer who had originally started his
own lobbying firm in 1985 with another Tory, former party
president Paul Curley.

It is interesting to note that Curley is a close friend of

Communications Minister Marcel Masse; not surprisingly, one of Curley's specialties was culture and communications. The connections didn't end there. At that time, Curley was attached to broadcaster Mary Lou Finlay; Finlay's sister, Patricia, became Masse's senior policy advisor. After Masse was moved to the Energy portfolio, Finlay continued working for him as a confidante and speech writer. It was said in Toronto that anyone needing help from the Communications Department in the early years of the Mulroney government was wise to hire Paul Curley, and now that Masse is once again the culture czar of Canada, the same is probably true.

Curley and Fortier folded their firm into PAI in 1987. A year later Neville left PAI to set up his own firm, William Neville and Associates. He was fed up with PAI's determination to compete head-to-head with GCI's aggressive lobbying techniques. Before the threat from GCI, PAI had done little actual lobbying and more advising clients how to understand and deal with government departments on their own.

Finally, in February 1989, PAI's parent company, Toronto-based Public Affairs Resource Group (PARG), run by senior Liberal David McNaughton, followed the pattern of so many other Canadian service industry firms and sold itself to a multinational. Included in the sale were PARG's polling arm, Decima, run by Tory punk pollster Allan Gregg, and a Washington lobbying firm, Government Research Corp. The sale, to Britain's WPP Group of London, the parent company of U.S. advertising giant JWT (in turn the parent company of J. Walter Thompson Ltd.), was worth $43 million with $12 million cash up front. The big winners were McNaughton and Gregg, who owned 70 per cent of PARG; the rest was held by other executives and employees.

A closer look at the books of PARG gives us an idea of the kind of money these firms make. McNaughton and Gregg bought PAI from its founding partners for $350,000 in 1979. At the end of the 1988 fiscal year PARG had earned $25 million, up 22 per cent from $20.5 million in 1987 and up 58 per cent from $15.8 million in 1986. Judging by its revenues, most Ottawa insiders believe GCI would be well ahead of PAI at this point because of their contingency fees. But Jon Johnson, whose two-year-old firm has grown from zero to $2 million in revenues, believes his company is the most profitable if you consider profits against expenses. Susan Murray's company has grown to revenues of more than $1 million in 1988.

Today PAI stands a chance to grow dramatically as part of Hill and Knowlton-PARG. Fortier is president and CEO of Hill and Knowlton-PARG in Ottawa (although the company will continue to be called PAI by everyone else), while Curley is vice-chairman of the parent company in Toronto. McNaughton continues to be the boss, while Gregg continues to run Decima.

In October 1988 ECL also sold a large chunk of itself, concluding a deal with the U.S.-based public relations giant Burson-Marsteller, which bought 49 per cent of the company. ECL also had a reputation as a Liberal firm, but during the Mulroney era it brought in Walter Grey's public relations firm, Henry and Grey, as an associate company. Grey, another very well liked Tory (with a formidable reputation as a piano player and foxtrotter), is a former Ottawa bureau chief for the *Globe and Mail* best known for his informative weekly newsletter, "Parliamentary Alert." This lists new government appointments, committee hearings, legislation and other Hill-oriented business. During the 1988 election campaign, Grey worked furiously at Tory campaign headquarters each morning, pumping out the party line of the day to all candidates by electronic mail. The Burson-Marsteller merger gave ECL access to the American company's offices in Toronto, Montreal and Vancouver as well as to its forty-five offices in twenty-two other countries.

One of the city's most powerful lobbyists, who usually isn't thought of as a lobbyist, is Thomas D'Aquino, the head of the Business Council on National Issues, an organization of CEOs from 150 of Canada's top corporations. D'Aquino has turned the BCNI into a major force for the big business community. A lawyer, D'Aquino comes from Trail, British Columbia, and went to the University of British Columbia. In 1969 he joined Pierre Trudeau's office as an assistant to Marc Lalonde, then Trudeau's principal secretary. After the Tories came into office in 1984 he made, as the saying goes, "a good transition," and today seems as conservative a business advocate as they come.

In the November election, several leading members of the business community, including D'Aquino, formed the Canadian Alliance for Trade and Job Opportunities, a high-profile business lobby group that campaigned for free trade. Its co-chairmen were former Alberta premier Peter Lougheed and former Nova Scotia Liberal premier – and former federal Liberal Cabinet minister – Gerald Regan. In the November election, the alliance's 196 members collected $5.2 million to sell the deal in a nationwide advertising campaign. Opposition parties cried foul, claiming that such expenditures, while not illegal, contravened the spirit of election spending rules. At first the alliance promised to open its books, but by May all it would say was that it would reveal its secret donor list but would withhold the amount each company contributed because of what they called corporate "sensitivity." Toronto *Star* reporter Tony Van Alphen contacted a group of fifty contributors in April 1989, but only fourteen of them were willing to tell him how much they had coughed up for the campaign. He found out that Alcan Aluminum, Noranda, Shell Canada and the Royal Bank gave about $1 million as a group, and that ten other companies, including Brascan, Ford of Canada and Texaco Canada, gave a total of $470,000.

No prudent public servant would dare criticize the government these days, but upcoming retirement can do wondrous things for a man's courage. Canada's chief electoral officer, Jean-Marc Hamel, who is retiring in 1990, blasted the alliance in April 1989, when he told reporters he was angry about large-scale election spending by interest groups. "It's totally unfair," Hamel told the Toronto *Sun*'s Michel Gratton. "It's as if two boxers get into a ring under the same rules, in the same weight category, with the same gloves and, all of a sudden, a spectator jumps in and starts hitting one of them with a hammer." Undaunted by criticism, the alliance planned a similar campaign against the deficit.

As the Tories move into their second term in office, new lobbying firms continue to blossom, especially those cashing in on the free trade agreement. Even the two top free trade negotiators set up shop as lobbyists. At the end of March 1989, Simon Reisman, the sixty-nine-year-old former senior free trade negotiator, set himself up as a consultant on free trade and government relations, calling his new company the official-sounding Trade and Investment Advisory Group. Without so much as a blush he told reporters that he thought it was time to cash in on his public service. "Having negotiated the agreement, I would like now to contribute to its successful utilization, and in the process add to my own activities and income," he said. The new company is affiliated with the Toronto law firm Smith Lyons Torrance Stevenson and Mayer.

Reisman is also planning to sell advice on subsidies to the government, and as far as International Trade Minister John Crosbie is concerned, that's just fine. "I see nothing wrong with someone of Mr. Reisman's great skills and background advising people on how to take advantage of the free trade agreement," he told reporters in April 1989.

Reisman was beaten to the punch six months earlier by his deputy negotiator at the Trade Negotiation Office, Gordon Ritchie, once a senior bureaucrat at DRIE. In October 1988, Ritchie had set up a trade consulting company called Strategicon. He then married it to the Ottawa law firm of Lang Michener Lash Johnston and took on Lang Michener's most visible partner, Jean Chrétien, as an associate. Another associate is former Liberal Cabinet minister Mitchell Sharp, one of Chrétien's strongest backers in his campaign for the Liberal leadership.

Senators are among the city's most powerful lobbyists. Even

though they are parliamentarians, receiving generous pay and benefits, they may sit on boards, work at other full-time jobs and lobby for clients. Montreal Liberal Senator Leo Kolber, the head of the Bronfman development company Cadillac Fairview, for example, has long been considered the lobbyist for Bronfman interests. Most recently, Conservative Senator Michel Cogger was exposed as the lobbyist for a Montreal businessman who wanted $45 million in government support for a high-technology project. According to testimony released by a Montreal court in June, Cogger called a senior DRIE official, Gabriel Voyer, and told him to "get moving" on the project.

And finally, no study of lobbying in Ottawa would be complete without looking at the emergence of another group of lobbyists, the generals and colonels and admirals and air vice-marshalls, all in their fifties, all in their prime, who are now streaming out of the Canadian military on full pensions.

In the United States, they call the system "rent-a-general." The FBI has spent the last two years investigating corruption in the defence industry, delving into the affairs of fifteen defence contractors. It has issued 275 grand jury subpoenas to companies and individuals, including Melvyn Paisley, as assistant secretary to the navy for research, engineering and systems from 1981 to 1987 and now a defence consultant for McDonnell Douglas Corporation. Like so many other former defence officials, Paisley left government to help a company win a piece of the procurement pie, a pie worth $80 billion a year.

Here in Canada defence procurement is worth $10 billion a year. Senior bureaucrats who have specialized in procurement are also lining up to join private industry. And some lucky guys (for they are all guys) have an extra card up their sleeve: they have worked for *both* Defence and Supply and Services, or Defence *and* Transport, and there is nothing anyone can tell them about procurement. When the *Financial Post* held a conference on the defence industry in November 1987, five hundred people showed up, and most of these were retired officers and bureaucrats now lobbying for contractors.

One group of retired officials have even formed their own consulting company, CFN Consultants in Ottawa. It was set up in 1983 by three former Defence Department bureaucrats: Lewis Crutchlow, the assistant deputy minister for matériel until 1982; C.R. (Buzz) Nixon, deputy minister of defence until 1982; and Major-General Maximilian Friedl, a former associate deputy minister for matériel. Other recruits brought in later include Vice-Admiral John (Jock) Allan, former Brigadier-General Bernard Roach, former air force signals Major-General Russell Senior, former Brigadier-General George Simpson, and Stanley Kerr, former director general of the federal government's procurement, aerospace and armaments products centre from 1976 to 1985.

In 1986 CFN set up a subsidiary company, CFN Management, and its brochure suggests they did this to give more specific management advice to hopeful bidders. The many services they offer are listed quite frankly; two are "assistance in proposal preparation and proposal review" and "liaison with key departments, agencies and officials in the Federal government acquisition process." In plain language, the old boys' system is alive and well and working in Ottawa.

The brochure also trumpets that CFN Management "has in-depth knowledge of Canadian government and military requirements, military specifications, contracting procedures and associated budgetary considerations." Can't be much more blunt than these old soldiers.

Most of the time CFN partners are working on retainer for multinational companies, but they also lobby for foreign companies; Nixon, for example, lobbied for Oerlikon, the Swiss arms manufacturer that won the government's $600-million low-level air defence contract.

Four other officials from Defence, all of whom were working on the low-level air defence project, abruptly quit their jobs to join Oerlikon a few weeks after it won the contract. They were Lieutenant-Colonel Gaston Lamarre, an engineer; Major William Matthews, a test pilot and technician; Dr. John Anderson, a research scientist; and Sergeant Roy Mongeon. There was no cooling-off period for these men; they turned up for work within a day or two of leaving Defence.

Oerlikon was taking no chances. As well as grabbing several Defence employees including former chief of defence staff General Bing Peart, they scooped up all kinds of well-connected Tories, including Peter Ohrt, Mulroney's scheduling director in PMO hired as deputy project manager and, as their publicist, Mulroney crony Roger Nantel, a Montreal advertising man and Mulroney's press secretary during the 1983 leadership campaign. Just a few days after the announcement that Oerlikon would build the low-level air defence system, the company dumped its internationally known law firm, Montreal's Lette and Associates (after its lawyers told Oerlikon that the land it wanted to buy had tripled in value in eleven days) and hired Montreal's Byers Casgrain, putting another Byers Casgrain partner and Mulroney crony, Jean Bazin, on its board. Bazin, who happens to be a cousin of Peter Ohrt, resigned when he was later appointed to the Senate. Another crony with Oerlikon links is Toronto lawyer Sam Wakim, the lawyer for Oerlikon subcontractor Litton Industries.

The hot military project for the past two years has been the $8-billion contract for new nuclear submarines, which was torpedoed in the April 1989 budget. While the project lived, everyone tried to get a bite. CFN's Jock Allan was hired by VSEL Defence Systems Canada, the Canadian arm of the British competitors for the submarines. And in May 1988 VSEL also hired GCI.

The British firm, which is built around Vickers Shipbuilding and Engineering, wanted to supply the government with at least eight Trafalgar-class submarines and, to ensure their bid got all the attention they felt it deserved, they used two Ottawa lobbying firms. Before they hired GCI, they had already brought in Corporation House, run by Sam Hughes, and put him on the VSEL board. When it was learned that GCI was now working on the submarine bid, Hughes made the best of it. The company was added, he told reporters, "because of its reputation for having access in certain areas . . . political areas," and he explained that the move "broadens the scope of VSEL's approach to Government."

Working with Allan and Hughes on the VSEL board were the Canadian company's president, retired Rear-Admiral W.B. Christie, who had also been a senior bureaucrat at Supply and Services, and John Killick, another former Defence Department assistant deputy minister for matériel and now a senior vice-president for Marconi.

The French were also fighting for the submarine contract, and had set up a Canadian subsidiary, SNA Canada, to help sell their Rubis-Amethyste-class submarine; like the British, they were not slow to bring the military on board. Their heavy shooters included retired Rear Vice-Admiral Daniel Mainguy and retired naval commander Keith Davies, director of the Canadian operations at SNA Canada.

The submarine bid was not, of course, the only high-stakes game in town. There was also the frigate program. Another big player who moved to private industry in March 1988 was Admiral James Wood, the former head of the Canadian Armed Forces Maritime Command, who is now vice-president of Saint John Shipbuilding as well as president of Saint John Naval Systems. Before he assumed the Maritime Command in 1983, Wood worked at Defence Headquarters in Ottawa – where he headed the committee that chose Saint John Shipbuilding to build the original six frigates. And Saint John Naval Systems is a new subsidiary of Saint John Shipbuilding with program support responsibilities for the new frigates. In other words, Wood ran the committee that chose the company to build new frigates, moved to the Maritimes as the senior naval officer, and then moved to work for the company that was buying the ships – and which got the contract to build six more.

Another former officer associated with the frigate program is John Henry, former deputy commander of the North American Aerospace Defence Command, who is now working as director of marketing for Paramax Electronics, which won the $2.5-billion contract to integrate all the electronic and combat systems on the new frigates. It is a member of the E.H. Industries (Canada) team for the new $2-billion Sea King helicopter replacement program and is working on bids for the nuclear subs. In August 1988 Paramax also hired Harold (Hi) Carswell as vice-president of government relations. Carswell, a former army lieutenant-general, had been assistant deputy minister at Public Works before moving to Paramax.

When the *Financial Post* held its defence conference, the place was full of stars. There was General Gérard Thériault, the chief of defence staff and Canada's single highest ranking officer from 1983 until 1987. He was representing the West German defence firm AEG Aktiengesellschaft. Another was former Mobile Command head Lieutenant-General C.H. Belzile, who left the armed forces in 1987 to work for SNC Defence Products. And there was Lieutenant-General Kenneth Lewis, who now works for the Aerospace Industries Association of Ottawa, and Rear-Admiral T.S. Allan, a former chief of engineering who became president of Control Data and is now with EHI, the British helicopter company.

Former Defence officials don't move just to defence industry businesses; like General Ramsay Withers, a few have moved into lobbying firms. Lieutenant-General Donald Mackenzie is one example; he moved to PAI after thirty-six years in the Royal Canadian Air Force and in the Canadian armed forces. He specializes in aerospace, military and defence policy and procurement.

Military officials at both the minister's office and Defence Headquarters in Ottawa refuse to discuss the conflict-of-interest issue here except to say there is normally a year-long cooling off period for retired officers. This has not appeared to be the rule for several who have made the move recently.

Despite the fact that Ramsay Withers, a former chief of defence staff and a former deputy minister of transport, moved to GCI as president and chief executive officer within days of leaving the government, the firm always insisted he never had any role in lobbying for the high-powered clients like Saint John Shipbuilding, VSEL, Airbus, Huang and Danczkay, Microtel, Mercedes-Benz or Bombardier (which had dealings with one or both of his old departments). Given Withers' excellent reputation in Ottawa, people believed him. But the gleeful invitation to his coming out party in Ottawa in April 1989 showed that the time for such caution was over.

GCI's notoriety embarrassed the government enough that it was decided to bring in legislation to govern this exploding industry. The Lobbyists Registration Act, expected to come into effect in September 1989, will divide lobbyists into two "tiers," with regulations for each. Tier-two lobbyists – and there are about ten thousand of these – are required to give only their own name and that of their employer. These are the obvious lobbyists, people who work for the Chamber of Commerce or the Canadian Medical Association or the Canada Labour Congress. The legislation is not really aimed at them. It is directed towards an estimated five thousand tier-one lobbyists, people like the Ouellets and Doucets, who, according to the act, "communicate with a public office holder" in trying to influence contract awards, policies, legislation or grants. They have to register their clients with an official registrar. They will have to list their clients' subsidiaries and parent companies and disclose which public servants they meet and "the proposed subject matter."

The problem with the act is that it will depend on an honour system: it does not force lobbyists to comply with the regulations. If the public is outraged, the act helpfully suggests that "anyone who has evidence of non-compliance may contact the RCMP." Sure.

9

· ·

Careful, Someone Is Listening

The students at the armed forces' language school on Woodward Drive in Ottawa's west end were fascinated. Every morning they watched men and women arrive for work at the plain grey three-storey building next door, a building that looked like a garage on the ground floor with two floors of offices above. No sign gave away the building's identity. The language students, most of whom are senior military officers there to learn Russian, Arabic, German, Chinese or other useful languages before being posted abroad as military attachés, would watch as the same people came out again shortly afterward, dressed quite differently, often far more casually, and drove off in nondescript unmarked cars. Teachers and students assumed that their neighbours were Ottawa's watchers, now officially called *surveillants*, in the spirit of bilingualism, who sit in cars and watch people come and go at certain embassies and certain offices.

Ottawa's intelligence community falls into two groups – the suppliers and the clients. The suppliers are the agencies and groups that collect raw data, work it into manageable shape and relay it to client groups. Suppliers are the electronic eavesdroppers from the Communications Security Establishment, known as the CSE. They are the quiet men and women from CSIS – the Canadian Security and Intelligence Service – who watch from buildings and unmarked cars. They are the people, in CSIS and at the CSE, who go through East Bloc scientific magazines and newspapers gleaning material that adds up to an understanding of a country's capability in fission or fusion.

An amusing note to this area of intelligence gathering appears in the annual report of the Security Intelligence Review Committee (SIRC), which tells us that CSIS does not make enough use of what they call open sources. "By open sources we mean such things as the mass media and scholarly and technical journals, both Canadian and foreign, as an alternative to intrusive investigation," the report states, before adding ruefully, "But a proclivity for investigative techniques is endemic in CSIS. The Service seems to give more credibility to information it has ferreted out through investigation than to information available to any astute reader."

Foreign governments, including the United States, also have their own networks of intelligence agents working in Canada. In Ottawa, they are usually put under diplomatic cover. It can be normal for a cultural attaché to be a senior KGB or CIA agent. (Canada, in contrast, is the only Western nation besides Sweden that does not have a foreign intelligence service.) Canada is considered an important post because it is so close to the United States and it is so easy to slip across the border. We are also important because we share secrets and defence strategies with the Americans and other NATO members, and are considered easy to penetrate. A telling anecdote in Peter Wright's *Spycatcher* underlines what other nations think of us. When the former assistant director of MI5 told a fellow British intelligence officer that he had briefed the RCMP and the FBI on a secret operation, the other officer hit the roof. "The Canadians! You might as well tell the fuckin' Papuans as the Canadians!" He was referring to Canada's outdated cipher machine.

The clients are the government departments like PMO, PCO, External Affairs, the Solicitor General's Department, National Revenue and National Defence, who take the tidy piles of data for their own purposes, further sorting and analyzing them.

Most Canadians know Canada has intelligence and security services, but if asked to name them they would likely mention only the RCMP and CSIS. The truth is that our intelligence network is wide and complicated and multilayered. One of its largest and most important components is the multimillion-dollar electronic eavesdropping and code-breaking agency, the Communications Security Establishment headquartered at Confederation Heights. The CSE is part of a worldwide network, usually known as UKUSA, incorporating the Government Communications Headquarters at Cheltenham in Great Britain, the Defence Signals Directorate in Australia, the Government Communications Security Bureau in New Zealand and the National Security Agency (NSA) at Fort George Meade, Maryland, near Washington, the major player in the group. The NSA, which employs up to 100,000 people and has been said to have a budget of $10 billion, also houses the world's largest computer complex. With a worldwide network of spy satellites, ships and listening posts, these agencies intercept thousands of telephone and telegraph transmissions using computers, some of which can even sift through and recognize voice transmissions, sorting out key words and phrases.

While the government has often said that the CSE does not spy on Canadians, other sources have maintained that the CSE works closely with CSIS and passes on results of domestic electronic intercepts to the agency. These sources also claim that the CSE has thousands of files on Canadian citizens. And as former solicitor general Robert Kaplan admitted to reporters in April 1984, the CSE may also eavesdrop on us without judicial warrants.

Normally it is illegal to eavesdrop on private communications unless a judge has issued a warrant to a law enforcement agency. CSIS must jump through twenty-six other legal hoops before it can place a wiretap or other electronic eavesdropping equipment. But Kaplan explained away the difference here by saying that the CSE doesn't need a warrant because it is only "gathering electronic impulses from the air, from the public domain, and analyzing them. Those electronic impulses that are floating around are in the public domain. Anyone who can pick them up is entitled to do so."

From a federal index of personal informational data banks, the *Globe and Mail*'s Jeff Sallot discovered that CSE keeps a data bank on people who are considered potential security risks. Quoting from the index, Sallot wrote on November 21, 1984, "This information is used to advise the government with respect to international affairs, security and defence." He said the index also noted that the Cabinet had been asked to designate the CSE data bank as one of the exempt banks under provisions of the Privacy Act. What this means is that if you suspect you might be one of the people listed in this bank, you cannot apply to see your file under the Privacy Act.

In the last few years perfectly ordinary people in Ottawa have started telling you that they don't want to "talk" on their phones. Bureaucrats, journalists, politicians and their aides seriously worry that someone is listening. They have surreptitious conversations in supermarket aisles about parabolic microphones and sophisticated listening bugs buried in lamps and picture frames and about men in parked vans using computers and monitors to watch top-secret memos as they are being typed in a government office. Some politicians and senior public servants routinely have their offices swept for listening devices.

Many others make fun of this paranoia. You're watching too many British spy movies like *The Whistle-Blower*, or reading too many Robert Ludlums, they'll say. They point out that it would take an expensive and enormous army of listeners to sort through all the boring lunch arrangements that form the bulk of Ottawa phone calls. They dismiss anxious questions about computers programmed to pick up key words and names in phone conversations.

Whatever the truth, people persist in worrying, and their worries have been raised repeatedly in Parliament, by members of all parties. In April 1984, for instance, Liberal Solicitor General Kaplan refused demands by both the New Democrats and the Conservatives to put the CSE under the legislative control of his new national security bill, Bill C-9. Saying it would be "damaging to national security," Kaplan also refused to give the House of Commons' Justice and Legal Affairs Committee a copy of the mandate under which the CSE operates. He asked committee members to accept instead his assurances that a Cabinet committee supervises CSE activities to make sure they are legal.

In March 1987, it was the Tories' turn to deny information on the CSE. Toronto Liberal MP John Nunziata said in the House of Commons that the CSE should be subjected to parliamentary review to protect the privacy of Canadians. His request was rebuffed by Paul Dick, then the associate defence minister, who said merely that "the CSE operates within the laws of Canada."

But British journalist and intelligence expert Phillip Knightley thinks the worriers are right. In the age of *glasnost*, he told a public meeting in Toronto in April 1989, the need for security and intelligence services is diminishing, so to perpetuate themselves spy agencies are turning to two new targets, terrorists and their own people. "They turn inward," Knightley warned his audience, "and watch and listen to their own citizens." Britain is the most secretive Western democracy in the world, he said, and the British government regularly brings outside experts, private phone tappers, to listen in on journalists, militant factions of labour unions, and environmentalists who belong to "green" parties.

Knightley and those in the security business in Canada warn us not to be so naive as to think the same thing isn't going on here. Although CSIS may have to get clearance to tap a phone, they don't ever have to make their actions public. Even if the wiretap is obtained with police help under the Criminal Code, which requires a court order (which is why, said one top government intelligence officer, security officials keep the names of friendly judges handy), you have to be informed within ninety days of the tap being removed.

But the paranoids point out that the wiretaps are never pulled off; they are renewed indefinitely so the subject won't have to be told. Furthermore, we're not talking about illegal taps by government agencies, they say, amused at one's innocence; we're talking about what Knightley is talking about, about spooks hired from private firms, sophisticated and discreet spooks with the latest high-tech equipment, hired through a maze of front companies.

For their part, commercial investigators insist all this worry is bunk. Few would use a parabolic microphone or tap a wire, because it is a criminal offence just to own such eavesdropping equipment, an offence that comes with a ten-year jail sentence. According to a top investigator for one of Toronto's largest private agencies, firms like his do work in Ottawa, but not for the government; the big jobs are checking out industrial espionage in the high-tech firms in Silicon Valley North, as Ottawa's Kanata suburb is called.

But Ottawa's spooks have all the toys, whether it is the full and latest range of NATO gadgets used by the CSE or smaller but equally sophisticated devices used by prime ministers. A former member of Pierre Trudeau's government remembers, for example, the small scrambling device used during all Cabinet meetings to confound possible electronic eavesdroppers. Shaped like a small radar antenna, it was placed on a desk in the office next to the Cabinet Room beside the prime minister's office in the Centre Block. When Cabinet meetings were in session, the device turned slowly, back and forth, to scramble the conversation in the room.

While few ministerial offices would have such sophisticated

toys, all of them have been buying a much more basic item, the shredder, symbol in today's Ottawa of someone who matters. Under the freedom of information legislation, journalists and other interested people like access consultant Ken Rubin are swamping government officers with five-dollar cheques and accompanying demands for government files. As a result, many top-level briefings are done orally. Very little paper floats around, paper that could come back to haunt the government in a later news story.

Government officials are quietly shredding paper at breathtaking speed. In January 1989 former Tory minister Pat Carney was outraged to discover that officials at the Department of International Trade, where she was minister from 1986 to 1988, had shredded all her files after she left to become president of the Treasury Board in 1987. There have been two schools of thought about Carney's case. One accepts the government's explanation that no damage was done; the shredded files were all duplicates and the originals had been safely lodged with National Archives. Others say this is a whitewash, that Carney, a former journalist, was not happy with much that went on when she was in the Mulroney Cabinet and that she intends to write a book about her time in office. She needed the files for the project and is now reduced to pulling together information from archival sources, a tedious and time-consuming job. Perhaps the government, mindful of the potential nightmare of Erik Neilsen's forthcoming memoirs, was prudently covering its rear end.

Neilsen, now head of the Canadian Transportation Commission, has been beavering away on a memoir of his years as a Tory MP for the Yukon and as a senior minister in the Mulroney government. He resigned as deputy prime minister in June 1986 and as an MP in January 1987 to take over the transport commission. In his case, no shredders got in the way of his memories. When he left office, reliable sources say, he took with him sixty-seven filing cabinets of documents, paper the government has been vainly trying to recover ever since.

Anyone in Ottawa can buy a plain shredder, which cuts paper into ribbons like fettucine. But if you mean business, you want a crosscut shredder that cuts paper both lengthwise and crosswise, and you have to order it from the government purchasing department, Supply and Services. Supply and Services buys only crosscut shredders, which must be used for all material labelled "confidential" and "secret." They cost between $2,000 and $12,000 each, depending on the power and sophistication of the model, and most come from an Ottawa firm called Datatech. In 1983-84, when the Liberals were sniffing defeat in the coming election and were destroying the evidence behind them, they bought a hundred crosscut shredders through Supply and Services. The following year, in the 1984-85 fiscal year, the government bought 162 serious shredders. How many of these were ordered by the fleeing Grits in their last four months in office in that fiscal year and how many by the victorious Tories in the remaining eight months is anyone's guess.

In 1985-86 the government bought 122 crosscut shredders, 142 in 1986-87 for $1.3 million, and 156 in 1987-88, a bargain at $1.05 million. It all adds up to nearly seven hundred crosscut shredders in the last five years at a total cost of nearly $10 million. And these figures apply only to standard government departments. They do not apply to the House of Commons, the Prime Minister's Office, Crown corporations and many other government agencies, boards and commissions.

There are only thirty-eight government departments ordering these machines, and the numbers show that each could now have up to eighteen crosscut shredders. What are they all used for? When asked, one senior mandarin confessed that he systematically shredded everything he thought he could get away with to avoid paper trails sought by investigative reporters under access to information law.

The CSE and CSIS are the largest intelligence agencies in

Canada, though the intelligence community also has branches in several government departments, including Transport, Employment and Immigration, Revenue Canada (Customs and Excise), External Affairs and National Defence. And there is the security and intelligence secretariat in the Privy Council Office, perhaps the most secretive and powerful of all our intelligence operations and one both feared and resented by some people at other agencies.

Many Canadians have heard of Reid Morden, the genial bureaucrat who runs CSIS; how many know who Blair Seaborn is? Even in Ottawa, Seaborn, who retired last year, was known to most public servants only as a smiling, quiet man with red hair and owlish glasses who worked at something obscure in the Privy Council Office. The truth is that Seaborn was, in some important ways, Canada's bureaucratic intelligence chief, and his background hints at the reasons. After serving with the Canadian army during the Second World War, he joined External Affairs and served in The Hague, Paris, Moscow and Saigon. He ran External's Eastern European Division and then their Far Eastern Division. After that he jumped to the upper mandarinate, becoming a deputy minister at Environment in 1974 and then chairman of the International Joint Commission in 1982. In 1985 he became intelligence and security coordinator to PCO, the secretary to the Cabinet Committee on Security and Intelligence. He was replaced in May, 1989, by Ward Elcock, a former assistant secretary to the Cabinet for legislation and House planning.

If you look at the chart below, first published in the Canadian Security Intelligence Review Committee's 1987-88 annual report, which shows each security agency and its reporting structure, you'll notice that this Cabinet committee reports directly to the prime minister, who chairs the Cabinet Committee on Security and Intelligence. The vice-chairman is Deputy Prime Minister Don Mazankowski. You'll see that several important intelligence committees report to it in turn.

At a Glance ... Major Components of the Intelligence Network

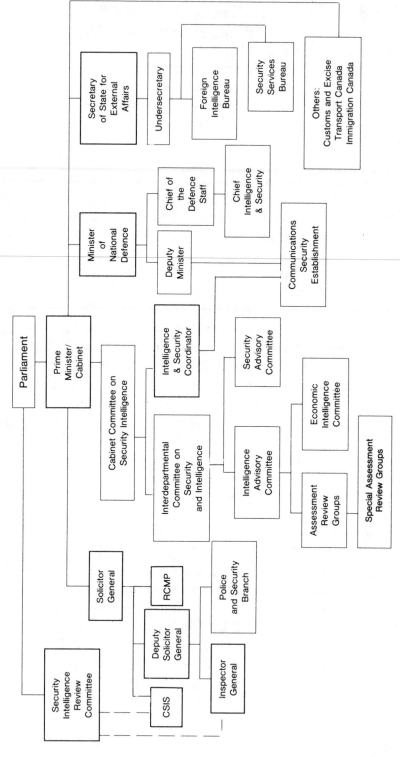

Notes: a) For simplicity's sake, only the most direct lines of authority are indicated.
b) Positions and departments with major statutory responsibilities are indicated by darker boxes.

Even the CSE reports to it, as well as to its putative masters at Defence.

In contrast, look at how the other security bodies, like CSIS and the RCMP, report; they report to a minister, either the solicitor general or the minister of national defence or the secretary of state for external affairs. Look, for example, at CSIS on the chart. It reports to the solicitor general and is checked by what is known as a review committee, in this case the all-party Canadian Security Intelligence Review Committee (SIRC) under the chairmanship of former Tory Cabinet minister Ron Atkey. His committee reports to the solicitor general, who delivers its report to Parliament. And another watchdog, this time for the solicitor general, is the inspector general; he monitors CSIS operations, policy, guidelines and internal controls. Needless to say, CSIS has often chafed at the supervision of two watchdogs, especially when Atkey's committee has been so critical of CSIS in its annual report.

Few Canadians know that only CSIS, of all these intelligence agencies, has a watchdog committee, although the RCMP recently acquired a new complaints committee, a kind of oversight body to investigate complaints againt the force. SIRC has absolutely no authority or oversight responsibilities for the CSE or the RCMP or any other security, intelligence or police branch of government. In contrast, in the United States there is an oversight committee to watch the NSA. Although the CSE's budget is hidden in Defence estimates and is classified, we do know that it is in the many millions every year. And we do know that the government has spent $100 million since 1984 to upgrade the CSE, buying it a Cray computer (the world's most powerful) and spending $30 million on an addition to the agency's headquarters.

In spite of these large expenditures, *only 1 per cent* of the information collected is processed and analyzed in Canada; the rest is handled in the United States. The source for this astounding fact is Senator Michael Pitfield, the Clerk of the Privy Council during the Trudeau years and the person who helped set up CSIS. Pitfield was speaking to Jim Littleton, a CBC producer who has written *Target Nation*, a fine book on the history of Canada's intelligence networks.

In the increasingly paranoid Ottawa atmosphere, there is a growing demand for CSIS security clearances at the top-secret level, and these cost $10,000 each. Even the gardeners at the prime minister's residences have to have top-secret clearances; so do the summer students working on the Rideau Canal, because there are some fortifications along the canal. "Too many people are seeking top-secret security clearances and too many deputy ministers are trying to get them; I guess they think it's like having an extra degree or something," grumbled Ron Atkey after a public discussion of intelligence agencies in Toronto in April 1989. (In fact, who gets one or who doesn't is defined in the Government Security Policy, a public document available from Treasury Board.) "CSIS keeps going back at people and asking if just 'secret' wouldn't do." Because of the demand, he said, it now takes seven months to do a minimal (known as a Level 1) check, and more than a year to do a Level 3 top-secret clearance. When a special international event takes place in Canada there is even more pressure; for the Calgary Olympics CSIS carried out 50,000 security checks. "In 1987-88," states the annual report, "CSIS dealt with 90,000 requests to check on prospective immigrants and another 90,000 for checks on applications for citizenship, 46,000 under the Government Security Policy (GSP), 14,000 for airport workers and 7,000 in other categories." Nearly 300,000 security checks for CSIS in that list alone. Even if only 100 of these were Level 3 top-secret checks, they would cost the taxpayers $1 million in manpower.

Security clearances have one unpredictable side effect. As Ron Atkey puts it, "One of the less attractive sides of security clearances is that sometimes the people being cleared get recruited as sources for the agency."

It must be said, in praise of Canada's security forces, that their work during the Olympics, the Francophone Summit in 1987, the Economic Summit in Toronto in 1988 and the Commonwealth meetings in 1987 was so thorough that no terrorists were able to slip through, despite many threats.

Another thing most of us don't know about CSIS is that it has its own training school, the Sir William Stephenson Academy, which reopened in April 1988. The school was moved to Ottawa from Camp Borden, Ontario, in 1987 and closed for a year to save money. The SIRC annual report shows its frustration with the tendency of CSIS, established as a civilian intelligence agency in contrast to the RCMP, to recruit former police officers instead of civilians; the academy, they hoped, would train what they tactfully call new blood. When the school reopened in 1988 with twelve students, CSIS made a point of saying they'd been recruited from outside the security and intelligence community.

Outside CSIS, people gripe about the academy, particularly about its name. They point out that although Sir William Stephenson was a Canadian, he was actually working for the British when he ran their intelligence operation, the British Security Coordination, in New York during the Second World War.

CSIS was set up in 1984 after the four-year MacDonald Commission on wrongdoing in the RCMP strongly recommended a civilian spy agency, one separate from the RCMP. The passage of the CSIS legislation, a special project of Michael Pitfield, in June 1984 was the last act passed by Pierre Trudeau's government. The agency had a rocky start, fuelled by the vicious in-fighting between the Mounties who transferred into the new service and the new civilian recruits. And ever since it was created, it has complained about underfunding and a lack of permanent headquarters. Currently it is scattered in offices all over Ottawa, although its headquarters are in the old Veterans' Affairs building on Wellington Street. In Toronto CSIS is housed beside the new SkyDome in an imposing, anonymous building on Front Street, with surveillance cameras panning the street.

There have been some spectacular failures in CSIS's short history, including its inability to prevent the 1986 Air India bombing, which took more than three hundred lives, most of them Canadian. Another screwup was the attempted assassination by militant Sikhs of Malkiat Singh Sidhu, a Punjabi Cabinet minister visiting relatives on Vancouver Island. The minister was seriously wounded in an ambush near Tahsis on May 25, 1986. Although a CSIS agent had information ahead of time that could have alerted officials to an assassination attempt, he failed to pass it on to the RCMP in time. The fallout of this episode was the resignation of CSIS's first director, Ted Finn, in 1988. Finn's resignation was caused not by the failure to pass on the information, itself a serious problem, but by the discovery that the agency had sworn a false affidavit in a warrant application.

Recently, the agency seems to be steadying itself. A critical assessment of CSIS, headed by former PCO Clerk Gordon Osbaldeston, has forced the abolition of the counter-subversion branch. This branch monitored groups and individuals in Canada suspected of promoting the illegal overthrow of the government. Many civil libertarians quite rightly worried that such monitoring often meant stepping over the line to bully or spy on legitimate groups. CSIS sheepishly admitted in the spring of 1989 that it had been interviewing the Innu of Canada's north, who were objecting to military air tests over their hunting grounds.

Eliminating counter-subversion won't put our spies on the pogey. The growth industry that keeps CSIS busy and which is keeping intelligence agencies all over the world busy is counter-terrorism. As the SIRC report states, "Most – though not all – terrorist threats to the security of Canada are related to conflicts in other lands." So our spies may keep an eye on local Arab fundamentalists to make sure they don't carry through orders from religious fanatics in Iran to kill writers. Separatist Sikhs who have imported their feud from India are another threat. IRA supporters, Lebanese, Turks and Armenians and Albanians, all carrying on their own national grudges, may be plotting against their traditional enemies even in Canada. In Ottawa, for example, Armenian terrorists murdered a Turkish diplomat in the late 1970s and later stormed the Turkish Embassy, killing a security guard.

CSIS is constantly under public scrutiny, but many Canadians agree with civil libertarian Alan Borovoy, who has said publicly that the CSE should also have a watchdog committee keeping an eye on it as SIRC watches CSIS. The CSE is the richest and yet the least known of Canada's intelligence agencies, but it has an extraordinary history. It was set up in June 1941 under the umbrella of the National Research Council as Canada's wartime code-breaking centre and was called the Examination Unit. In 1947 it changed its name to the Communications Branch of the National Research Council and then became the Communications Security Establishment in 1975 under National Defence.

Most Canadians have never heard of the CSE, although its name gets raised in Parliament from time to time, usually by naive MPs who never mention it again after their party comes into power. No one knows how many people work there, but a good guess is between six and eight hundred. Today the Chief, as he is officially called, is Peter Hunt.

Home to the CSE is the Sir Leonard Tilley Building, a large, plain L-shaped brick building surrounded by barbed wire on Heron Road in Confederation Heights, once a leafy suburb of Ottawa and now just a few hundred acres of ugly government buildings. The CSE building is on the ceremonial route into Ottawa from Uplands Airport, and VIPs pass it all the time without knowing what it is or who works there. One of the many reasons people hate working there is that it is in the middle of nowhere; the nearest place to go for lunch is the dreary little Billings Bridge shopping plaza, a five-minute drive away.

Casual passersby don't notice the thicket of antennae cluttering the building's roof. They fail to see that employees must pass through a guardhouse before they enter the building, a guardhouse where their faces and their passes are carefully scanned. Another security desk carefully scrutinizes them again at the front door. No other office window is closer than a few hundred feet away, but new CSE employees worry they're being spied on by neighbours with zoom-lensed cameras and high-powered telescopes. Some CSE workers have even refused to work next to windows.

The history of the birth of the CSE was held under a top-secret classification by the Department of National Defence until 1986, when it was released under freedom of information law to Mr. X of Wolfe's Island, near Kingston. Mr. X, also known as Scott Foster (he had his name changed legally to X several years ago), collects espionage history, among his many other interests. From his studies of British, U.S. and German intelligence work during the Second World War, he knew Canada was heavily involved as well. He took the Defence Department to court and, acting as his own lawyer over a two-year period, won a difficult judgement that these historic documents be released to the public under freedom of information law.

In 1941, as the war progressed, Ottawa's mandarins and military chiefs were anxious to be involved with the main players of espionage in Washington, New York and London. After all, Bill Stephenson was a Canadian. Stephenson, then forty-five, was responsible for British intelligence gathering in North and South America and served as the chief liaison with the U.S. security service, the Office of Strategic Services run by General William (Wild Bill) Donovan.

But the British, too, needed to expand their code-breaking operations. According to Toronto historian David Stafford in his 1986 book, *Camp X*, the British wanted to move some of their top code breakers from the cipher centre at Bletchley Park in England to North America. Stephenson wanted to expand operations in Canada. Even though the British at first objected to a Canadian operation, it was agreed to set up a code-breaking unit in Ottawa.

The godfathers of the new Canadian service included Lester Pearson, who had just returned from a senior posting in London to take up the second-in-command's job at External Affairs, and Charles Ritchie, now celebrated for his diaries but then an aide to Vincent Massey, Canadian high commissioner to London. Ritchie was the liaison between Pearson and Massey; Ritchie was also getting advice from the British intelligence chiefs at MI6.

Other Canadians involved were Arnold Heeney, then the Clerk of the Privy Council, General W.W. Murray, then the head of Canadian military intelligence, and Norman Robertson, later the Clerk of the Privy Council but then under-secretary of state for external affairs and Pearson's boss. Pearson and Robertson arranged for two University of Toronto mathematics professors to go to Washington to talk to American security experts about how to start our own code-breaking unit, often called signals intelligence. (Spy jargon today refers to the CSE and its fellow agencies as SIGINT, for signals intelligence.)

Pearson said later in his memoirs, in the only reference to the new spy shop, "Our unit was concerned with breaking enemy codes, not with the more glamorous work of snaring and shooting spies, but it did outstanding work in its own field."

The professors came back from Washington full of news about a famous American cryptographer called Herbert Yardley, recommended by General Mauborgne, the U.S. signals chief, who would be willing to come to Ottawa to set up a modest cryptography unit. Yardley, a brilliant self-taught cryptographer, had set up the U.S. Army's first signals intelligence unit in 1917 and had remained as head of the secret American cryptographic department from 1919 to 1929. He set it up in a New York brownstone in 1918 and called it the Black Chamber, after France's famous First World War code-breaking unit, the Chambre Noir.

But in 1929, uncomfortable with what it believed to be warlike activity, the U.S. government disbanded the unit, despite Yardley's pleas to expand it into a large-scale operation. Enraged, Yardley took his revenge in 1931 by publishing *The American Black Chamber*, a book that described the development of the U.S. War Department and military intelligence cryptographic work. Because the book tipped off foreign powers, especially the Japanese, that their codes had been compromised, it was the military's turn to get angry. They took him to court to prevent him from publishing a second book about Japanese battle codes in 1933, but he used the material anyway – in 1933 he simply turned it into a spicy novel called *The Blonde Countess*. In 1938 he went to Chungking, China, travelling as a hides trader under the name Herbert Osborn, but his real job was training some of Chiang Kai-shek's officers in breaking Japanese battle codes. By 1940 he was back in Washington and bored; the offer from the Canadians delighted him.

To avoid setting up another branch of government, Pearson and Murray decided to tuck it under the wing of the National Research Council, and found them a stately old house on Laurier Avenue in Sandy Hill, right beside Mackenzie King's house. Yardley's pay was set at $550 a month; his assistant (and later his wife), Edna Ramsaier, received $250. Seven Canadians joined them, including Norman Robertson's sister, Mary Oliver, who was hired to run the office. Using training pamphlets he'd wheedled from Mauborgne, Yardley trained his fledgling cryptographers in the arcane art of code breaking. Much of what they were decoding was the transmitted radio garble sent on from British Security Coordination in New York, which itself, according to David Stafford, received much of the material from the wireless facilities at Camp X. Some material came from listeners at army headquarters in Ottawa.

The material originated from three main sources. First there was traffic between Vichy, France, and the French Embassy in Ottawa, material that Stephenson's people found dovetailed neatly with traffic between Vichy and the French Embassy in

Washington. Then there was a great deal of communication between German Abwehr agents in South America, especially in Brazil, and their masters in Berlin. The Abwehr agents often cabled terrified messages about imminent discovery and capture. Finally, there was a great deal of Japanese wireless traffic.

Even though Yardley complained about his pay, whined for American "smokes" and asked Pearson to get some Camels brought back in the diplomatic pouch from Washington, the Examination Unit was doing good work. The only problem was a lack of cooperation from the British, especially Stephenson's outfit in New York.

The explanation came unexpectedly from Massey, who warned External Affairs Minister Louis St. Laurent on July 5, 1941, that the British were worried about Yardley and the Americans were still angry about Yardley's 1931 book. "There is a feeling Osborn is money-grubbing, unreliable and untrustworthy," wrote aide Charles Ritchie on Massey's behalf. Pearson fired Herbert Yardley on November 22, 1941, and one of Pearson's colleagues, Tommy Stone, a senior diplomat who was one of Canada's best intelligence experts, who was present at the interview, described how painful it was. "We had a most unpleasant half-hour. Yardley accused us of bringing him up here and picking his brains dry and turning over into other hands various new methods of cryptographic problems which he had developed."

Yardley fought hard against his expulsion, even writing to Eleanor Roosevelt, the wife of U.S. President Franklin Roosevelt, to ask her to help him, but it was no use. By the end of December 1941 he and Edna were gone.

The unit survived Yardley's forced exit; indeed, it thrived. By 1944 it had grown to about fifty people, headed by an English intelligence officer, Oliver Strachey. They worked closely with Stephenson's New York office. They brought in a talented young Oxford-trained historian called Herbert Norman to translate Japanese battle codes. Norman, a Communist before the war, joined External Affairs in 1939, but moved over to the unit in 1942 as head of a Special Intelligence Section, set up, writes David Stafford, at the urging of Stephenson, who had unsuccessfully tried to hire Norman for the British Security Coordination. Norman hired an assistant and three support staff, including his brother, who was only nineteen but spoke Japanese, to analyze the intercepted Japanese traffic and prepare reports on Japan and the Far East. Just before the Japanese attack on Pearl Harbor, the unit picked up signals that made it clear an attack was imminent, but no one realized the significance of the messages and they were not decoded in time.

In later years, Herbert Norman's life was not a happy one; although he became ambassador to Japan after the war, he fell under suspicion of being a Communist spy and was questioned by RCMP security services and the FBI. Pearson always protected Norman, but a renewal of charges against him in the U.S. Congress finally broke him. In March 1957, when he was Canadian ambassador to Egypt, he threw himself off the ninth-floor balcony of the Canadian Embassy in Cairo. Some questioned his death, wondering if it was foul play; most saw it as the final act of a distraught man.

After the war, the government planned to wind up the affairs of the Examination Unit, but just as the place was being disbanded in 1945, the Gouzenko story broke. Igor Gouzenko, a Soviet cipher clerk working at the Russian Embassy, defected in September 1945 with 109 documents proving that Soviet spies were very busy in Canada. His revelations resulted in the convictions of twelve people and the establishment of a royal commission to investigate his case. The government discovered there was at least one Soviet spy ring operating in Canada and possibly more. (Gouzenko was given a new identity, wrote two books about his adventures, appeared on many television shows with a bag over his head, and died in 1982.)

The Gouzenko affair convinced the government that the Examination Unit should not only be saved but moved to larger quarters and beefed up. So the unit changed its name to the Communications Branch of the National Research Council (CBNRC is how it was known), rented an old Grey Nuns' convent on Echo Drive and set up shop concentrating on the Soviet threat instead of the German and Japanese. In the late 1950s the CBNRC outgrew the convent and moved to a specially designed new building at Confederation Heights.

In 1975 the unit changed its name to the Communications Security Establishment and moved over from the NRC to tuck itself under the umbrella of Defence, where it remained hidden until 1983. That's when a CBC program and some questions in the House brought the agency unwelcome publicity. And that's when we found out it had 683 unionized employees (computer technicians, scientists, cryptographers and security and intelligence experts) and about eighty managers. Since 1983, however, it has again dropped out of the public consciousness.

Two years after the war, in 1947, the CBNRC formally joined the international network of electronic eavesdroppers coordinated by the United States National Security Agency. Staff came from demobbed military men, many of them British. Among the most valuable new employees were linguists who could listen to faint voice transmissions, smothered in layers of static, coming in from Siberian airports and fishing trawlers on the Pacific coast and embassies around Ottawa, and make some sense of what they were hearing.

What the CSE actually does still baffles many people. Sources told former *Globe and Mail* Ottawa bureau chief Jeff Sallot that the CSE guards government secrets by installing special shielding devices around sensitive electronic information sources such as computers, and that the shielding also protected telephone and radio systems. The shielding devices are code-named Tempest by NATO, and a *Globe* investigation into questionable CSE support for an Ottawa manufacturer of Tempest equipment in March 1987 caused one of the few little runs of CSE stories. The *Globe*'s Peter Moon discovered that the CSE had been using equipment service contracts to prop up two financially shaky Ottawa companies, known collectively as Mist.

In the old days, the Mounties were the CSE's best clients. The Mounties had the glamorous job – as Pearson would have put it, the "snaring and shooting of spies." The Mounties got to follow people and pick locks and open mail and were at their peak of power and prestige in the mid-1950s. Peter Wright remembers coming to Ottawa in July 1955 to help the RCMP bug the new Russian embassy; although he praises the group, he forecast the problems that would bring the unit down:

> I was met at the airport by Terry Guernsey, the head of the RCMP's Counter-espionage Branch, B Branch. With him was his assistant, a Welshman named James Bennett. Guernsey was a lanky Canadian whose outwardly unflappable manner was constantly betrayed by the nervous explosive energy underneath. Guernsey was trained in Britain by both MI5 and MI6 and returned to Canada in the early 1950s convinced that the RCMP was unsuited, as a uniformed police force, to the delicate work of counter-espionage. Guernsey began to recruit civilian intelligence officers and single-handedly built up B Branch into one of the most modern and aggressive counter-espionage units in the West. Many of the ideas which later played a major role in British and American thinking, such as computerized logging of the movements of the Russian diplomats in the West, began as Guernsey initiatives. But he constantly ran up against the oppressive restrictions of the Mountie tradition, which believed that the uniformed RCMP officer was inherently superior to his civilian counterpart.

With help from defector Gouzenko and from the contractor who was putting up the new embassy and was willing to have Mounties disguised as workmen on his site, Wright wired the building, a job they called Operation Dew Worm. He installed microphones in six rooms at the northeast corner of the building, rooms that would house the embassy's intelligence offices and the cipher rooms. Eight years later, Wright wrote, microphone sweepers arrived in Ottawa and pulled them out; obviously they knew exactly where to look in the forty-two-room building.

The same thing happened in 1957, he said, when he went to Montreal to help the RCMP bug the Polish Embassy, only this time the microphones were pulled out almost immediately by Polish officials. The implication was clear; someone in Canadian intelligence must have been telling the Soviets and the Poles where the bugs were. Later, the Mounties thought it might have been Bennett, but he was cleared; no one ever really knew who.

Over the years, though, Mountie prestige faded. The striped-pants set at External Affairs would sneer over their Pouilly Fuissé at the blundering oafs in the thick-soled black shoes who burned barns and had no, well, finesse. They failed to see how a bunch of high-school graduates (as most RCMP recruits were in those days) who were trained to ride horses and catch fur poachers in the north could transform themselves into intelligence experts. They winced at the Mounties' ham-handed efforts to be part of the international intelligence game, playing against far more sophisticated and often better educated experts from the CIA and British Security's MI6.

The barn-burning and other excesses of the 1970s and the resulting MacDonald Royal Commission on RCMP wrongdoing gave the Trudeau government just the ammunition it needed; in 1984 it separated intelligence and security from police work at the RCMP, setting up CSIS instead. It has been a painful and difficult transition, but many of the tough old give-no-quarter Mounties have been pensioned off or have quit in disgust, and smoother, silkier personnel have been brought in. There are still plenty of detectives in the RCMP. They work on white-collar crime and drug smuggling and other sordid areas of low-life behaviour. What skulking there is to be done is handled by the folks at CSIS.

10

··

The Press Gang

If you want to see Mike Duffy, and most visitors to Ottawa do, whether or not they'll admit it, you have to drop by the Press Club at 150 Wellington at lunch time. There the former top CBC Ottawa correspondent, now of CTV, will be, large as life, gossiping with the Toronto *Star's* Val Sears, twisting secrets out of Bruce Phillips, once Mulroney's main media man, or flirting with a wide-eyed parliamentary intern. Mike Duffy is the most famous journalist on Parliament Hill. For whatever reason, people like to tell him things, and he always has gossip that nobody else knows. If Duffy is appointed to the Senate – the rumour that makes its way around the circuit at least twice a year – not even his fellow journalists, usually an envious lot, will mind.

In 1988 Mike Duffy, long the king of Hill reporters, was not enjoying life at the CBC. A troika of "broads," as the male reporters of the Ottawa Press Gallery liked to call them, Wendy Mesley, Anna Maria Tremonti and Catherine Wright, were brought in by the corporation as a nod in the direction of affirmative action and to even the male-female on-screen ratio. These ladies were cramping Mike's style. He didn't get the lead story every night; sometimes he even dropped down to the third or fourth item.

Suddenly an opportunity came up. Duffy picked up his marbles and went over to Baton Broadcasting to host "Sunday Edition," his own news and current events show. Now we miss Mike giving us the real poop on "The National" and we yearn for his shameless upstaging of other reporters on pundits' panels. And he probably misses the clout that comes with his former job.

Make no mistake about it: just as there is an inner, inner Cabinet – the prime minister's new eight-person Spending Review Committee – and an inner Cabinet – the nineteen-person Planning and Priorities Committee – there is a similar pecking order among journalists on the Hill, and Mike Duffy lost his place when he left "The National." Although the Ottawa Press Gallery membership grows every year and now numbers about 350, which includes dozens of cameramen, soundmen, producers and photographers, only the handful of jobs listed below really count.

- The *Globe and Mail*'s Ottawa columnist, or "the bottom corner of page six," as it is known, currently held by Jeffrey Simpson. Before Simpson's tenure, the column was written by such distinguished journalists as Michael Valpy, Geoffrey Stevens (who wrote the column for nine years and is often considered the best writer to have held the job) and George Bain.

  Simpson is widely respected for his even-handed, academic style and his articulate summaries of parliamentary business on CBC Television's Sunday night news. His job is not to break news stories but to analyze them, and he often gives the impression among his colleagues of scorning the poor wretches who pick and shovel their way through interviews and paper trails to produce a major story. Simpson rarely offends anyone and is as much a part of the city's Establishment as the most senior of deputy ministers.

- The national column for the Toronto *Star*, now held by
  Carol Goar. The *Star* made news itself when it replaced
  Richard Gwyn, a widely respected and well-liked journalist
  who had been transferred to London, with Goar, the first
  woman to be appointed to the job. Goar's appointment
  enraged some of the boys in the Ottawa bureau, but she was
  used to that. The same thing had happened when Goar was
  appointed Ottawa bureau chief for *Maclean's* magazine, the
  posting she held before she took over the Gwyn column.

  Goar, a shy workaholic, is at heart a reporter rather than a
  columnist. Her solidly written columns are crammed with
  research and information instead of being pumped up lazily
  with opinion. As Larry Zolf puts it, "She is the best
  explainer in Ottawa. No one can explain something complicated like the deficit better than Carol Goar." She will
  occasionally write a profile of someone, as she did of Alberta
  Tory Senator Martha Bielish, which provides a moving,
  humane picture of a politician under unfair attack. Bielish
  was being widely criticized for her lengthy absences from
  the Senate. Goar discovered that Bielish was coping with a
  gravely ill husband while taking over his chores on the
  family farm.

  Goar is sometimes accused of being *too* fair, of lacking the
  columnist's necessary edge. In profiles of three new MPs
  elected in 1988, for example, she failed to mention that one
  of them, Calgary Tory Lee Richardson, a former aide to
  both Alberta Premier Peter Lougheed and to Prime Minister
  Mulroney, had been forgiven loans of $410,000 by the Bank
  of Montreal in 1983. The terms were extraordinary: Richardson was required to pay back only $50,000, interest-free,
  over nine years. Goar is too good a journalist not to have
  known about the uproar this caused, but probably felt
  Richardson deserved a break. This compassion is one reason
  Goar is among the few powerful journalists on the Hill
  without enemies.

- The senior political correspondent at CBC Television, a job held by David Halton. Halton, a fluently bilingual Ottawan – and son of legendary reporter Matthew Halton – lends his comfortable, respected authority to CBC broadcasts. Like Simpson, he is primarily a news analyst and he is uncomfortable with scandal. In private he is a funny, cynical man who lives in the elite mandarin habitat of Rockcliffe Park.

- The senior parliamentary writer for *Le Devoir*, a job now held by Michel Vastel. *Le Devoir*, a Montreal paper with a circulation of less than forty thousand, has an influence far beyond its size, and its Ottawa writer is always a key member of the Ottawa press corps. *Le Devoir* is considered the leading French-language opinion-maker on constitutional issues such as the Meech Lake Accord and on language questions like Quebec's Bill 101.

  Vastel is not French-Canadian, but French, and he sometimes looks down with Gallic hauteur not just on English Canada but on Quebec as well. He is a gritty, hard-working reporter to be found in the middle of every scrum and every brawl, whipping his tape recorder under the loose lip of every passing politician. Despite his tough exterior, he is generous with other reporters who need his help in making a vital link in a Quebec story.

- The senior parliamentary correspondent for CTV, the job held by Craig Oliver. Oliver, a seasoned veteran who has hosted CTV's "Canada AM," offered the only peppery coverage of the bland 1988 Tory election campaign. Clearly impatient with the Tories' cautious say-nothing program, Oliver often delivered commentaries etched in acid.

- The senior parliamentary correspondent for CBC Radio, the job held by Jason Moscovitz. Moscovitz may well be the best investigative reporter in Ottawa. Bilingual and a native Montrealer, he spent four years in Quebec City covering the provincial legislature during the Parti Québécois years. He broke one Quebec scandal after another on "The National" during the first years of the Mulroney government. As a result and quite predictably, say CBC insiders, CBC bosses received call after call from senior Tories about Moscovitz. Reliable sources say the CBC brass even tried – unsuccessfully – to move him to Vancouver. It must be remembered that the CBC suffered $85 million in cuts from their budget soon after the Tories came to power, and most Conservatives were convinced that CBC reporters were a nest of left-wing Liberal sympathizers. As the CBC brass were in the middle of negotiating a new licence with the Canadian Radio-television and Telecommunications Commission for an all-news TV channel, Moscovitz's exposés became more trying.

Finally, in a clever manoeuvre, CBC insiders say, the brass assigned him to every reporter's dream – investigative stories. Because investigative work is painstaking and time-consuming, Moscovitz rarely appeared on the news. As the Mulroney years rolled on, CBC Television in Ottawa broke fewer and fewer stories of any kind, preferring instead to follow events of the day on the Hill, expanding on Question Period dust-ups and PMO press releases. When "The National" dared to stick a toe into a controversial story it was often only to cover a print story, broken by hard-scrabble reporters from the *Globe and Mail*, the Toronto *Star*, the Montreal *Gazette* or the Ottawa *Citizen*. Only the reporters and producers at CBC Television's "fifth estate" actually tried to break stories. Their biggest triumph in the last five years was the 1985 tainted tuna story.

No wonder Moscovitz finally left television for the CBC's senior radio job in Ottawa, replacing Brian Kelleher, who had moved to CBC Radio's Washington bureau. Today we hear Moscovitz on CBC radio regularly, but his wit and his edge are best enjoyed when he is a guest or guest host on Judy Morrison's weekly CBC radio show, "The House," on Saturday morning.

- The national column for Southam News, held by Don McGillivray and offered to all fifteen Southam papers across Canada and is also marketed to non-Southam papers through

Southam Syndicate. McGillivray could well be the best-loved journalist on the Hill. An RCMP nut who collects Mountie paraphernalia, ephemera and junk, he seems to live in his book-lined office at Southam News headquarters on Sparks Street, which is crammed to the gunnels with *Hansards*, files, press releases and encyclopaedias. In fact, McGillivray does as much lurking in parliamentary corridors as do the most starry-eyed new Hill reporters.

McGillivray also teaches at the Carleton University School of Journalism and brings his large journalism classes to his house for dinner a couple of times a year. He's seen it all, many times, and while he never patronizes eager juniors, he can guard them against excessive zeal because he knows the traps. But McGillivray loves a good story and will always throw himself into the pit as a researcher for even the most junior reporter who needs advice.

At least twice a week McGillivray stuffs his pockets with cash and travels up and down the Sparks Street Mall to Morrow's Nut Shop and to Marks and Spencer's food shop and to Shoppers Drug Mart gathering bags of treats: chocolate kisses when Allan Fotheringham worked there, licorice allsorts, jujubes, jelly beans, Smarties, cookies and assorted gourmet teas for other colleagues. It's amusing to see even the most dignified and stately correspondents ambling around to McGoo's candy jars for a sugar hit in the late afternoon and snivelling like a four-year-old when they are out of their favourite. Someone once estimated that McGillivray's generosity costs him $2,000 to $3,000 a year.

- The Ottawa bureau chief and columnist for the *Financial Post*, Hyman Solomon. Solomon, a tall, lanky man with a thick thatch of greying hair, is an unnervingly good listener, slow to judge but ruthless when he makes up his mind – after fastidious weighing of the evidence – that a deputy minister is an idiot or that a policy is trash. He is particularly well liked by the senior mandarins in Ottawa who trust him implicitly; they know that he is not a hungry young reporter slavering for a news hit and willing to burn them to do it. They also know he is one of the few reporters in the city interested in the public service as a beat. Solomon distills his patient, thorough research into one of the best-informed columns in the city.

- "The House," hosted by Judy Morrison. Morrison, who endured polite hostility to her presence from an all-male radio news staff for years, has emerged as one of the Hill's stars over the past few years. Her CBC Radio show runs every week and is now the best radio program on national politics in Canada, crisply delivered with humour and style. She can be merciless with her guests, as she was in a January 1988 interview with a stumbling Multiculturalism Minister Gerry Weiner, who could not deliver three clear sentences in a row on government immigration policy. Speaking out for impatient listeners, she accused Weiner of waffling and tried to pin him down again and again. Finally, disgusted, she dismissed him. "You're sitting on both sides of the fence," she said before closing down his microphone.

- Parliamentary columnist for the Ottawa *Citizen*, Marjorie Nichols. Nichols, an outspoken westerner, is one of the Gallery's most colourful figures, principally because she has courage and because she does not give a damn about what people might say. Nichols is willing to tackle any politician. Her contempt for Mulroney and his gang shows through clearly, but it is always based on meticulous research. Most recently, Nichols has been battling lung cancer. A heavy smoker, she was diagnosed in 1987 and given a few months to live, but she told friends that she was determined to be one of the small percentage of people who survive. With nothing to lose, she submitted to a ferocious regime of experimental drugs, then hauled herself back to her three columns a week. Perhaps the most emotional moment at any Press Gallery annual dinner in years was the welcome back for Marjorie Nichols and the Thomson chain's well-liked Ottawa columnist, Stewart MacLeod, at the 1988 dinner after both had been on sick leave fighting cancer.

Speaking at a political dinner in Vancouver in 1987, Marjorie Nichols cracked the joke that will live forever in Canadian politics: "Despite what you may hear, Bill Vander Zalm is not stupid. They bring him to the federal-provincial relations meetings so he can explain Meech Lake to Don Getty." Don Getty was *not* amused and one of his staff wrote an angry letter to the paper when the joke was printed as a Quote of the Day in the *Globe and Mail*. Bill Vander Zalm didn't complain probably because he didn't get it.

- Parliamentary columnist for Thomson Newspapers, Stewart MacLeod. MacLeod has held this spot for many years, but people in Ottawa rarely get a chance to read him because Ottawa has no Thomson papers except the *Globe and Mail*, which doesn't run MacLeod's column. However, MacLeod's columns are widely read in the dozens of smaller Canadian newspapers in which they appear.

Almost all the journalists working on the Hill are among the top reporters in their organizations. A Hill assignment is for most the peak of their careers. *Globe* reporters might hope some day to head for bureaus in Washington, Beijing or London, but until then – and only if they are very good – they might get to Ottawa. Newcomers to the Hill these days often have law degrees or M.A.s or Ph.D.s. Most are bilingual and have years of experience in different areas of reporting. What so many lack, however, is institutional memory. No matter how bright the rookie reporters are who come into town for the *Globe* and the CBC, Ottawa's smalltown rules and historical connections are difficult to master. When Norman Spector, the secretary to the Cabinet for federal-provincial relations, gives Quebecer Florence Ievers a senior job as an assistant secretary to the Cabinet, new reporters think nothing of it. Old hands are surprised: they remember that Ievers was once a political staff member of Trudeau's PMO, responsible for processing patronage appointments.

To most MPs, the reporters who really count are not the Ottawa stars but the ones in their ridings who write for the hometown paper. After all, that's where the MP gets re-elected. As Jack Ellis, the former Conservative MP for Belleville, Ontario, once said, "The major reporters and the major papers are not important to me. What's important to me is the Belleville *Intelligencer* and the reporter who is important to me is their political reporter who works out of Belleville."

Another group of important journalists are those working at slaveship Canadian Press, where the unofficial slogan is "Have you written your ten stories today?" Only a few Canadian newspapers and broadcasters can afford their own Ottawa bureaus; they depend on the team of reporters and photographers and rewrite people at CP.

Canadian Press reporters are the unsung heroes of Canadian journalism. All day long they feed stories to Canadian newspapers and broadcasters, updating them constantly. They cover Question Period brilliantly, always extracting the real news quickly and succinctly from all the hot air. Less than an hour after Question Period ends, editors across Canada can count on CP filing its stories. If an 11:00 a.m. Cabinet shuffle is on, you can count on CP to start filing the names on the wire by 11:03. Their leads are sharp and tight. These stalwart journalists are usually anonymous. Most editors remove the CP reporter's byline before the story goes into the paper, or marry it, with the credit "and Canadian Press," to a story written by one of their own Ottawa bureau writers.

CP reporters are enraged by reporters for other newspapers who sit at their computer terminals, which are all wired into Canadian Press, and wait for CP reporters to file. Then these other reporters, without an ounce of conscience or remorse, pick through the CP reporter's story, pulling out facts that might have escaped them and rewriting them into their own stories. One Ottawa reporter working for a big paper used to sit at his terminal as the clock ticked on, screaming at it, "File, goddamnit, file! These guys are just screwing me around!"

Reporters like this justify their behaviour by saying their editors will do the same later anyway. This is why CP reporters cannot contain their glee when one of their stories, complete with byline, makes page one of a major paper like the Toronto *Star*. It means their story was judged by *Star* editors to be better than the one filed by the *Star* reporter. Naturally the *Star* reporter will be wild. Many CP reporters become stars who are picked off by big papers; good examples are the terrible twosome Bob Fife and Tim Naumetz, who now work for the Toronto *Sun*. During the first three years of the Mulroney government Fife and Naumetz were names that made the Mulroney press office shake. Often working together as a team, they broke scandal after scandal.

Southam News service is an auxiliary wire service that files to all fifteen of Southam's papers and to its weekly *Financial Times* as well as to a few other papers. Southam News tends to offer background and analysis to complement CP's hard news. Every Ottawa reporter dreams of working at Southam's, which has about twelve staff in the parliamentary bureau, another half dozen across the country and another six or seven around the world. They have the most lavish expense accounts, the most interesting trips, the merriest farewell lunches.

Southam stars have included Christopher Young (a former managing editor of the Ottawa *Citizen* and the Southam News Service, now the service's Moscow correspondent), Charles Lynch and Allan Fotheringham. In the past Southam News rarely gave jobs to women in Ottawa, although they do have a few women correspondents outside Ottawa, such as Aileen McCabe. Women who have worked there complain of being ignored at story meetings and excluded from the martini and tennis outings. Today there are two women in the Southam Ottawa bureau, Juliet O'Neil and Joan Bryden.

(The national Press Gallery was once just as much an old boys' club as the House itself, and the rare female reporter who worked there was usually tolerated – if she was willing to put up with the sexist jokes – but never really accepted. Today there is a small minority of thirty-nine women covering Parliament.)

Outside of important regional reporters like the Halifax *Chronicle-Herald*'s Don MacDonald, the Winnipeg *Free Press*'s Joan Cohen, and the *Edmonton Journal*'s Geoff White, there are the mavericks, the Press Gallery freelancers who wield plenty of clout. The most famous is Claire Hoy, whose column, distributed by Southam Syndicate, runs three times a week in about twenty Canadian papers. He also writes a weekly City Hall column for the *Citizen*. Hoy's 1987 bestseller, *Friends in High Places*, about Brian Mulroney and the scandals and pratfalls of his first three years in power, is still selling well and its royalties kept him afloat when he lost his job at the Toronto *Sun* in 1988. When Hoy was working at the *Sun*, he said that he was not writing for his peers, as so many Ottawa journalists do, nor for the country's powerbrokers, but for "the little guy on the Queen streetcar."

Like Marjorie Nichols, Claire Hoy is not afraid of anyone. He refuses to play the game and does not socialize with politicians or with their staff. He despises Ottawa's sleazy lobbyists and hustlers. He believes that when reporters get too cosy with politicians they will pull their punches or ignore a potentially damaging story.

Hoy is convinced that his hostility to the man he dubbed "Lyin' Brian" and to Mila got him fired from the *Sun* in 1987. He believes that *Sun* publisher Paul Godfrey, a staunch Tory, had taken so much flak from Mulroney over Hoy's persistent rants against the Mulroneys that he ordered Hoy back to Toronto. Hoy claimed this order amounted to constructive dismissal. He sued Godfrey and the *Sun*; the case is still awaiting trial. Even Hoy's admirers wince at his visceral hostility to homosexuals, the pro-choice movement and to human rights commissions and believe these attitudes didn't help his case with the *Sun*.

Another *Sun* reporter who left abruptly after one too many

snipes at the Mulroneys was Derik Hodgson. Hodgson printed one unflattering Mulroney story after another and finally his bosses had had enough; they demoted him and ordered him back to Toronto. Hodgson quit in disgust and is now working for the Canadian Labour Congress.

Freelancer and author John Sawatsky is another important Press Gallery figure. A gentle, soft-spoken former Hill report- er for the Vancouver *Sun*, he is best-known as an expert on the RCMP and espionage. With his long-time research col- league, Harvey Cashore, Sawatsky is now in the middle of a four-year project, a full-scale history of how Brian Mulroney won the Conservative leadership in 1983 and the federal election in 1984.

A meticulous researcher, Sawatsky leaves nothing to chance. He has even programmed computers with specially designed software to index and cross-reference all the names and facts for the book.

Then there is another group of influential journalists who are unknown to the public, yet who play critical roles behind the scenes. These are the editors and producers who call the shots on the stories. One of the most powerful has been Elly Alboim, the tough, well-respected producer of the Ottawa section of the CBC's "The National," now a journalism teacher at Carleton. And there is David McCormick, the Ottawa producer for "The Journal," a good-natured, quiet Winnipeg- ger who, in some ways, is the most fawned-upon journalist on the Hill because he's the one who picks the politicians and journalists who talk to Barbara Frum every night.

Whether or not the House is sitting, the *Globe and Mail* and *Le Devoir* often set the agenda for the day on the Hill. Every morning official Ottawa grabs these papers to see what's on page one, what issue columnist Jeffrey Simpson has tackled on page six, what Quebec Liberal backbench revolt is brewing under Michel Vastel's byline in *Le Devoir*.

If the House is sitting, Opposition MPs huddle in their

tactics meetings each morning to decide what questions to ask in Question Period that afternoon; more often than not, their questions are based on *Globe* or *Le Devoir* stories. Often there will be stories in the *Gazette*, especially by Montreal reporters Claude Arpin, Bill Marsden and Rod McDonnell, who often do a brilliant job of Ottawa reporting from Montreal, or in the *Citizen* or the *Star*, that will trigger questions as well, but rarely does a radio or television news show break a story or raise an issue that will surface later in the House. A momentous exception, of course, was Global Television's Doug Small and his celebrated news break of Michael Wilson's leaked budget on April 26, 1989.

For Gallery newcomers, the press theatre is a chamber of terror. Like an MP standing in the House to make a maiden speech or ask her first question, the first time a reporter gets up to ask the prime minister or a Cabinet minister a question, it is hard to keep the voice from quivering or the hand from shaking.

Outsiders would be surprised to know how closely Gallery reporters work with Opposition politicians on certain stories. During their years in Ottawa politicians and reporters often develop useful working relationships and strong friendships. A reporter covering External Affairs or the environment or the Supreme Court will often become close to an Opposition MP who is the party's critic for that department. A reporter chasing a good story about a dubious fishing licence issued in Halifax or a strange stock deal in Vancouver will naturally look for help from the Opposition MPs who represent ridings in these areas.

Reporters and Opposition MPs need each other. A reporter wants the story, the MP wants good publicity and to make the government look incompetent, sleazy or stupid and preferably all three. When an MP gets a hot tip on a good story, he or she will often pass it on to a favourite reporter; the deal is that no other reporter will get it and the two will share information as the story is nailed down. If the story looks as if it will work, the two must come to an agreement on how it will be handled.

Nothing makes a print reporter more furious than to have an MP say he will give the story to only two people: the print reporter and a television reporter. If the MP gives them both the story at the same time, say in the late afternoon, the TV reporter can get it on the national news that night. The print reporter will be scooped because the earliest he or she can get into print is the next morning's paper. A worse sin is to leak the same story to more than one print reporter. But it works both ways. An MP can do what a reporter cannot – advance the story in the House during Question Period. All House communication is "privileged." In other words, an MP cannot be charged with libel or slander if he or she reviles another member or anyone else in the House. Outside the House, out in the corridors, for example, an MP is subject to the same rules as any other citizen. Government spokespeople, of course, become skilled at dodging embarrassing questions, but even just asking the question and getting it on the record provides the reporter with what he needs to get a story rolling.

"Will the minister tell us if John Doe, the minister's brother, received an untendered contract from Supply and Services of $50,000 for widgets?" an Opposition MP may ask. "And if so, will the minister explain how this happened and how many other widget contracts his brother has received?" (The cardinal rule for setting up a question like this is to know the answer.) This question may have come from a tip given to a reporter from an unhappy widget maker who never had a chance to bid on the contract. But because the reporter can't get his calls returned by the minister, he gets the Opposition MP to call the minister to account during Question Period. Advancing the story this way allows the reporter and other interested journalists to harass the hapless minister in a scrum in the House lobby after Question Period, unless the issue is so hot that the minister's staff has arranged for him or her to duck out a back entrance.

If the issue is a major scandal, a rolling scrum may develop: a mob of reporters surrounds the minister, who tries to avoid them. The minister's aides push forward in a flying wedge while reporters press in, trying to capture the victim's words on their tape recorders. The television cameramen walk backwards in front of the whole procession, frantically trying to keep their own reporter in the picture with the minister.

The most memorable rolling scrum the House has seen in recent years was on Monday, May 12, 1986, the day Sinclair Stevens resigned. Stevens, the minister of regional industrial expansion, had been under attack for several days in the House after two *Globe* reporters, David Stewart-Patterson and Michael Harris, revealed that Stevens' wife, Noreen, had received $2.6 million in loans for the Stevens' cash-strapped companies from a businessman connected to Magna International, the auto parts manufacturer that had received millions of dollars in government grants from Stevens' department.

As the days went on and more and more details of the loan and the Stevens' business dealings were revealed, the cries for Stevens' resignation grew among Opposition MPs. Finally Stevens resigned, but he wanted to leave the House with his head held high, so he decided to go out the centre doors under the Peace Tower. Normally everyone from the prime minister to his Cabinet to reporters uses the West Entrance because it is closer to the Chamber. Hundreds of reporters, cameramen, photographers, editors and producers, all kinds of people who would not normally have left their offices, followed the minister in his procession out of the House. It turned into an ugly scene. People tripped and fell over each other and reporters close to Stevens were worried that the diminutive minister, who had been off on sick leave for months following heart surgery, might even have a cardiac arrest.

After Question Period, having figured out what the main story or stories will be, reporters usually head for the lobby outside the Chamber and lunge for Opposition MPs who will summon up some pithy outrage for the reaction needed for the story. Many Opposition MPs trawl the lobby looking for action, hoping to get a few seconds' exposure on "The

National," but reporters tend to go for the high-profile members who have the best quotes, people like Liberals Sheila Copps, Brian Tobin, Dave Dingwall and Don Boudria or the NDP's Nelson Riis, Jim Fulton or Lorne Nystrom.

When ministers or Opposition leaders stop to give reactions or comments, two or three of their own staff are always at their sides, one always taping the questions and answers just in case the minister later wants to prove he or she was misquoted.

Reporters also prowl the lobby after Question Period; maybe they don't have a definite story they're chasing, but if they see a reporter stop an MP for a comment, they'll sidle up themselves, tape recorder turned on, to see if there's anything interesting going on. Sometimes a mob of reporters will boil up around a bewildered MP who is giving a scheduled interview to a hometown reporter. Once they realize what's going on, they melt away to resume the search for fresh meat.

Many reporters prefer to cover Question Period by watching it on television from the comfort of their own offices. By doing this they miss a lot. They miss the Opposition leaders' staff, who sit anxiously in the galleries above, mouthing the answers for their bosses, taking notes on details, glancing at the Gallery for their reaction. And they miss the scrums afterwards and the corridor gossip. They miss delicious vignettes like the one in which Fisheries Minister Thomas Siddon, Ph.D., flounced into the Chamber for Question Period wearing his academic gown and hood. Mulroney looked up, noticed the Gallery snickering and turned to Siddon. Obviously furious, he ordered the minister out with a curt jerk of his thumb. The mortified Siddon crept off to remove his costume.

Unfortunately, the Press Gallery spends too much of its energies on Question Period. Day after day after day, press coverage is QP-driven. Someone may give a reporter a tip about a great scandal, but if the tip requires a three-week paper chase the reporter who is preoccupied with Question Period just won't have the time to follow it up. If reporters don't have a tip to chase during the dog days when the House isn't sitting, they often turn to old chestnuts like Senate reform or House committees for real yawners to fill the space.

The Press Gallery is such an integral part of the political system that its main building at 150 Wellington actually belongs to the House of Commons. They keep it up, staff it with its commissionaires and organize the leases on its nine floors. Because the Press Gallery is considered part of Parliament, Gallery members enjoy dining privileges in the Parliamentary Dining Room.

It used to be the Press Gallery was so small it could live happily in the House itself. Reporters worked in the "Hot Room," a long, untidy room with rows of desks wedged together, overflowing with yellowing press releases, sandwich wrappers, yesterday's papers and cigarette butts. Today the Hot Room is used mostly by the correspondents of distant papers and some freelance Gallery members like John Sawatsky and Claire Hoy. With bulky camera equipment and computers and all the new paraphernalia of the business, not to mention its swelling numbers, the press corps has outgrown all its spaces and you'll find journalists' offices all up and down Sparks and Wellington streets.

Still, the Press Building is the hub of the action. The Toronto *Star* is on the ninth floor; the *Globe* has a suite on the third. The CBC's national news has a couple of floors, which they share with "The Journal"; Global News and CTV also have suites here.

Outsiders sometimes confuse the Press Gallery and Press Club. The Gallery includes the working journalists covering Parliament; the club is their watering hole, which takes up the second floor of the Press Building. Here you can buy terrible food cheaply and let your out-of-town friends stare at some of the better-known members of the media. In fact, though, the club is used more by business and government flacks – "communications" or "information" officials who work for every-

thing from the Post Office to Air Canada – than it is by
practising journalists. If it weren't for these associate members,
the club would go broke. Some senior bureaucrats use the
club, as do some politicians and diplomats.

Down on the main floor, sharing space with Global Television and the commissionaire who knows more intriguing
secrets about journalists and politicians than anyone else in
Ottawa, you'll find the press theatre, the room with the desk,
the water jugs and the blue curtains that viewers see so often
on the nightly news. The reason you always see a journalist
sitting on the politician's left, hosting the event and choosing
the questioners, is that this is Gallery territory and the
politician is there theoretically at the invitation of the Gallery.

Rarely does the Press Gallery examine itself publicly except
under the off-the-record rules for the annual black-tie Gallery
Dinner, and even at this event politicians are roasted more
often than reporters. In 1985 both Don McGillivray and Allan
Fotheringham wrote columns about the dinner, the first for
Mulroney as prime minister. "Brian Mulroney bombed Saturday before the toughest audience a Canadian politician can
face," wrote McGillivray. Fotheringham's review of the event
described Madame Sauvé as the "boffo queen of one-liners."
As a result, the Gallery executive forbade both to come the
next year. That just fired up McGillivray; ever since then he
has run around interviewing every dinner attendee he can find
for his annual column on the event.

The Gallery Dinner is the biggest social event of the year for
most reporters. It used to be a drunken spree but today it is
quite sedate. The last time anyone got revoltingly drunk and
offensive was in 1985; the columnist and his equally drunk
date, who had heckled Mulroney and Turner throughout
their speeches, were carted off and forbidden to return the
next year.

Women spend a fortune buying evening dresses for the
dinner. Usually there is no one there better dressed than
CTV's Pamela Wallin, unless it is Flora MacDonald. In 1985

Toronto Liberal John Nunziata showed up in a snappy dinner jacket, wing collar, red cummerbund and red Reeboks.

Reporters can invite politicians, bureaucrats, diplomats and other notables to the dinner. If you ask a politician, the theory goes, you get a better table than if you take a deputy minister or a political aide. Captains of industry who wing in on the late afternoon flight from Toronto are disconcerted to find themselves seated at the fringes while obscure backbenchers are front and centre. Everyone would like to ask International Trade Minister John Crosbie, but he can be disappointing company. The wittiest public speaker in the city is, in private, a shy man with minimal small talk. They should ask his effervescent wife, Jane, instead. Other guests in great demand are Finance Minister Michael Wilson (let's see how many invitations he gets next year, in the wake of the budget leak fiasco), Employment and Immigration Minister Barbara McDougall and Mulroney's principal secretary, Stanley Hartt. Most people assume the luminaries have already been asked by the Gallery's bigshots. The day before the dinner panicky senior aides and ministers quietly let it be known that they have not yet been invited. That's why heavyweights sometimes end up at the dinner with extremely junior reporters or a laconic cameraman who hadn't gotten around to asking anyone. Some Ottawans lobby outrageously for dinner invitations. One of the most persistent was always Gaetana Enders, the wife of former U.S. ambassador Thomas Enders. She would usually call up her friend, John Grace, then the editor of the Ottawa *Journal*, and coax him into asking her.

Before dinner everyone meets for drinks in the Hall of Honour in Parliament's Centre Block, and before drinks most news organizations hold their own cocktail parties. There is even a fair bit of pushing and shoving to get invited to the most important of these. God help a poor reporter who can't take his or her guest to a pre-cocktail cocktail party thrown by Southam's or the *Globe* or the *Star*.

After the Hall of Honour reception, guests cram the

elevators for the sixth-floor Parliamentary Dining Room. Here the tables are desperately crowded and for once, because of the number of people, the food is execrable. But everyone's really here for the speeches. For the last four years Governor General Jeanne Sauvé has led off with a priceless speech. It is the one time all year when she can abandon vice-regal reserve and voice her opinions. Most of her best jokes take a sly dig at Mulroney. In 1985 she delicately flayed him for the Quebec City Summit snub when he excluded her from his first meeting in Canada with U.S. President Ronald Reagan. But like all the best Gallery Dinner speakers, Madame Sauvé pokes fun at herself more than at anyone else. In 1988 she gave out imaginary Oscars to politicians, reserving one for herself as the best actress in a leading role in *The Incredible Lightness of Being*. This was rueful recognition of her own lack of real power, but it was also a slip of the stiletto into Mulroney.

She is followed by the three leaders. John Turner gave a brilliant speech in 1985 and, according to all the reports, won everyone's hearts when he made fun of his own housing humiliations. Not only were damaging leaks coming out of PMO about the renovation expenses of Stornoway, but John and Nicole Bosley had evicted him from the Speaker's residence at Kingsmere where he had been living while Stornoway was being finished. At that time a group of protesters were squatting in a raggedy tent on the lawns of Parliament Hill, and Turner joked that he was hoping they'd find space for him. Ed Broadbent is always funny. A sort of uneasy atmosphere lies over the crowd when Brian Mulroney speaks.

His first speech as PM laid an egg because he did not understand the culture of the event and saw fit to rub Opposition noses in his massive majority and in their troubles. The next year someone coached him and this time he knew enough to make jokes at his own expense about ministerial scandals and patronage excesses.

After the dinner, people move to the West Block of the House of Commons to watch the Gallery Show. The show used to be the jealously guarded property of people like Charles Lynch and Don Newman; now a younger group have moved in and the amateur days are gone. One of the best performers is, without question, Michel Gratton, who can sing like Robert Charlebois and, for reasons known to no one but himself, often chooses to do so in the top half of a rubber wet suit. CBC Radio's Jeannette Matthey sings with a clear voice of professional calibre and the *Sun*'s Joe O'Donnell, now in Washington, used to ham it up in the smoky tones of a lounge singer. The funniest is always the *Citizen*'s Robert Lee, who has perfected the role of the gormless dork for any occasion.

Every year the skits and songs are based on the major stories of the year; reporters and politicians alike sit tensely in the audience, bracing themselves for a cold dose of satire. When it is all over, many of the crowd go to the Press Club where, if they are lucky, they can join the prime minister in a round of "When Irish Eyes Are Smiling."

PART FOUR

UPSTAIRS DOWNSTAIRS

11

Location, Location, Location

Does it matter where you live in Ottawa? "Definitely," says Dennis Mills, Liberal MP from Toronto's Broadview-Greenwood riding and a senior aide to Prime Minister Pierre Trudeau from 1980 to 1984. "If you want to get into the game in Ottawa you have to live in Rockcliffe or the Glebe. I mean, if you're an aide in Ottawa and you live in one of those highrise towers with everyone else you'll get treated one way by the bureaucrats; if you live in a house on Linden Terrace in the Glebe you'll get treated another way. They'll take you seriously."

Another way of making Mills' point is to say that Ottawa is like any other small town. If you are important enough you can live anywhere, but if you are a newcomer, people will judge you, to some extent, by where you live. Linden Terrace, for example, is one of the very best streets in the Glebe, a fashionable community that begins just twenty blocks due south of the House of Commons. The large brick houses have generous verandahs and deep gardens, but best of all, they have no neighbours across the street. Instead, they turn their complacent faces to Patterson Creek, a picturesque little branch of the Rideau Canal from which was pulled, several years ago, a poor dead priest with multiple stab wounds.

The highrise towers that Mills scorns are places like the Queen Elizabeth Towers, a downtown highrise stuffed with politicians and political aides, sleeping two or three to a room to save money. The most famous threesome in a downtown highrise are Deputy Prime Minister Don Mazankowski; Defence Minister Bill McKnight, a farmer from Wartime, Saskatchewan; and Tory backbencher Jack Shields, a former businessman and star of the Fort McMurray, Alberta, Shriners and Kinsmen. They have been sharing an apartment for years. These are the kind of people who broke Ottawa real estate agents' hearts back in 1984 when it became clear that the new Tories were thrifty commuters, not house-proud new settlers.

One Tory MP who did buy an expensive new home after the 1984 election was Winnipeg's right-wing, anti-French Dan McKenzie, but he bought it in Oakville, Ontario, which is admittedly very fashionable but a good 350 miles from Ottawa. In Ottawa he roughed it in a downtown apartment. His home in Oakville is in the most expensive condominium in town, Ennisclare-by-the-Lake. He and his wife also used to spend a great deal of time at their holiday home in the southern United States.

According to well-informed Winnipeg Tories, McKenzie announced he wouldn't run again in 1988, so they turned over his riding, Winnipeg-Assiniboine, to an upcoming star, Dorothy Dobbie; when he started making noises that he had changed his mind, he was offered a $50,000 (plus expenses) one-year contract from Joe Clark at External Affairs to study closer economic ties with the Turks and Caicos Islands in the Caribbean. His contract was extended in June 1989.

Like most communities, Ottawa prefers settlers, and Linden Terrace means you're not just passing through. Nearby, comfortingly, are the other great streets of the Glebe: Clemow, perhaps the grandest, set with occasional embassies but sadly diminished since it lost its splendid elm trees to Dutch elm disease back in the 1960s; Monkland and Powell and the Queen Elizabeth Driveway, which meanders along the canal. These are streets to compete with the toniest streets in Rockcliffe.

Monkland was like a village of its own when it was populated by the merry canon of St. John's Anglican Church, Borden Purcell (now a member of the Refugee Determination Board in Toronto) and his wife, Carter, and the Mitchell Sharps, and the CBC's Terry Hargreaves and his wife, Jodi White. Hargreaves and White are almost the only people left in Ottawa who still throw interesting parties. CBC producer Larry Zolf and his wife, Patsy, moved to Monkland in 1970 for two years. They spent much of their time defending their two small children from Auditor General Maxwell Henderson, who kept chasing the youngsters off his lawn. The real estate agent who found the house for the Zolfs was Irene Norman, the widow of former Ottawa diplomat Herbert Norman, who threw himself off the embassy roof in Cairo in 1957 after questions were raised in the American Congress about his being a Soviet spy. "Did you know my husband?" Irene Norman asked Zolf. "No," he replied. ("You learn fast in Ottawa," he said many years later.)

Influential Tory lobbyist Pierre Fortier, president of Public Affairs International, lives on Monkland; so does a legendary former mandarin, Robert Bryce, who was made Clerk of the Privy Council in 1954 and deputy minister of finance. Down near the end of this short street live David and Chris Dodge; an assistant deputy minister at Finance, he is the government's tax reform genius, while Chris works at Treasury Board. Their Boxing Day parties, at which they serve fresh oysters and Black Velvets (stout diluted with champagne) are famous.

Another well-known Monkland couple are Sylvia Gold and her husband, Jack. Mrs. Gold is head of the Advisory Council on the Status of Women; her husband has been engaged in an extremely nasty lawsuit with the government after being bounced out of a public service job for security reasons. Mr. Gold, a self-confessed supporter of the New Democratic Party, says he won the job fair and square in a competition but lost it when it was discovered that he belonged to an anti-apartheid group.

But even the Glebe, while admittedly fashionable, is not everyone's cup of camomile. Others prefer Sandy Hill or New Edinburgh or Centre Town. The Glebe is Ottawa's granola-land, where old hippies go to become respectable. Bank Street, the main shopping street, gives the impression of being lined with stores selling unsulphurated apricots and salt-free California mix. The locals come out every Saturday morning dressed in Birkenstocks and Indian gauze and pick through the tapes of flute music in the record shops. This is a community devoted to its schools (noncompetitive sports encouraged) and to its churches: committees saving Nicaragua and saving whales fill basement halls, night after night. When asked if the Glebe had a funeral parlour, one wag responded, "I don't know, but if it did, it would be called Death 'n' Things."

Unfortunately, the Glebe is, on the whole, a dour place. The architectural style, except for some interesting renovations, is best described as late-Taft-early-Wilson. Most of the houses, set too close together on narrow lots, are built of nasty oxblood brick that never ages to a mellow pink. The windows are small, allowing the stingiest helpings of light inside, just enough to keep the spider plants alive. The grass grows only in bad-tempered spurts around gravel driveways. To many, the Glebe is a lonesome land of rooming-houses and basement flats, of students and widows and separated wives.

Nevertheless, some powerful people live in the Glebe. Superspy Reid Morden, the head of the Canadian Security and Intelligence Service, for one. International Trade Minister John Crosbie, for another, with his wife, Jane (although their permanent home is in Newfoundland). Others include Privacy

Commissioner John Grace and his wife, Ruth, and Economic Council of Canada head Judith Maxwell and her husband, Tony, who works with Treasury Board's privatization branch. Then there are former CBC mandarin Gordon Bruce and his wife, Jean, a talented writer and senior official at the National Gallery. The *Globe and Mail*'s Jeffrey Simpson, and his wife, Wendy Bryans, a lawyer with the Department of Justice, also live in the Glebe, as do the *Financial Post*'s Ottawa bureau chief, Hyman Solomon, and his wife, Starr, who runs her own public relations company.

But the Glebe and every other other fashionable area in Ottawa are always compared with Rockcliffe Park. Established as a village in 1926, and no more than ten minutes' drive from Parliament Hill, Rockcliffe is the most beautiful and most elitist residential community in Canada. And surprisingly, Rockcliffe does not include Rideau Hall or 24 Sussex Drive; these official residences are actually part of the neighbouring community of New Edinburgh.

No commercial buildings are allowed within the village borders – no Becker's, no 7-Elevens, no video shops. The only exceptions are the two private schools, Elmwood, established in 1915 for girls, and Ashbury College, built in 1910 as a boys' school but now coeducational. No churches are allowed; worshippers have to go next door to New Edinburgh, where the smart church is tiny St. Bartholomew's. An Anglican church built in 1868, it is attached by tradition and proximity to Government House and is used by the royal family on their trips to Ottawa.

Rockcliffe does not allow salt on the streets in the winter, only fine gravel, which is pleasant for the community's dogs (salt stings their paws). Another bylaw allows dogs to run free in the village. No garage sales are allowed in Rockcliffe, although this is one rule people often flout. No apartments either, although one house on Buena Vista was duplexed many years ago. There are almost no sidewalks. And Rockcliffe may be the only place in Canada where everyone places little hinged green wooden teepees over their evergreens and bushes in the winter to protect them from snow and ice.

Rockcliffe tags and monitors every single tree in the village. A village bylaw ensures lots are at least eighty by a hundred feet to keep the density down. Today there are about eight hundred houses, including nearly fifty embassy residences, and 2,500 people living in the community. A small house here – and there are a number below Maple Lane – costs a minimum of $350,000, while most medium-sized houses cost about $500,000. Anything big and impressive, the kind of house that boasts a butler's pantry and a library and several bedrooms and bathrooms and a large garden, will cost between $700,000 and $1.5 million. One reason the community is so charming is the variety of the houses, from palatial diplomatic residences sporting portes-cochère and flagpoles to modest old country houses, many of which were originally just large cottages.

Sadly, many of the cottages are being torn down to make way for ugly bunkers masquerading as homes. The village council has been so alarmed over these megahouses that they have recently passed bylaws restricting their size and established a high-powered "Taste Committee" to vet designs on new developments. The Taste Committee is not a group you'd care to cross, and includes lobbyist Thomas D'Aquino; Cynthia Baxter, co-owner of the children's bookstore The Bookery; Tim Murray, a local architect and brother of Rockcliffe reeve Pat Murray; and Polly King, former social columnist of both the *Globe and Mail* and the Ottawa *Citizen*.

Rockcliffe Park is a community that cherishes its traditions and the nice little eccentricities that make it unique. But these nice eccentricities and all this independence bear a steep price; taxes here are the highest in the Ottawa area, with most families paying at least $5,000 a year.

Even in Rockcliffe there are areas that are more fashionable than others. If you could afford to buy anywhere here, you'd want a house somewhere between Lisgar Road on the west,

Mariposa to the south and Lansdowne Road to the east. To the north the boundary is the Ottawa River, and the houses on the northernmost streets – Coltrin, Thorold, Hillsdale and the top of Acacia – are among the village's most expensive. The residence for the Japanese ambassador, facing Rockcliffe's prettiest park, The Rockeries, is the grandest and most impressive diplomatic residence in Ottawa, outshining even the American. Its stone fences and iron gates keep the curious away from the broad lawns surrounding an immense stone house with the rising sun emblem of Japan shining like a huge gold coin embedded into the porte-cochère.

Nearby to the east on Crescent are several impressive houses. One of the loveliest is the large Georgian-style house built by the Hughson family in the 1920s and now owned by the New Zealand High Commission. It had its problems in the mid-seventies with its neighbour, the ambassador of Gabon, who lived there with his three wives and twenty-seven children. It was a lively household, to say the least, and even though New Zealand High Commissioner Edward Ladder loved children, he and his family found it noisy next door. But the Ladders' problems were nothing compared to the Bill Terons' on the other side. The multimillionaire developer had built a large, very modern house beside the Gabonese residence. Obviously, a houseful of thirty people produces more garbage than an average home. It was the Teron side that got whiffs of the Gabonese garbage.

Even worse, the ambassador installed a metal garden shed, the kind you find at Canadian Tire, on his lawn. It must have been handy for all the trikes and hockey sticks, but such a visual blight had never before been seen in the village. When the ambassador was recalled to Gabon, the shed disappeared. But the ambassador's own disappearance was even more extraordinary. He and his wives and children just walked out one day, leaving all the doors and windows open. The oil ran out, the pipes froze and burst and all hell broke loose. Only a strong protest from the village council prevented the Gabonese from levelling the house; instead, they were persuaded to gut and restore it.

West of the Japanese ambassador's residence, on Acacia Lane, which winds like a country road through the top of the village, you'll find the most beautiful residence in the village, now that of the papal nuncio but once called Rockcliffe Manor, Annie Keefer's old house. Set well back on its acres overlooking the Ottawa River, it can be seen only through the arch of its gatehouse, a pretty, sunwashed building covered with ivy and almost as appealing as the main residence.

Acacia Lane wanders along to the back of the American ambassador's residence before it joins Lisgar Road. If you walk back here, you'll see the incredible view the Americans enjoy, a view over the Ottawa River, up the mouth of the Gatineau River and across the rolling Gatineau hills. The Americans have a wonderful three-storey stone house sitting high on a hill, surrounded by eleven acres of beautifully groomed lawns and gardens. The only odd thing about it is the neo-colonial pillared porch added a few years ago by Paul and Martha Robinson, making it a strange mix of Tara and limestone Loyalist.

The village is divided by McKay Lake and its little adjunct body of water called the Pond. On the other side are some large and attractive fifties-style Cape Cod houses and bungalows, as well as a new development that has old-time village residents cringing at its vulgarity. The houses, often mock-Tudor designs, are huge and graceless, with massive garages. There are only two exceptions to the rule of tastelessness that reigns on this side of the Pond. One is a development of two-storey condominiums built of soft pink brick that hug the shoreline of the Pond and house many of the elderly residents of Rockcliffe who did not want the chores of their big houses but could not bear to leave the community. The other is a pair of stunning contemporary black houses, outlined like a Mondrian painting with sharp colours around the windows and doors, designed by local architect Stefan Hensel.

Now here's the way to tell a newcomer to Rockcliffe, Someone Who Does Not Belong. Watch him put out his garbage on garbage morning. The garbage collector will come thundering up to the front door to inform the hapless householder that garbage cans (never bags) are to be kept in a garbage hut at the back or side of the house and that the men will walk back and pick it up. The only stuff picked up at the curb is *trash*. No one will tell the newcomer the difference between trash and garbage, but when other people in Rockcliffe put out trash it appears to consist of broken Chippendale chairs, or a wicker loveseat in need of a fresh coat of paint, or maybe a slightly outdated *Encylopedia Britannica*. Garbage, on the other hand, is mostly stuff that smells, although even that is changing; Rockcliffe is the only community in Ottawa in which kitchen garburetors are legal.

One of the best stories about Rockcliffe garbage comes from Larry Zolf, who, back in 1974, was producing a satirical CBC television show called "Up Canada." According to Zolf, he was approached by Terence Belford, then a *Globe and Mail* reporter. Belford, says Zolf, came up with a great idea for a television feature. Distinguished Rockcliffe resident Beryl Plumptre (later the village reeve) was then chairman of the Food Prices Review Board. Why don't we steal her garbage? suggested Belford to Zolf. We can go though it and see what she eats compared with the common man. We can even hire a dietician to evaluate it. We can measure the thickness of her pork chop bones. It had been a long time since Zolf had heard an idea he liked better. The two rented a van to haul away the stolen garbage and booked the show. Belford's mistake was telling a colleague, who promptly warned Mrs. Plumptre. Within twenty-four hours the doughty mandarin had a padlock on her garbage hut and the plot was foiled.

Rockcliffe has its own police force, a branch of the Ontario Provincial Police with headquarters in the Rockcliffe Park Public School building, known as RPPS. Because of the high proportion of diplomats in the community, the streets are constantly patrolled by gentle cops who know most of the residents by name. A few years ago, Rockcliffe police were annoyed when Ottawa city cops started dumping homeless drunks off on the streets within the village's borders. Obviously, the city police thought it was time the spoiled village police got a taste of real life.

At one time, RPPS had two police forces operating in the building. Because Pierre Trudeau's children were there for years, the RCMP bodyguards had their own room where they could smoke and drink coffee. During lunch hours and recess, the cops were outside with the kids, often refereeing games, stopping fights and comforting children with scraped knees and bruised feelings.

Aside from the school, the police and a meeting hall, RPPS also houses a tiny one-room public library, one of the best in the city. It's open only from 3 to 5 every weekday afternoon and stocks only the latest bestsellers, including political books, biographies, crime fiction and novels. Except for librarian Barbara Mirsky, a long-time village resident and a member of a distinguished Ottawa family, the staff are all volunteer workers; they include two Supreme Court judges' wives and wives of other important bureaucrats. Although retiring mandarins may move out of the village, usually to apartments in nearby communities, they rarely give up their library memberships. As they are the first to admit, the place is a hive of gossip, and they would never know what's going on if they didn't come in to borrow books from time to time.

One of the hottest topics in the library for the past year or two has been the fate of Berkenfels, the old eleven-acre Perley-Robertson estate. Berkenfels was originally the property of Warren Soper, an Ottawa lumber baron who first built the house next door, which is now the American ambassador's residence. Soper called his house Lornado, Sandra Gwyn tells us in *The Private Capital*, after his favourite heroine in fiction, Lorna Doone. When his daughter married, Soper gave her the land next door and built a fine, deeply gabled stone house called Berkenfels. This house has been passed down to Soper descendants Michael and Timothy Perley-Robertson. "The Boys," as they are known in Ottawa, want to develop their inheritance, dividing it into seventeen house lots. The Taste Committee is poised for action.

Peter White, Prime Minister Mulroney's principal secretary, has led a secret campaign to have the government buy the property, renovate the old stone house and give it to the British government as a site for their high commissioner's residence. In return, the British would cough up Earnscliffe. The reason for this swap is simple: the Tories want their own political shrine. The Liberals, after all, have Laurier House, dedicated to the memory of Laurier, King and Pearson as well as Kingsmere, dedicated to King, so many Conservatives feel they too need a chunk of Ottawa real estate dedicated to one of their own. (The fact that it was a Tory prime minister, R.B. Bennett, who passed up the chance to acquire Earnscliffe many years ago, is something they airily dismiss while Liberals chortle.) White's efforts became complicated when he put forward a bid (estimated at about $10 million) for Berkenfels. White needed approval from Treasury Board, who would presumably guarantee, if not provide, the funds, although White was doing this out of nationalistic pride and there was never any question of personal profit. Treasury Board officials pointed out, however, that as the PM's principal secretary, White could be seen to be exerting undue influence in the matter. So he redrew the bid, this time putting in a London, Ontario, lawyer, Allan Patton, as the purchaser in trust. White was trying to line up private donors to contribute to the costs; some said his old boss Conrad Black was a sure touch. In July, 1989, it was revealed that Patton was trying to buy the house on behalf of Vauxhall Gardens Development Ltd., a firm owned by White, and gave the Perley-Robertsons an offer – approved by Cabinet – of $11.3 million. White's plan was to sell it to the NCC without profit but the deal collapsed when the British High Commissioner, Sir Alan Urwick, turned down the idea. Patton had originally agreed to close the deal with the Perley-Robertsons on January 6, 1989; when the deal fell through, they sued Patton and Vauxhall for $400,000. The whole plan is now in legal limbo.

The biggest fight the village has ever seen, over the proposed site for the new U.S. Embassy, lasted two years. Because the Americans had outgrown their Wellington Street building, the government promised them a large new location that would have the prestige of the old one. The Americans let us have that wonderful site on Pennsylvania Avenue for our new embassy in Washington, the reasoning went; they need something just as good. And they also required a site that met tough U.S. security requirements. Underground parking, for example, posed a security risk. Something just as good proved to be a park at the edge of the Ottawa River in Rockcliffe known as the Mile Circle because its circumference is exactly a mile. It is next to the RCMP Musical Ride headquarters, and local joggers and dog walkers grew accustomed to the sight of terrified novice riders gripping their reins as they cantered around the Circle.

The National Capital Commission under Jean Pigott not only said they were going to let the new embassy go up here but that they were going to turn the site into a diplomatic compound and planned to permit at least five more embassies. The community went bananas. Furious residents of Rockcliffe, New Edinburgh and especially Manor Park, the neighbourhood just east of Rockcliffe, fought the decision tooth and nail with protests and lawn signs that stayed up for well over a year. They muttered that Pigott, who had grown up in a more modest Ottawa neighbourhood, had a complex about Rockcliffe and was gleefully sticking it to the community. The American ambassador, Thomas Niles, and his family were the unfortunate targets of abuse during this campaign, even though he had no say in the decision and his posting would end long before the building would be up. Malicious children at Elmwood taunted Mary Niles, the ambassador's daughter, about the "Niles' Circle," and the Niles family couldn't go anywhere without being lobbied on the issue. Eventually, the government caved in and decided to offer the Americans land to the east of the Mile Circle, in some of the riverside pasture land used for the horses of the RCMP's Musical Ride. Last anyone heard, budget considerations had forced the U.S. government to cancel plans for the new embassy altogether.

Who lives in Rockcliffe today? Besides most of the senior diplomats in the city, you'll find former Conservative leader Robert Stanfield and his wife, Ann, just down the road from his old residence, Stornoway. A few houses north of the Stanfields are Joan and Gordon Henderson. She is a dynamo in business and cultural circles (she is on the boards of the Stratford Festival and of Selkirk Communications), while he runs the enormous law firm he built up over many years, Gowling and Henderson, which has branches in Kitchener and Toronto. South of the Stanfields are Paul and Adele Deacon. Now retired, Paul Deacon was the publisher of the *Financial Post*. His wife works hard for many local charities and is involved in Toronto on the board of the National Ballet.

The man John Turner beat twice in Vancouver Quadra, Bill Clarke, lives in a beautiful white clapboard house where the flag of British Columbia flaps in the sunshine. Clarke's wife, Sheila M'Gonigle, was a village councillor and ran for reeve, but was defeated by jovial Irish architect, Pat Murray. Margo Roston, the Ottawa *Citizen's* social columnist, lives with her husband, Gordon, in a large stone house here, just a few blocks away from the one she grew up in. Business Council on National Issues president Thomas D'Aquino and his wife, Susan Peterson, also live here, in a stunning house cantilevered out over the hill that slopes down to McKay Lake, originally built by architect Hart Massey for himself.

Then there is former Liberal Cabinet minister Jack Pickersgill, a powerhouse in Canadian politics during the late Mackenzie King years and throughout the St. Laurent and

Pearson years, who lives just a few doors away from the New England-style clapboard house once inhabited by his old enemy, John Diefenbaker. Diefenbaker had hoped his house would be turned into a museum, but the trustees of his will could not find financial backers for the project and finally sold the house.

In the old days, Rockcliffe was stuffed with the government's top mandarins. Today, despite generous salaries, many cannot afford homes here. One who has been here for many years is Arthur Kroeger, the deputy minister of employment and immigration, and another is James (Si) Taylor, the under-secretary of state for external affairs.

For those who want to cosy up to the best things about Rockcliffe but don't want to pay the freight, the answer is usually New Edinburgh, the little community just across the grounds of Government House. New Edinburgh is even closer to the Hill than Rockcliffe and shares the same schools, churches and shops. The rule of thumb in the Burg, as people call it, is that the closer you are to Government House grounds or to Sussex Drive, the better.

The wrong end of New Edinburgh is the east end near Beechwood, which is close to Vanier, a rough and ready Francophone community. But what's been happening down at the "wrong end" of New Edinburgh, and even across the street in Vanier, is a yuppiefication of brick townhouses, like the one on Ivy Crescent in which decorator Giovanni Mowinckel held court, all bulging with skylights, bristling with new fireplace chimneys and surrounded with yards and yards of latticed fencing. The sure giveaways are the Volvos and BMWs parked in the Unilock brick forecourts.

If you have the money you will prefer to find a spot at the other end of the Burg, perhaps on the west side of Stanley Street where the houses back onto a park and the Rideau River. And anyone who has a view of the Minto Bridges, the lovely little wrought-iron confections built across the Rideau in 1901 in the Earl of Minto's days as governor general, considers himself lucky. The earl found it a nuisance to mush his carriage up to Rideau Street from Government House in the winter when the weather was bad and the route that is now Sussex Drive was impassable, so he ordered the bridges built.

New Edinburgh's houses may be small but many are Victorian architectural treasures with deep gables, mullioned windows and wrought-iron details. On many, ribbons of glossy gingerbread festoon the porches and gables. Most people here are keen gardeners and fill their old-fashioned pocket-handkerchief gardens with roses and lilacs and irises and clematis, and they keep their grass borders and lawns immaculately barbered.

New Edinburghers also love their laneways. This community is one of the few in Ottawa to have little lanes running through each block in the main section of the neighbourhood; the lanes are given names like River Lane and Avon Lane, and many are the streets for tiny cottages that have been shoe-horned into large back yards over the years. On summer evenings and Sunday afternoons, the lanes are crowded with young families pushing strollers along; the rest of the time they are wonderful playgrounds for all the neighbourhood children.

New Edinburghers also treasure their #3 bus, perhaps the most famous bus in Ottawa, a travelling cocktail party immortalized in Heather Matthews' funny political cartoon strip, "On the #3 Bus," in the Ottawa *Citizen*. This bus means not having to say you're sorry you don't have a second car. It picks up its cargo of powerbrokers block by block through the Burg every morning, winds them through the market and drops them off near the Hill. Some get off at the Château to grab a quick power breakfast at Zoe's; others wait till it can deposit them in front of the heavy doors of the Privy Council Office and the Prime Minister's Office. Some sit tight until they're close to 50 O'Connor or the Royal Bank Building at 90 Sparks, where all the bigshot lobbyists go to make money.

Whatever their destination, as riders mount the steps their eyes quickly swivel around the bus, avoiding contact with neighbourhood bores and zeroing in on empty seats beside anyone powerful or interesting. Scooting quickly into place as the bus lurches along, they launch immediately into gossip. A stray remark overheard at the Arts Centre the night before hints at a deputy shuffle. A "cabdoc" is getting a little traffic from some other departments that want the project stalled. Someone flipped that little house on Crichton for a neat profit.

Aside from the prime minister and the governor general, New Edinburgh's most famous resident is undoubtedly Margaret Trudeau Kemper, who lives in a long, narrow brick house on Union Street. Tall fences guard her privacy, but it has been many years since she has been a novelty in New Edinburgh. She and her husband, Fried Kemper, a wealthy real estate developer, live here with their two small children, Kyle, five, and Alicia Mary Rose, born in February 1989, and with her and Pierre Trudeau's three teenaged sons on the weekends.

New Edinburgh is full of diplomats, journalists, bureaucrats, politicians and business people. One of the more intriguing residents is Martha Robinson, the wife of former U.S. ambassador Paul Robinson. She rents a two-storey apartment from fashionable local renovator Robin Benitz on Charles Street, at the "good end" of the Burg. She liked the city so much and made so many good friends here that she found it hard to leave; in fact, she found it impossible, which led to a minor diplomatic incident. The Americans' policy on ambassadors is simple: two U.S. ambassadors cannot be on duty in the same country at one time. So the Nileses were perched on the tarmac in Washington waiting to come to Canada while the Robinsons took their departure. The trouble was that the ambassador could not persuade Martha to leave. The flight was delayed and delayed until finally, so the story goes, he left without her. While today Mrs. Robinson does spend time in

Illinois with her husband, she maintains the home in New Edinburgh.

Rockcliffe, New Edinburgh and the Glebe are all expensive and central, but many influential powerbrokers prefer to live even more centrally in slightly raffish areas. Lower Town is a landlocked island bounded by Rideau Street on the south, Sussex Drive on the west and north and the Rideau River on the east. Lower Town used to be where the poor people lived, but now it has become terribly smart. Its main streets, like Clarence and William and Dalhousie, bustle with cafés, bookstores and interesting clothing stores, but the main attraction is the Byward Market, whose heart is a big brick building, beautifully restored about fifteen years ago, where farmers sell their own cabbages and lettuces and parsley and maple syrup and eggs. On the area's residential streets, recent homebuyers have renovated the shabby old houses the poor people had to leave behind. This is not a community for families with little kids and dogs, it's for single professionals. Several senior mandarins, such as Sylvia Ostry, the prime minister's ambassador at the Multilateral Trade Negotiations and his senior organizer for international economic summit meetings, live in one of the city's most exclusive apartment buildings, the Sussex on Boteler Street.

The Toronto *Star*'s Val Sears lives nearby in a wonderfully renovated old house on Cathcart Square. While he prefers to have people think of him as a curmudgeonly bachelor, he is a good cook and generous host who throws lively parties at which he stands around and insults his guests, who know enough not to take offence.

The Whites are another interesting pair of Lower Town residents. Huguette White, an actress and writer, lives with her husband, Stanley, an NCC restoration architect, in an intriguing two-storey apartment above the Ritz 3 Restaurant on Clarence Street. Their apartment is daringly contemporary and full of personal whims and quirks. The living-room sofa is a real – yes, dead – cow, contentedly lying on her side, her feet folded under her. The Whites spied this example of the fine art of taxidermy wedded to moulded fibreglass in Italy at a furniture fair and couldn't resist. Their television is suspended from the ceiling by a chain, and their twin Eames chairs are arranged on an angle, just so, for comfortable viewing. Huguette White is a gifted gardener. Inside the apartment she devotes hours and hours to the care and feeding of weird little desert plants, lithops they are called, which she orders from specialty mail-order catalogues and fertilizes with the aid of Q-Tips.

Ottawa's Roman Catholic Archbishop Plourde lives in Lower Town too, just two blocks north from the Whites in the Bishop's Palace at St. Patrick's Cathedral on St. Patrick Street. Archbishop Plourde won his fifteen minutes of fame in 1987 when he was convicted of shooting a neighbour's trespassing dog at his summer cottage. "It was a case of 'an eye for an eye and a dog for a cat,' " sniped one observer.

South of Lower Town and across Rideau Street is Sandy Hill, perhaps the most historic and most interesting neighbourhood in Ottawa. The oldest residential neighbourhood in the city, it has many large nineteenth-century houses, even though a sad number have been lost to make way for highrise apartment buildings. Some of the old houses are now embassies or ambassadors' residences. One magnificent house was turned into an exclusive private club, Le Cercle Universitaire.

Laurier Street is the main street running through Sandy Hill. New Democratic Party leader Ed Broadbent and his wife, Lucille, live on Laurier in a big and sunny book-filled house across from Le Cercle. And just around the corner from Le Cercle is one of the most interesting buildings in Ottawa, the Russian Embassy, a great grey mass squatting on the side of the hill with the Rideau River running below. Outside are the usual parade of demonstrators and the discreet watchers sitting in unmarked cars across the street. A few years ago the Soviets were fit to be tied when the next-door property was sold to developers; part of the old Senator Norman Patterson estate, it was turned into condominiums with underground parking. As the backhoes dug away just yards away from the Soviet compound, the Soviets became more and more agitated. Visions of security devices being planted in the new foundations terrified them. One of the most interesting sections of Peter Wright's book *Spycatcher* is devoted to his efforts to plant microphones in the embassy walls during its construction.

Almost all of "Old Ottawa" came from Centre Town or Sandy Hill. In the twenties, thirties and forties, Rockcliffe was still just a pleasant suburb with only a few old families living in a few grand houses. Today, Sandy Hill is a raffish sort of place; many of the fine old houses are now rooming houses for students at the University of Ottawa, which takes up a large chunk of the area. A great deal of infilling and restoration is going on now. Perhaps the most beautiful houses in Sandy Hill are in the terraced stone row on Daly Street known as Philomen Terrace. These three-storey houses contain classically proportioned drawing rooms, high ceilings, magnificent mouldings, deep window sills and fine marble mantels. The butternut bannisters and wide staircases sweep majestically down through all the floors, even to the high basements. Today the most famous resident of Philomen Terrace is the lawyer David Scott, the tough-minded counsel for the 1986-87 Parker Commission into allegations of conflict-of-interest against former Tory Cabinet minister Sinclair Stevens. A partner in the old Ottawa law firm of Scott and Aylen, and brother of Ontario's attorney general, Ian Scott, Scott is a descendant of Sir Richard Scott, the leader of the Irish Catholic community, a member of Parliament and the mayor of Bytown in 1852.

Sir Richard Scott was one of the strongest lobbyists for the choice of Ottawa as Canada's new capital and lived in a vast old house at the other end of Daly Street, a house he had bought from Sir Charles Tupper, a physician and one of the Fathers of

Confederation. That house eventually became the Elizabeth Residence, a genteel retirement home for ladies like the late senator from Prince Edward Island, Elsie Inman, who preferred to dine alone at her own table and was nicknamed the Queen by the other residents. The women crammed their bedsitters with their favourite pieces of old family furniture and pictures and silver and crockery; every morning they'd gather in the drawing room for sherry and every afternoon tea was served on a silver tray. Sadly, after a sudden fire that destroyed the kitchen, the trustees decided the Elizabeth Residence had had its day and turned it over to developers to make a swanky condominium. The ladies disappeared, probably into nursing homes where tea, if it came at all, arrived in a styrofoam cup.

One of the Scotts' neighbours in Philomen Terrace is Joan Askwith, the well-loved owner (with Cynthia Baxter) of The Bookery on Sussex Drive, perhaps the finest children's bookstore in Canada. Mrs. Askwith is the widow of Charles Askwith, former Gentleman Usher of the Black Rod in the Senate.

The only other fashionable part of downtown Ottawa is Centre Town, which is around Parliament Hill. Today Centre Town is half commercial and half residential; the closer you get to the Hill, the more highrise office towers and commercial buildings you'll find. But starting around Somerset Street, there are some fine old houses. Although many are now cut up into smart doctors' and lawyers' offices, bookstores and antique stores and restaurants, or have been turned into embassies, there are several private homes left. McLeod, Waverly and Connaught streets offer many houses with stained glass, high ceilings, elaborate mouldings and cornices and lavish woodwork. And two highrise towers, 10 The Drive and 20 The Driveway, house many important diplomats and bureaucrats in spacious luxury. Politicians don't live in these elegant towers; they are too expensive.

Elgin Street, a bustling, hustling few blocks of restaurants, delis and trendy clothing stores, is the main street in this neighbourhood. And Elgin Street is the hangout for a large population of Ottawa's gay community, who have given the street life and style. Certain apartment buildings, but only the oldest and most beautiful, like the Art Deco masterpiece the Blackburn, are almost solidly gay. Lesbians are among the strongest supporters of Elgin Street's Ottawa Women's Bookstore; just a few blocks to the north and just off Elgin is the Gays and Lesbians of Ottawa headquarters, which is always busy with meetings and counselling sessions and people manning telephone advice lines.

For newspapers and magazines, everyone goes to Mags and Fags, the saucy little shop put together by the irrepressible Arthur Inglis, who also owns Vanilla, a popular women's clothing store just down the street.

But a lot of people don't want to live downtown, despite the convenience. One area that stays steady and reliable, with a name almost as boring as Centre Town, is the west end's Civic Hospital area, which is full of attractive, middle-class, two-storey brick houses built after the Second World War, when building lots here were going at $500 apiece. It's a well-to-do neighbourhood of doctors and dentists, but it is somehow characterless, like a street in a 1950s television sitcom. (In fact, if you had to identify Ottawa neighbourhoods by sitcoms, the Civic Hospital is "Father Knows Best," Centre Town is "Family Ties" and New Edinburgh or Sandy Hill would be home to the Huxtables on "The Cosby Show.") The only interesting house in the area is Bayne house on Fuller Drive, which belongs to bakery heiress Grete Hale.

This large stone house was bought by Grete Hale's father, Cecil Morrison, in 1928 when it was a derelict farmhouse. He and his wife, Margaret, repaired it and furnished it with treasures, including an elaborately carved sixteenth-century Italian mantel from Crook Castle near Edinburgh. It's the only private home in Ottawa in which you will find brochures describing its history and its furnishings.

258 OTTAWA INSIDE OUT

Bayne House competes with the Billings house in Alta Vista for the title of the oldest house in the city of Ottawa. Mrs. Hale says her house, named after the Scottish settler who built it, has been officially dated 1828.

When Bayne House was built there were only four other farmhouses between it and Nepean Point, where the Parliament Buildings sit today. The stone was quarried nearby on what is now Fairmont Avenue, and Agriculture Canada has confirmed that in its day the farm was the best dairy farm in eastern Ontario. A few years ago, during one of the regular rounds of hand-wringing over the lamentable state of Stornoway, there was talk about selling Bayne House to the government as an official residence for the leader of the Opposition, but nothing ever came of it.

Farther west, there's only one residential area of real interest, and that's Highland Park. Beyond that are endless suburbs, a no-man's land of municipalities and subdivisions like Nepean and Kanata and Britannia and Glen Cairn, all providing clean, pleasant and often luxurious housing, but so unfashionable that interesting people who live here are regarded as individualists.

Highland Park is different. It's the poor man's Rockcliffe Park, a green and cosy neighbourhood with some wonderful old houses. Former residents Toronto *Star* political columnist Richard Gwyn and author Sandra Gwyn brought glamour to the area when they lived here on Cole Avenue. Neighbours on their street got used to seeing Cabinet ministers' black Buicks and Chryslers parked outside, jostling for space with journalists' Hondas and bureaucrats' Volvos. Former Liberal Cabinet minister David Collenette and his wife, Penny, a law student and well-known human rights activist, live in Highland Park; so does Frank Iacobucci, the new chief justice of the Federal Court of Canada, with his wife, Nancy, who is also a lawyer.

The old days when just about everyone who mattered lived in Rockcliffe, the Glebe or Sandy Hill are gone. Today powerful people live all over town. And some daring ones did it, even when it wasn't quite the thing to do. When Pierre Trudeau announced that Gordon Osbaldeston was succeeding Michael Pitfield as Clerk of the Privy Council in 1983, the media was hot on Osbaldeston's trail. Although he had been a deputy minister for years, his profile had been low compared to many other high flyers and there was a scramble to find out something about him. CTV sent a camera crew to his house in Bell's Corners, quite possibly one of the most unfashionable neighbourhoods in the Ottawa area, known principally for its strip malls, doughnut shops and the only IKEA in Eastern Ontario. The Osbaldestons had lived there for many years, happy to be near a church they liked and good schools. They had even built their own home there.

"That night on the news they showed a picture of my house," remembers Osbaldeston, laughing merrily. "They said I lived in 'fashionable Bell's Corners.' The neighbours were thrilled; they said that had done more for property values in the community than anything before."

12

· ·

Power Decorating

As with other great eras in human history, the Paleolithic Age and the Bronze Age, for example, the history of Ottawa's decorating game falls into two distinct periods, BG and AG: Before Giovanni and After Giovanni.

Giovanni Mowinckel was one of the city's great personalities, a man too big for Ottawa, a man no one really ever knew well or understood. He arrived mysteriously one day in 1978 and disappeared suddenly and in a swirl of scandal nearly ten years later. He left his stamp on the lives and drawing rooms of the city just as surely as some of the city's most famous politicians and bureaucrats. Before Giovanni, Ottawa was not a great town for decorators; most people, through thrift and inclination, preferred to "do" their own houses. While other designers hated Mowinckel for pinching the few clients they did have and for all the publicity he garnered, there is no denying that he raised local standards.

Many Ottawans used to depend on risk-free design services in the local department stores; that's why so many of the houses look so much alike. This is changing now. One of the city's best interior designers, John Swain, recently opened a wholesale design centre, Design Source, in the Byward Market area patterned after Designer's Walk in Toronto where rare, expensive fabrics, carpets and wallpapers can be ordered. People no longer have to go to Toronto to find Fortuny cottons or Scalamandré silks; Swain and his partner, Michael Courdin, have them, along with matching wallpapers.

And there is Patrick McCarron, a talented designer whose own gracefully restored home on Philomen Terrace, which he sold several years ago, testified to his ability to mix imagination and wit with classic design sense. Another popular firm with established Ottawa was Caris Interior Decorations, run by Mme. Caris out of a cluttered, charming little shop on Beechwood just at the edge of Rockcliffe. Her clients include the Sauvés at Government House. The design firm of Timm Robinson earned its bread and butter from the up-and-coming doctor or lawyer in Alta Vista or microchip millionaire in Kanata. The two partners split recently but the firm remains. Its design team now includes John Grice, one of the young talented people Giovanni Mowinckel nurtured in his business.

Another designer who seems to be doing well is Constance Reisman, the wife of former free trade negotiator Simon. Her best-known job was decorating the sumptuous Trade Negotiations Office in the top floors of the new Metropolitan Life Building. A few eyebrows were raised when it was discovered she was doing the job, but she was not the only well-connected wife to get a good decorating contract. Huguette Langevin, the wife of Pierre Paul Bourdon, once the chief of staff for former public works minister Roch LaSalle, was hired to do LaSalle's ministerial office at DPW, a two-storey extravaganza in pink and grey, and junior defence minister Paul Dick's office at Defence.

The only real action, the only work in Ottawa that could go into *City and Country Home* or *Architectural Digest*, tends to be public work or institutional work – the interiors of great

public houses like 24 Sussex Drive and Rideau Hall, the offices
of the prime minister, the residence of the Speaker of the
House, the interior of the new Rideau Club, to name a few
examples. And in the 1980s Giovanni Mowinckel snapped
almost all of it up, leaving the rest of the city's designers to pick
up the crumbs.

Mowinckel's past was, well, always fairly unclear. He moved
to Montreal about 1975 from England, but he was not British.
He told people that his mother was Norwegian and his father
Hungarian, that he had grown up in Italy, near Genoa, had
Italian citizenship (which was to prove handy later on) and had
studied law in England. He claimed he was a specialist in
marine law, which he'd studied in Paris. It was in Paris, he used
to say, that he became interested in the decorative arts, so he
switched to interior design, which he studied at the École des
Beaux-Arts.

Now fluent in English, French and Italian, Mowinckel
moved back to London in the 1960s and worked as an interior
designer, eventually going into business with well-known
British designer Alastair Colvin. There he prospered, earning
enough to buy a picturesque stone house in the Cotswolds.
But around 1975 he moved abruptly to Montreal. He never
explained why he left England except to say he was tired of the
restrictions and snobbery and wanted to live in a more open,
entrepreneurial society.

In Montreal he quickly found financial backers to start a
new business. One was well-connected Westmounter Toppy
Eberts, who introduced him to top-of-the-line clients and to
the best suppliers; another backer was Montreal businessman
Aubrey Schwartz. When Mowinckel's Ottawa firm failed in
1987, Schwartz was one of many creditors.

In 1978, disenchanted with Quebec's drive towards separa-
tism, Mowinckel moved to Ottawa. Ottawa was a strange
harbour for him. No one knew him. Few people had the
money his kind of work demanded and those who did
preferred to decorate their own houses. Getting started all

over again was not easy. He found a partner, German-born architect Reinhold Koller, and they set up a little shop called Colvin Design over a store in Byward Market where they sold beautiful English antiques and carried some exclusive fabric and wallpaper samples. He also carried a breathtaking assortment of antique Persian kilims obtained from his friend Dale Whiteside, an officer at External Affairs who had lived for years in Iran with her husband.

Ottawa had rarely seen a flower so exotic. His stuff was gorgeous, but then, so was he. Mowinckel is one of the world's charmers. Very tall, handsome as a movie star, funny and clever, he always dressed like an old-fashioned Ottawa gentleman. He looked as if he had picked up his clothes casually over the years from places like Turnbull and Asser and Hermes and the shops along London's Jermyn Street. His shoes were always burnished to a deep mahogany glow. Despite his sophistication he liked simple people and simple things. He liked dogs and cats and children. Pretence enraged him; he would much rather spend a lunch chin-wagging over spaghetti and cigarettes with a neighbouring farmer or with one of his favourite workmen than with a wealthy namedropper. He didn't patronize ordinary couples who came to admire his lovely old English desks and tallboys, or to gaze at Dale Whiteside's kilims. He educated them tactfully and never pressured anyone to buy. He lived in the back of a scruffy old house on a mean little back street in the market, but his apartment was exquisite, full of treasured architectural drawings from Italy and bits of old English furniture.

Slowly the clients started signing up. The first of note were Bob and Fran Andras, who had hired him to help with their Rockcliffe house on Cloverdale. At that time Andras, a Liberal Cabinet minister from Thunder Bay, was president of the Treasury Board. Later, after Andras left politics and moved to Vancouver to head up Teck Corporation, Mowinckel commuted to the West Coast to do their new house there. Then came the Tory interregnum of 1979 and a couple (now divorced) from Alberta, David and Dreena Jenkins. Jenkins, a wealthy land developer, was an aide to Prime Minister Joe Clark. He and his wife bought an expensive house in Rockcliffe and turned to Mowinckel for help.

Other commissions followed quickly and before long Mowinckel closed the antique shop and concentrated on design work alone. Old international connections helped him land a job advising California millionaire Walter Annenberg, the former ambassador to the Court of St. James, on his art collection. Canadian television star Peter Jennings, now anchorman at ABC in New York, became another client, partly through the influence of Jennings' sister Sarah, an Ottawa broadcaster, and her husband, Ian Johns, a developer, who became close friends.

Mowinckel once explained that what his clients wanted was "the old money look" and no one knew better than he how to give it to them. He knew how to put together the down-cushioned sofas and botanical prints and faded oils and antique lamps with soft silk shades, fringed in pink. He knew where to find the antiques, the wing chairs, the button-back sofas, the ashtrays and silver cigarette boxes. He understood deep crown mouldings and old Crown Derby and swagged valances. He had a reputation for knowing just the right "little woman" to slipcover a chaise longue, just the right "chap" to make some Roman shades for the bathroom, just the right French polisher for Granny's credenza.

No one gave him more trouble than the people with *real* old money who finally succumbed to his charm. They liked everything just as it was, he used to complain affectionately. Their Persian rugs were so old they had holes and their ancient Chippendale chairs were cracked and broken. That was fine with them. All they wanted him to do was slipcover patched and threadbare old sofas with chintzes that looked just like the original.

Although Mowinckel's client list grew in importance and size, his partnerships soured. After a couple of years together, he and Koller split and today Koller speaks of his former partner with some bitterness mixed with amusement. He found Mowinckel to be an extremely shrewd businessman, but one who preferred not to bother with the nuisance of filing income tax returns. Koller tired of doing most of the dogsbody work while Mowinckel basked in the adulation, but he acknowledged that without Mowinckel's charm the firm would never have mattered. After the rupture with Koller, Mowinckel hired a talented London-trained designer from Ottawa, Lesley MacMillan, who was only twenty-four but had excellent social connections. For a while the relationship worked well, but the two eventually fell out because Mac-Millan had decorated a new apartment for Post Office boss Michael Warren and won great acclaim and publicity for it. Mowinckel was piqued. When MacMillan then bought and renovated an old Ottawa house with a friend who was attached to Warren, Mowinckel, spoiling for a fight, accused her of moonlighting against his interests. Understandably furious, MacMillan quit and opened her own competing company; she now works in Toronto.

Partners aside, Giovanni Mowinckel understood Ottawa's smalltown mentality well. He volunteered his design talent for local cultural events, helping to decorate rooms at the National Arts Centre for galas with high hopes and low budgets. He served as the unpaid chairman of the decorating committee for the new Ronald McDonald House on the grounds of the Children's Hospital of Eastern Ontario. It was Mowinckel who brought together Ottawa's other decorators to donate their imagination and furnishings for the bedrooms, kitchens, sitting rooms and bathrooms of this hostel for families of children dying of cancer.

He was invited everywhere, accepted everywhere. His friends were people like David and Diana Kirkwood and Hamilton and Marion Southam and Bob and Peppy Landry. He decorated the Southams' house at 9 Rideau Gate, a stately old house whose nearest neighbours were Rideau Hall, 24

Sussex and the Government Guest House. At Christmas friends would find him on their doorsteps, beaming with his great delight in the season, dressed in his big raccoon coat, bearing huge poinsettias. He returned their hospitality with small dinner parties and cross-country ski outings and lunches at his Gatineau home, Farrelton House, a modest Quebec farmhouse set high on a slope with a spectacular view of forests and hills. Inside, the house was simple but attractive. Sofas and walls were upholstered in blue denim piped in red and the furniture was a mix of old bamboo pieces mixed with Canadian pine and English mahogany. It was pleasantly cluttered with books, pictures and records, but the clutter was arranged like a Dutch still life. In the summers, guests would gather on his broad verandah and gaze out over the view. He conducted his long-standing relationship with graphic artist Richard Sainte-Germaine with casual dignity. Among his friends, there was no question that people would disapprove, and Sainte-Germaine became a close friend to many of Mowinckel's circle as well.

Mowinckel also made friends with many members of the diplomatic community. Friendships with Italian diplomats were particularly close and one special chum was Rosemary Balancino. She was married at the time to the embassy's first secretary, and after their marriage broke up she stayed on in Ottawa for a while. At the time Balancino owned a small house on Stanley Street in New Edinburgh. Even after she returned to Rome and found a job at Bulgari's, the ultra-exclusive Via Condotti jewellery store, she kept the house and rented it out. Mowinckel's office managed her property for her and forwarded the rents; even today, Marie Dorion, his former bookkeeper, is burdened with this chore.

By 1983 Mowinckel was well settled in Ottawa. Needing a city office, he bought a sow's ear of a house at 33 Ivy Crescent in New Edinburgh and turned it into an elegant little building, decorated with rich silk curtains, yellow walls and antique furniture. In true Mowinckel style, he threw a chic party to celebrate the new headquarters. Home was always the Gatineau farmhouse, however, where he and Richard lived with their black Labrador, Spook.

Mowinckel eventually won the one commission every interior designer in Ottawa would have killed for, designing the $800,000 interior of the new Rideau Club. The old club, which was right across the street from the Parliament Buildings, burned to the ground in 1979. After sitting around with their insurance money – as well as the money from the priceless site from the government – club directors decided to take over a floor of the new Metropolitan Life Building on Bank Street. Before the fire the club had become almost moribund because Pierre Trudeau and his cabinet had always disdained it. Now, club directors needed to attract a new generation of members, including women, and they knew the new quarters had to be as splendid as the old club. The only real fight was over the squash court. Old-timers felt the club must have a billiards room, while the new guard said a squash court was essential to attract the kind of members they needed. The old-timers won.

The new club was a success beyond anyone's imagination, and much of the credit was due to Mowinckel's design work. The moment people walked into the foyer with its domed ceiling, they were captivated. On the walls he used an English fabric he obtained from Toronto designer Bud Sugarman. Distinctively patterned with ribbons and bows, the pattern was so appealing that he used it on one too many houses. To her chagrin the Mulroneys' friend Pierrette Lucas had her living room furniture upholstered in it, then saw it at the Rideau Club, then found it on the sofas and chairs at Stornoway, when he did the house for the Mulroneys. When Mowinckel later did 24 Sussex Drive, his contract stipulated "exclusivity" of fabric: he had to promise not to use the same stuff on other peoples' sofas after he used it at Sussex Drive.

By the time Brian Mulroney was elected Conservative leader in June 1983, Mowinckel was already famous and a sure bet to get the Stornoway commission. But did the house need "doing"? Many thought not. After Joe Clark and Maureen McTeer moved back in 1980, Cecilia Humphreys and her sister Maureen Lonergan fixed up Stornoway for the family for the second time. This time, however, Clark and McTeer were fed up with trying to win brownie points for thrift, and they did the house the way they wanted. Pierre Trudeau had had the house redone for $133,934 but had taken some of the furniture back to 24 Sussex with him, so they found the place fairly spartan. Clark and McTeer spent about $36,443 of taxpayers' money on it.

Three years later, the Mulroneys did a complete redecoration, spending $150,000 of public money on decorating, furniture, repairs and a new porch. Mowinckel and Mila Mulroney combed the shops of Montreal and Toronto, filling the house with colour and warmth. The living room chintz was the Bud Sugarman ribbons-and-bows fabric in a deep rusty red with walls to match. The sunroom walls were softly padded and then covered with the same green cotton used for the curtains and upholstery. The kitchen was modernized, again. The children got a new playroom on the third floor with child-sized sinks and toilets. Mila Mulroney and Giovanni Mowinckel celebrated the finished work in December 1983 with a big press reception. Print media were allowed in from 12 to 12:30; the television crews from 12:30 to 1. At the door, Mrs. Mulroney's assistant, Bonnie Brownlee, handed out printed sheets listing which items of furniture belonged to the house and which to the Mulroneys and how much everything cost. Mila steered reporters to her dining room, where a footman stood by to pour coffee into fine china, then walked them around the rooms showing each detail and posing cheerfully for every photographer. Donna Thacker, a gifted cook from Alberta who is married to Tory MP Blaine Thacker, had given the Mulroneys some heart-shaped gingerbread cookies decorated with "Brian loves Mila," and these hung on the Christmas tree in the dining room.

The whole event was quite simply a triumph for Mila

Mulroney and for Mowinckel. Mulroney revealed herself as hospitable to the press and even eager to detail the costs to the public. She promised that when they inevitably moved into 24 Sussex Drive and redecorated there, she would repeat the exercise with another press tour. (It never happened.) And a day or two after this event, the Mulroneys threw a series of cocktail parties for nearly two thousand friends, caucus colleagues and other senior Tories.

In 1984 Mowinckel's clients included the embassies of Morocco, Brazil and Sweden. Imperial Oil (Bob Landry was vice-president) and the law firm of Gowling and Henderson employed him; so did Lawrence and Audrey Freiman, developer Pierre Bourque and architects Murray and Murray.

John Turner won the Liberal leadership in June 1984 and moved very briefly into 24 Sussex Drive. While he was there he and his wife borrowed several pieces of furniture from several sources, including Harrington Lake, Rideau Hall, External Affairs and the Museum of Man. In November, after the Tories won the election, Public Works officials tried to recover these pieces, writing Mowinckel to ask for help in retrieving them. Whether they were successful no one knows, but there was an odd footnote to their request.

After Mowinckel went bankrupt and fled to Italy in 1987, his basement storage rooms below the Old Spaghetti Factory in Ottawa contained many bits and pieces of furniture. One was an antique upholstered bench for the foot of a double bed, part of a set, which was waiting to be reupholstered for the Mulroneys' room. The DPW letter, and Mowinckel's records and photographs, showed the bench belonged to Rideau Hall. But as far as the Royal Bank of Canada, Mowinckel's receivers, were concerned, everything in the warehouse belonged to them, the bench included.

The fact that Mowinckel had not given the bench back to Rideau Hall by 1987, despite a written request from Public Works in 1984, shows just how chaotic the inventory system is for the antiques and other furnishings that have been acquired at public expense for the nation's official residences. When a senior functionary tried to enforce some bureaucratic rules about one residence she was bluntly told in 1985 that they were transferring her to Saskatchewan. She buttoned her lip and the transfer was eventually quashed. In 1988 the *Globe and Mail* tried to obtain an inventory of publicly owned furnishings for 24 Sussex Drive and Harrington Lake. After months of stalling, two sheets of paper arrived simply listing such items as "four chairs, three sofas, two tables, six lamps, three chairs," without any descriptions. It seems there is no careful inventory for prime ministerial furniture purchased by the public. Prime ministers are free to move it around as they choose and if they take things, who will dare to chase them?

After the September 1984 election, decorating became a growth industry in Ottawa. Much to the annoyance of the new House of Commons Speaker John Bosley and his wife, Nicole, Liberal Leader John Turner and his wife Geills were living at Kingsmere in The Farm, the Speaker's official residence, while they waited for Maureen Milne, their Toronto decorator, to finish the work on Stornoway. The Bosleys, who wanted to redecorate The Farm as well as the Speaker's office and private quarters in the House, had hired Mowinckel to do the job and were itching to get started. The Mulroneys had asked Mowinckel to take on 24 Sussex Drive for them as well as their new summer residence at Harrington Lake and their three offices – Mila Mulroney's office in the Langevin Block and the prime minister's offices in Langevin and in the Centre Block.

Although these should have been dream assignments, Mowinckel confided to a friend that he was reluctant to take on the Mulroney work. He had found the Stornoway job stressful and was not sure he could cope with 24 Sussex Drive. His friend advised him not to take it, but he could not resist. He agreed to do the work for 10 per cent of all the costs, charging only a fraction of his usual fees in exchange for the publicity he would receive. Normally his margin was 60 per cent; he would buy furniture, fabrics, carpets, papers and other materials at wholesale cost and then add 60 per cent to cover his fees and overhead and profit. Even though he was still just running a one-man shop with the help of two talented assistants, Karen Large and John Grice, one bookkeeper and one delivery man, Gary Peters (the son of his curtain-maker), he believed that the job would take only three months and that he could afford three months at 10 per cent. In fact, the job took a year and a half.

Mowinckel signed contracts in September and October 1984 to redecorate 24 Sussex, Harrington Lake and the three Mulroney offices. The Prime Minister's Office gave him a plastic identity card that entitled him to government discounts when he was travelling. According to his staff, he used this card frequently, especially in hotels.

Mowinckel had also agreed to redecorate the Bosleys' house and John Bosley's Commons offices. While he made these plans the Turners were unhappily surveying Stornoway and not liking what they saw. The house, which had built up an inventory of basic furnishings over the years, had been stripped by the Mulroneys to help fill the rooms at Harrington Lake. Harrington, it must be admitted, was an eyesore. Though the old clapboard farmhouse is large and picturesque, most of the furniture was the kind of "modern rustic" maple atrocities you might find in a Sears basement. The living-room rugs were cheap braided ovals. In the bedrooms the curtains, bedspreads and upholstery clashed the way leftovers from other households always do, and the floors were covered in worn linoleum.

The only furniture left at Stornoway was an antique mahogany dining-room table, with matching chairs and sideboard, which belonged to the house. When the Turners raised a fuss they were told they could tour the government warehouses and choose anything there they liked. What they had to choose from, not surprisingly, were the discarded bits of furniture from Harrington Lake thrown out by Mowinckel.

At that time Stuart Langford, a lawyer, former CBC Television reporter and an old Ottawa hand who had grown up in Rockcliffe, was Turner's executive assistant. His advice to his boss was to forget Stornoway. Buy your own place in Rockcliffe, he urged Turner. Stornoway will bring you nothing but grief. Turner ignored this excellent advice.

By January 1985 Turner was still living at Kingsmere and Public Works had done $206,000 worth of repairs to Stornoway and was about to start on another round of work. A mischievous PMO source leaked these figures to the press, adding that the total costs were estimated at $500,860.

On February 5, 1985, Turner ordered all work halted until the newly appointed Official Residences Council could go through the house and see for themselves what was needed. He asked them and the prime minister to decide how much more should be spent. Piously, Mulroney tossed the ball back into Turner's court, saying he did not want to be responsible for ordering a further $300,000 worth of publicly financed decorating, but if Turner wanted to, it was on his head. In March members of the Official Residences Council trooped through Stornoway. In the middle of April Bill Fox, then Mulroney's press secretary, announced that the government had approved another $191,960 in renovations and repairs, bringing the total to $398,000. Ultimately, the total cost of the Stornoway work from September 1984 until December 1986 was more than $700,000.

Meanwhile, the Bosleys were becoming more and more impatient to move into Kingsmere. It was exasperating to Nicole Bosley to have Mila Mulroney showing off all the beautiful furniture and fabrics Mowinckel was helping her pick out when the Bosleys couldn't get started on their own official residence. In the interim, House of Commons furniture refinishers working in the Wellington Block put in 750 hours of work on pieces for Bosley's office and official residence, and the Bosleys picked out more furniture during a trip to England. By early April the Bosleys finally decided enough was enough. They asked Turner to leave Kingsmere. Mortified, he complied and moved into the Château Laurier hotel.

Unfortunately, Mowinckel's work on The Farm began to attract attention about the same time John Bosley started to irritate the prime minister and a noisy faction of right-wing Tories. Although the Official Residences Council toured The Farm and made recommendations for improvements, the word went out from PMO that the $400,000 planned costs were outrageous. Eventually, by the end of the summer of 1986, the prime minister decided Bosley had to go. Joe Clark, Bosley's oldest friend in caucus, was given the dirty job of firing him. Clark told Bosley that if he did not agree to resign, the government would release all the details of the Bosleys' decorating expenses, even the costs of the furniture refinishing done by House workmen. Bosley was unwilling to subject his wife to such public heat and agreed to step down.

During the eighteen months Bosley and Turner were under attack for their decorating plans, Mila Mulroney and Giovanni Mowinckel were busily transforming the offices and the two residences. Mulroney was the first prime minister's wife to have a suite of offices in the Langevin Block; most worked at home with the help of a secretary seconded from their husband's office. She took over a small three-room suite at the side and back of the Langevin Block, where the RCMP used to work, and the Mounties moved across the hall. Contractors drilled through the stone floors to install plumbing lines so they could fit in a small bathroom. The total cost of the work, without furniture, was $30,583, which covered new carpeting, paint, wallpaper, curtains and the bathroom.

Documents obtained under access to information state that in October 1984, $50,000 was budgeted for Brian Mulroney's offices in the Parliament Buildings and in the Langevin Block across the street. One bill shows that Public Works paid $13,378 to recover seats in one of them while another shows that it cost $31,565 to install bullet-proof glass in the Centre

Block offices. In 1988 it was revealed that Denys Labelle, vice-president of Verval Ltée., the Hull firm that installed this glass (with personal approval from Public Works Minister Roch LaSalle clearly noted on the contract), paid $5,000 to Tory MP Michel Gravel, as well as building him an $11,000 sunroom, in exchange for this and other Public Works contracts. In January 1988, when Labelle had sold his shares in Verval to his partner, Armand Turpin, Verval won federal government contracts worth $813,203 for interior glazing at the Museum of Civilization. Labelle formed a new company, Marbel Enterprises, which won two federal government contracts in 1987 worth $213,262 and ten more in 1988 worth $283,980.

While Mila Mulroney's office is attractive and functional, Mowinckel turned the prime minister's Centre Block office into a spectacular showcase of antiques and art. "The 1984 renovations were undertaken to maintain the heritage character of the Centre Block office," wrote Robert Giroux, deputy minister of public works, in a letter explaining the costs. According to Giroux, the office had not had a major renovation since 1968, when Pierre Trudeau moved in. Mowinckel's 1984 job "involved replacing the plywood floor base with hardwood flooring, acquiring additional furniture to supplement the existing collection and, wherever possible, re-upholstering existing pieces."

Documents obtained under access to information legislation show that the government spent more than $70,000 in the fall of 1984 decorating Mulroney's Centre Block office; the costs included $3,100 for Mowinckel's fees, $1,679 for new curtains, $314 for Greeff fabric from Bud Sugarman, one camelback sofa for $1,250, one Chippendale wing chair for $1,200, one swivel tilting chair for $1,500. As well there were two armchairs covered to match the wall fabric at $2,629, a new hardwood floor for $4,322 and new carpets for $8,422.

From the Paisley Shop in Toronto, one of the most expensive antique stores in Canada, came an eighteenth-century mahogany side table for $3,800, four Gainsborough armchairs for $6,000, a figured mahogany Regency cabinet for $2,850, a rare Georgian "patience" (gaming) table in figured mahogany for $2,400, a mahogany Regency mirror for $2,350 and another Georgian figured mahogany table for $1,950, for a total of $19,350. Mowinckel also chose a $6,000 antique globe from the Paisley Shop for Mulroney as a gift from Montreal businessman Paul Desmarais, the head of Power Corporation.

Henrietta Antony's Montreal shop provided more antiques: a seventeenth-century Dutch chandelier for $8,500 (plus $300 to install it), two silver candlesticks with shades for $940 and a bronze and brass lamp for $1,590.

Another valuable addition was an antique Agra carpet from Toronto's Persian Carpets, for $10,165. Odds and ends for the PM's desk from Montreal's Ferroni Inc. added up to $477.50; they included a leather blotter for $168, ashtrays for $171, $39 for a wastepaper basket and $95 for a memo box and "desk tub."

Finally, $6,500 worth of cabinetry was done by Montreal's Patella Construction to make a television cabinet. The total, including the bullet-proof windows, adds up to $102,124.

All in all, the Mulroneys had every reason to be happy with their new offices. Mowinckel and a team of painters, carpenters, plumbers, antique experts and gallery curators had produced graceful rooms for both the prime minister and his wife, filled with the finest fabrics, pictures, rugs and furniture they could find.

A few weeks after the work started, Joseph Martin, the director of the National Gallery, became incensed by the treatment of artworks from the gallery that had been hanging in 24 Sussex. While other senior politicians and bureaucrats may rent artworks from the Canada Council's Art Bank, only a few people, among them the prime minister, may borrow pictures from the National Gallery.

In a long letter dated October 17, 1984, Martin wrote J.A.

Langford, the NCC's design project manager, that Mowinckel had informed Charles Hill, the gallery's Canadian Art curator, that the Sussex Drive renovations would require the removal of nineteen paintings and two sculptures on loan from the gallery to avoid damage. Gallery policy dictates that only trained gallery personnel can move artworks, but when Hill tried to arrange the removal an official at 24 Sussex told him – after many calls and much obstruction – that the works were gone. Boyds Moving and Storage had taken them to their warehouse.

The official said he knew of the gallery policy, but, wrote Martin, "he felt he was capable and justified in having the works moved by Boyds." Hill immediately took the works out of the warehouse, where they had been stored with the furniture.

"The warehouse was cold and there were no climatic controls in the building," fumed Martin. "The frame of one work (J.W. Russell: *Mme de B and Son*) was slightly damaged at the corners and abraded along the bottom edge. David Partridge's sculpture *Channelled Configurations* was more seriously injured. A number of the nails forming the visual element of this work were bent, the artist's plywood support was chipped along the back of one edge and tape had been wrapped around the nails at two points.

"We were informed," Martin thundered, "that the bronze sculpture *Le vieux pionnier Canadien* by Marc Aurèle de Foy Suzor-Côté had been taken to the prime minister's residence at Harrington Lake. After having looked for it there, it was subsequently located in the basement of 24 Sussex with a mover's sticker affixed to the sculpture."

Unheated warehouses, Martin explained, created a serious and sudden alteration in temperature and humidity levels and can "lead to serious structural damage to the works [which] may not be detected for years but is all the more dangerous for its apparent invisibility." Finally, so outraged by the sloppy handling of the twenty-one pieces, Martin threatened to "question the continuation" of the gallery's lending policy with the board of trustees.

Mowinckel quickly took the blame for the art debacle. In a sheepish letter to Martin, he explained that he had personally tagged all the furniture in 24 Sussex for removal to Harrington or a warehouse while the renovations were underway, and that he had left written instructions for anything not tagged to be taken into storage. Apologizing for the "inconvenience," Mowinckel added, "I was only trying to expedite the work I am carrying out on behalf of the Prime Minister."

But scoldings from crosspatches like Joseph Martin were rare indeed. For Mila Mulroney and Giovanni Mowinckel, little happened to mar the even tenor of their days of shopping and watching the work progress. In the beginning, an effort was made to set a strict budget for the work at Sussex Drive and Harrington Lake. Back on September 28, 1984, Art Wilson, then an assistant deputy minister at Public Works, received a telex from J.A. Langford, the manager of design and construction, saying he had received "verbal instructions from [Fred] Doucet to spend up to $97,000 on 24 Sussex and $25,000 on Harrington Lake." (These budgets were based on written estimates for plumbing, wiring, millwork and painting both houses.) Later, on October 26, Mowinckel wrote to Michael Plasse-Taylor, the project designer, to say the budget was not to exceed these amounts and any bills that went beyond them should be sent to him personally.

Mulroney himself announced the two budgets and said any money spent above and beyond these figures would come from his own pocket. The truth was that he had had private assurance from his close friend David Angus, a Montreal lawyer at Stikeman Elliott and the chairman of the PC Canada Fund, that these "above and beyond" bills from Mowinckel would be covered out of party funds. During the first eighteen months in power, Angus sent Mowinckel cheques adding up to $324,000, and senior Tory sources said the arrangement was not known by the PC Canada Fund board of directors. The only people who knew, the sources said, were Angus, PC Canada Fund executive director Nicholas Locke (who had to co-sign the cheques with Angus), the Mulroneys and Mowinckel. "It was a personal and private agreement," said Mr. Angus on April 14, 1987; "a private gentleman's agreement" is what Mulroney's press secretary Marc Lortie called it in April 1987.

Interestingly enough, most of the cheques to Mowinckel from David Angus were for under $25,000 each. Sometimes two or three cheques adding up to well over $25,000 would go out at the same time. Clearly, Angus had signing authority only for cheques up to $25,000 before he needed PC Fund board approval, so he paid in small amounts. The only cheque that was higher was for $108,000, which was probably the one the board, as the story broke in the news media, said they approved. (No member of the PC Fund board would discuss it, nor would Angus. One member who had discovered the system and was horrified by it did say off the record and after the story was out that "it was the chairman of the fund who brokeraged the money and the husband and wife [the Mulroneys] who spent it.")

Later, both Angus and Lortie said the prime minister had only "borrowed" the money and had paid "more than half" of it back. But they refused to produce any evidence of this repayment.

It is important to realize that the money spent by the PC Canada Fund was only a portion of the money lavished on the two residences during Mulroney's first eighteen months in office. Documents supplied by the Privy Council Office on April 15, 1987, show that the government spent a total of $945,904 between September 1984 and December 1986 on the two houses. These figures included capital costs and operating and maintenance costs – everything from cutting the grass to shovelling snow to wiring up a dishwasher as well as buying goods and furnishings.

PCO Clerk Paul Tellier played an interesting role in preparing these documents. On Friday, April 10, 1987, he called me from an airport saying he had heard that the *Globe and Mail* was about to print a story on Mowinckel and the decorating costs. (The story was planned for Saturday and he had been tipped off by the PM's principal secretary, Bernard Roy; Roy in turn had been told by Donald MacSween, then the director of the National Arts Centre. MacSween guessed because I had called his wife, a prominent local retailer, over one of the decorating bills.) Tellier said his office would like to make sure our figures were accurate and asked if we would delay printing the story until Monday. He promised his staff would begin to gather the documents immediately from Public Works and the National Capital Commission and would get back to us within hours. Despite these promises, there was no material forthcoming in time for the Monday paper, so the story was held until Tuesday. On Monday, PCO officials said they still had not gathered all the relevant information. The same thing happened on Tuesday. Finally, at 3:00 on Wednesday afternoon, April 15, Tellier's executive assistant, Rick Cameron, arrived at the *Globe*'s Ottawa bureau with the documents. On Wednesday at 3:00 the House rose for a ten-day April break. This meant that no uncomfortable questions about the *Globe* story would be asked in the House.

Were we out-snookered by Tellier? Certainly. But PCO was too clever by half. The extra days were spent combing through files; on Monday and Tuesday we found all the cancelled cheques from the PC Canada Fund. If PCO had not delayed us hoping to spare Mulroney a roasting in Question Period, a weaker story would have run, missing the most important evidence.

Mila Mulroney had no intention of letting Mowinckel's taste dominate the decor of 24 Sussex. Notes and lists and memos poured in from her assistant, Bonnie Brownlee, conveying her wishes, including explicit details of where all the Stornoway furniture should go. Mila spent the Christmas of 1984 in Palm Beach sorting through fabric swatches; the work on 24 Sussex was supposed to be finished by January 5, 1985, and no delay would be brooked.

But Mila herself caused delays. After Felix Schwartz, the painter, finished painting the living room at Sussex Drive a pale peach and then rag-rolling it, a painstaking procedure that gives a subtly dappled finish, Mila said she hated it. The room was repainted beige. This colour change necessitated a new rug; the pink carpet that had just been installed no longer matched. There were problems with a second and a third custom-made carpet and finally a fourth acceptable carpet was installed.

Mila and Mowinckel toured antique shops together to find the right kinds of accessories and furniture for the houses. One favourite stop was Phyllis Friedman's in Montreal. Mila's mother, Bogdana Pivnicki, worked there and they bought several pieces from her, including an old piece of Canadian earthenware with a beaver pattern for $375, two eighteenth-century carved wooden stands with *putti* for $1,600, three Spode platters for $690, an eighteenth-century mahogany clothes press and a mahogany chest of drawers for $7,000, two milk cans (turned into lamps) for $275, a Quebec pine mirror for $525, a nineteenth-century *cheval* mirror for $760 and a collection of majolica plates, wicker and folk art for a total of $568. (These prices do not include the standard 15 per cent discount the Mulroneys received. Most stores gave them discounts of up to 40 per cent.)

David Brown of Mountain Street sold them a French bronze lamp for $525 and Henrietta Antony sold them many pieces including at least $3,741 worth of lamps and shades. (She also sold them an antique French baker's rack for $4,800, although inexplicably she later told the *Westmount Gazette* that the price was "nowhere near $4,800" as reported in the *Globe*. Mowinckel's records include a receipt from her store, however, made out in her hand, showing the price as $4,800. Antony also told the *Gazette* that to her knowledge the prime minister and his wife had acquired their antiques "on a shoestring.")

Some of Mila's friends in Montreal asked local antique dealers to donate items for the house, in much the same way that White House First Ladies have solicited donations for the White House rooms, but at least one dealer, asked for some porcelain plates, coldly turned the request down.

Mila and Mowinckel again patronized Toronto's Paisley Shop, which had supplied so many antiques for Mulroney's office. Here Mowinckel purchased a nineteenth-century mahogany partner's desk for the prime minister's study; it cost $12,400 and was one of the items paid for by the PC Party. Other Paisley Shop purchases, all English antiques, came out of government funds; they included a figured walnut box for $850, a painted tray for $1,075, a reproduction mahogany side table for $825, an 1810 Georgian mahogany work table for $3,200, an 1810 figured mahogany tripod table for $975, a mahogany Pembroke table for $1,950, an 1800 Sheraton side table for $1,600 and a piece of old Coalport china for $450. The store also repaired several pieces of furniture.

Toronto designer Bud Sugarman supplied more than the overused ribbons-and-bows chintz. He sold them two 1870 English crystal vases with silver mounts for $3,400, as well as a pair of "semi-antique" Chinese frogs, dated 1920, for $495. Another special order from Sugarman was twenty-four malachite place mats, handmade by an eighty-six-year-old woman called Mrs. Shline; these were $200 each and, according to Mowinckel's staff, Mila gave a dozen to the Desmarais as a present.

Canadian furniture was the Mulroneys' choice for Harrington Lake, and at R.G. Perkins in Toronto they bought chairs ($2,120) and lamps ($2,350) and at Ruth Stalker in Montreal they bought a pine harvest table ($1,275). Patricia Fleet in Ottawa sold them an armoire for $850 and an old rope bed for $400.

In the spring of 1985 Mila Mulroney accompanied her husband to the Bonn Economic Summit. When it was over she flew to Rome, accompanied by Bonnie Brownlee and an RCMP bodyguard, on a private visit to shop with Mowinckel. (He took his assistant, Karen Large, on the trip.) Keith Hamilton, a senior aide in PMO, wired the embassy in Rome to arrange for a $3,500 advance for Mrs. Mulroney. Cables flew back and forth between External Affairs and the embassy to arrange for hospitality. While documents obtained under access to information law showed that the government paid the party's bills for meals and accommodation, the costs were removed from the documents; the excuse was that the visit was a private one. Under Section 15(1) of the Access to Information Act, "personal information" is exempt, but the government did not explain why it paid the bills for a private visit.

Mulroney and her party stayed at the Hassler, the most exclusive hotel in Rome, situated at the top of the Spanish Steps. The Via Condotti, Rome's world-renowned shopping street, starts at the bottom of the Steps, and Mowinckel and Mulroney dropped into Bulgari, considered the most expensive jewellery store in Europe, to visit Rosemary Balancino, who was working here. Here Mila ordered one of the store's least costly items, a steel necklace with gold clasps and topazes. It cost about $3,200. Stories abound about how she paid for the jewellery, but receipts show that Mowinckel paid for it four months later in August 1985. When asked about this in an interview in April 1987, Marc Lortie said that Mila had paid Mowinckel in Rome "on the spot, on the street, in cash." Why? Why did he pay at all? Didn't she have travellers' cheques? The cash advance? A credit card? "You know how Mowinckel is. That was how he wanted to do it," Lortie insisted.

Over the following months questions about the necklace remained. Well-informed Ottawans gossiped like mad about this relatively small purchase. Many professed to "know" that Mila Mulroney had bought a "fabulous" piece of jewellery in Italy and that Mowinckel had disguised the cost in the house bills. Mowinckel had told his staff to keep all the receipts "just in case he ever needed them." "He was afraid of Mila," one former staff member said. The Toronto *Star* sent a reporter to Italy in March 1988 to interview Bulgari staff and to London to talk to Mowinckel, who was there on business.

But the truth comes from the documents themselves, aided

by on-the-record interviews with Rosemary Balancino and with Danielle Letarte, a young woman who worked for a few weeks as a temporary bookkeeper for Mowinckel in August 1985. (Mowinckel, to his credit, refuses to discuss this incident or the problems he had with the Mulroneys later in 1986. "They were clients," he said grimly, in Italy in the spring of 1988, "and the relationship with a client is bed on trust. I can't discuss it.")

The receipts and documents from Bulgari show the necklace was ready in early August 1985. Rosemary Balancino telephoned Mowinckel to say it was ready and to have him send the money; she also sent a bill addressed to Mr. M. Mulroney, 24 Sussex Drive, which someone sent over to Mowinckel's office for payment on August 8. Mowinckel told Danielle Letarte that they needed to send a cheque off to Bulgari that day, but that he was waiting until he received a cheque himself. Just before the bank closed at 3 p.m., she said, he rushed upstairs to her office and gave her a cheque for $5,000, which had just come in from the PC Canada Fund. "I remember it was from the fund because it had the logo," Letarte said. "We got a lot of cheques from the party and they always had that logo on it." (There is, however, no evidence that anyone at the PC Canada Fund intended the money to be used for jewellery.)

She ran off to the bank and bought a bank draft for $3,237.75. She doesn't remember what she did with the balance of the money, but the fact that Colvin Designs' bank records do not show a deposit for the leftover money that day suggest she brought it back to the shop.

Once he had the bank draft, Mowinckel called Purolator to come and pick it up; Purolator sent it to Rome the same day, August 8. Karen Large, on Mowinckel's instruction, rewrote the Purolator receipt showing a charge of $21.75, attributing it to "Charges to send staff uniforms from Rome." A close examination of the bill shows this makes no sense. The Purolator coding indicates clearly that the bill is for sending an airmail letter *to* Rome. Mowinckel did admit, during conversations in Italy in April 1988, that the Purolator document had been doctored, and confirmed a hunch that the only reason the Purolator bill ever surfaced was because he was annoyed with the Mulroneys. He had planned to absorb the charge himself as a personal cost; it does not show up on any of the bills he sent the Mulroneys for expenses incurred in August 1985. It was only the following summer, during the terrible wrangles about bills, that he got angry and included it. It was this doctored Purolator bill that caused the *Globe and Mail* to take a second look at the whole issue of the necklace.

In an interview from Rome, Rosemary Balancino said that the bank draft arrived, but because she herself was coming to Canada in a few days, she decided to bring the necklace with her. (Mowinckel's staff remember helping him plan a big supper party for her at Farrelton House.) She admitted not declaring the necklace at Canada Customs, and said that to her knowledge Mrs. Mulroney did not declare it later.

The Prime Minister's Office was upset when the *Globe* printed this story in the spring of 1988. This time both Marc Lortie and Communications Director Bruce Phillips said Mila had sent cash over to Mowinckel's Ivy Crescent office on August 8, 1985, to pay for the bank draft and that they could prove it but wouldn't. The version that had Mila peeling off the lire on the Via Condotti was forgotten. They refused to discuss why Mowinckel was involved in the transaction and alleged that the *Globe* story was a lie.

While work progressed on the official residences, Mowinckel picked up a raft of influential new clients, including Mulroney's principal secretary, Bernard Roy, his executive assistant, Hubert Pichet, Bill Neville, Dalton Camp, Thomas D'Aquino and his wife, Susan Peterson, Paul Desmarais, the Saudi Arabian Embassy and Olympia and York's new president, Mickey Cohen. He was earning revenues of more than $1 million a year, but his expenses were enormous, and he was still earning nothing from the Mulroney work. He bought condominiums in Toronto and in Florida and a MURB in Ottawa. He also owned a small country house (which he had bought years earlier) in Great Rollwright, England. He brought a fine old Bentley in from England and talked an Ottawa car dealer into buying it and then leasing it back to him. He owned a Jeep and a Buick as well. Although he maintained a large loan at the Royal Bank and his property was heavily mortgaged, his bank manager was not worried.

Cash flow became a problem in the summer of 1986. At this time the Mulroneys owed Mowinckel $51,000 for design fees and furnishings they'd charged on his account at various stores and they had owed this amount for eight months. For the first time since he set up shop in Ottawa, Mowinckel was unable to pay his creditors, like Bill Jackson at the Paisley Shop and Paul Lavergne at Neander in Montreal. Upset at being embarrassed in this way, he finally wrote the Mulroneys to threaten legal action if they did not pay and sent copies of his letter to Hamilton Southam and National Capital Commission chairman Jean Pigott. The Mulroneys were enraged that the letter had been sent to Southam, who was head of the Official Residences Council. Mrs. Mulroney's assistant, Bonnie Brownlee, told bookkeeper Marie Dorion that "you do not threaten the prime minister." The warning was clear, Dorion said; if Mowinckel took legal action he would lose the contract to decorate Manoir Desmarais, the Desmarais' vast 35,000-square-foot country estate on the Saguenay River. So he did nothing and lost the contract anyway. A Desmarais spokesperson, Francoise Patry, said merely that Mowinckel was only one of several decorators being consulted and that he had no right to expect the contract.

As the summer of 1986 dragged on, Mowinckel took to his bed at Farrelton House for three months with a bad case of shingles and brooded. Although the NCC finally paid $38,000 towards the Mulroneys' bills and David Angus kicked in another $5,400 from a secret PC Canada Fund account in Montreal, Mowinckel felt wronged. He knew the relationships with the prime minister and with Paul Desmarais were over. John Bosley was on the verge of resigning, so he had no heart for The Farm project. Although things were souring rapidly, in the fall he went ahead with plans to open an antiques and accessories store on Laurier with Joy Large, Karen's mother.

But by late autumn, rumours were starting to leak out about the lavishness of the residences. On November 17, 1986, Liberal MP Don Boudria asked Public Works Minister Stewart McInnes the following question in the House: "Did the Government employ the services of Colvin Designs Ltd. and/or Giovanni Mowinkle [sic], interior designer for the period September 4, 1984, to June 30, 1986, to supply furnishings, improvements, interior decorating or advice on same for the Prime Minister's residence at 24 Sussex Drive in Ottawa or the Harrington Lake residence, and if so, by residence, what was the cost of each contract?"

"No," answered McInnes.

"Was all of the work paid for from government funds and, if not, who paid such costs and what was the amount involved in each case?"

"Not applicable," was the terse reply.

These questions were answered in written form at 6 p.m. at what is known as "the late show," the time set aside for questions that cannot be answered during oral Question Period.

Lying to the House is an offence punishable by a minister's resignation. Six months later, on April 27, 1987, after the *Globe* published stories of how the Mulroneys used party funds, McInnes apologized to the House, admitting his answer "was inappropriate and inadvertently misleading." He blamed officials for supplying him with incomplete information. Incredibly, all McInnes acknowledged was the $38,000 worth of work on 24 Sussex, not the other thousands spent by the government on the offices, Harrington Lake or other Sussex Drive work. Then Don Mazankowski tried to soften McInnes' damaging admission by reminding the House that Mulroney paid for his own groceries and had established an Official Residences Council to advise on the houses. He neglected to add that the council was made up almost entirely of Mulroney friends and had no real power.

Just before Christmas Mowinckel started planning his escape from Ottawa. He quietly began to liquidate his real estate holdings. During the late fall he arranged shipment of all his furniture and goods to Italy. He plodded through assignments and the store opening, but all the time he was planning how to get his money out of Canada.

Finally, in February, he laid off his staff and slipped out of the city after a frantic dash to the bank to cash a large cheque from a real estate sale. He fled to Rome, where Rosemary Balancino comforted him, and then to Tuscany. His companion, Richard Sainte-Germaine, joined him at the end of March. Mowinckel and Sainte-Germaine now live in an old Tuscan farmhouse that they rent from an Ottawa friend. They press their own olive oil from an olive grove on the property, they shop for groceries in nearby Porto Ercole and sometimes see the few friends from Canada who know how to reach them. From time to time they go to Rome or Florence. Although they occasionally work with Giovanni's oldest friend, London antique dealer Dennis Leroy, on various projects including shipping Italian antiques to England, how they support themselves is anyone's guess.

Back in Canada, Mowinckel left chaos in his wake. Creditors, including old friends Paul Lavergne and Henrietta Antony and the Peters family, were left high and dry. He had taken goods he had not paid for and left enormous debts behind him, something like $400,000 worth, including a quarter of a million dollars to the Royal Bank. The bank pushed the company into bankruptcy and then called the RCMP in to trace him. Though the police eventually found Mowinckel in Tuscany, they could not extradite him because he had retained his Italian citizenship. All they could do was issue a warrant for his arrest on charges of theft and fraud.

Exit Giovanni, the prince of chintz. His departure did not mean the end of decorating at Sussex Drive and Harrington Lake, of course; it has carried on under the direction of Richard Raycroft. Robby McRobb, the Mulroneys' first butler at 24 Sussex Drive, conveniently moved to a job as "household liaison" at the National Capital Commission in the fall of 1985 and for the next two years, until he moved to the Prime Minister's Office under the direct supervision of Derek Burney, then Mulroney's chief of staff, he acted as Mila's purchasing agent. Burney personally authorized payment of bills for loveseats, cookie sheets, paella pans, wrought-iron furniture, beach umbrellas.

What else did they buy? More of the same, more wicker, more cushions, more china and silver (in fact, $4,684 worth of silver including "candelabrum, dome cloche, jam holders, napkin rings and cruet" purchased from the National Arts Centre). They bought forty-eight Madeira place mats and forty-eight napkins from Ogilvy's for $3,036. "Aesthetic" plexiglass baby gates installed for staircases in both residences – $500 for Harrington Lake and $1,304 for 24 Sussex – were an innovation. Purchases in 1987 included upholstery costing $3,694, a new washroom floor for $925, another tile floor for $1,900, some patio furniture for $465, a pressure-treated floor for the wine cellar for $320, a new carpet for $10,773, some curtain tassels for $434 and some tiebacks for $378, a wall unit for $950, another television and VCR for $1,500 . . . The list goes on and on and on. There is no sign of it abating.

In the summer of 1988, the Official Residences Council released its "master plans" for the six government houses, recommending $67 million be spent on them over the next ten years. A confidential council document prepared in 1986 and revised in 1987 spelled out more details. The plans are to spend $5.2 million on 24 Sussex Drive between 1987 and 1997 for such things as furnishings, landscaping and capital expenditures. The forecast operating budget added to a grand total of $9.8 million over ten years. Harrington Lake would get $1.9 million in the same period for its master plan of furnishings and landscaping; operating costs would bring its total up to $3 million between 1987 and 1997.

In early May 1989 the Toronto *Star* reported that the NCC had spent $150,000 on plans alone for more renovations at 24

Sussex, including a new kitchen, more closet space, reorganizing the living room, replacing the sunroom, improving the gardens, adding new lighting, improving the access for handicapped people and changing the outside of the guardhouses "so that they are more in keeping with the appearance of the main and chauffeur's residence."

A spokesman for the Prime Minister's Office said his boss knew nothing about the plans and had no control over the property, which was administered, he told *Star* reporter Patrick Doyle, by the autonomous Official Residences Council. The spokesman was wrong. The prime minister controls the house completely and the council is a toothless advisory body. This assessment is borne out by the experience of one NCC functionary.

A *frisson* of exasperation popped up in some bureaucratic correspondence between the NCC's Agnes Jaouich, the head of the Official Residences Division, and the Prime Minister's housekeeper, Luciana Jovanovich, in December 1987. A big push was on to get another decorating bout over in time for the Mulroneys' Christmas at Harrington. But this time, "the occupant," as officials have now taken to calling Mrs. Mulroney, had gone too far. The Official Residences Council guidelines designated the halls, stairs and certain rooms at Harrington as "state" areas, Jaouich reminded her, and their guidelines allow the NCC to choose appropriate carpeting. But Mulroney did not like the NCC choices. She wanted white wool carpet, even in the children's TV room; Jaouich called white wool "inappropriate" for such "high traffic areas" and recommended green. Mulroney wanted brass stair rods holding down the carpeting; brass stair rods, fussed Jaouich, were "inappropriate" for a summer cottage.

The white carpeting and brass rods were in place for Christmas.

13

Looking Good, Feeling Good

A group of men who met regularly at the Gays and Lesbians of Ottawa downtown headquarters were worried. Here they were, all hard working, well educated and many of them bilingual. Cultivated men with good taste. What were they doing wrong? Somehow, no matter how hard they worked, they just couldn't make it to the top layers of the city, neither socially nor professionally. They seemed to be doomed to remain at mid-level jobs, attending mid-level dinner parties, invited only to second-rate embassies.

They decided to Take Steps. They invited Carol Reesor, a local image consultant, to analyze their situation and tell them what they were doing that offended the straight male community who, ever so subtly, made the decisions that affected the gays' social and professional lives. Reesor thought it was a wonderful challenge. "Many of these men are very senior people, but because Ottawa is so ultra-conservative – it's the most conservative city in Canada – they sense they don't make it past a certain level because of their lifestyle." She thought it over carefully and put together a list of suggestions.

"One thing straight men find offensive," Reesor says, "is men in fur coats. Especially mink coats. Other men laugh at them behind their backs. You see, men are not as cold as women, which is why women wear them. When a man wears a fur coat the message he sends out is mixed. So I was going to start by telling them to cut back on furs and jewellery."

Armed with this well-meaning advice, Mrs. Reesor arrived at Gays and Lesbians of Ottawa one evening and was ushered into the cloakroom, where, as she says, "I hung my little mink on a peg, then looked at the other twenty-five fur coats hanging beside it and lost my nerve."

Another knotty problem she found was how the gays introduced their partners, their significant others, at cocktail parties. "What do we call them?" fretted the men. "I suggested 'mate' because I thought it had a nice nautical ring to it – as in 'ahoy there, mate!' " she muses, "but they rejected it. They thought it sounded too . . . macho."

Ottawa's gay community is not the only group who think they need help climbing social and professional ladders. Newcomers often find the city hard to fathom. They arrive feeling gauche and ill-informed, ignorant of the unwritten rules, unaware of the code words. Some learn by native instinct, some never learn, and some simply decide to shortcut all the pain and get a little help. A friendly deputy minister can guide a new Cabinet minister through most minefields of Ottawa's political and bureaucratic games; so can an experienced press secretary or chief of staff. But that's not enough. In Ottawa, mastering the social games is critical to professional success. Reesor has made a living delivering advice on appearance, communications skills and behaviour to Cabinet ministers without offending them. Over the past few years she has taken on many well-known Toronto clients and now she spends as much time in Toronto as she does in Ottawa.

Reesor is discreet. She won't name her clients but does rhyme off some of the jobs they've held: a former justice minister, a top-level RCMP man, a former minister of regional and industrial development, the former president of the Treasury Board and the former minister of supply and services. There have also been ordinary MPs and political candidates as well as some local businessmen. Her favourite in the latter category was an Ottawa plumber with a Grade eight education and a little stint in reform school who now calls her with delight every time he gets invited to join a country club or sit on a board of directors. "He used to wear Laredo cowboy shirts," she remembers with an indulgent chuckle. "The first time I took him into Harry Rosen's to pick out a navy blue suit and watched him try it on, it was like a metamorphosis."

Carol Reesor is a "character." We all know characters: men and women who look odd, wear comfortable shoes and battered overcoats and keep smelly dogs and are very amusing and have murky pasts. They get invited everywhere, smoke too much, drink too much, and know where all the bodies are buried. Truth to tell, usually they're embarrassing bores. Carol Reesor is none of the above. She's slim, pretty and preppy with long, streaky blonde hair, usually pulled back in a loose chignon. The kind of woman who wears winter white wool sweaters with smartly tailored slacks, and elegant silk suits that look as if they cost a great deal of money. In a community that usually communicates through innuendo, Reesor's candid, matter-of-fact wit is refreshing.

Image consultants abound in today's Ottawa. In recent years, the best known have been Gabor Apor and Henry Comor, that weather-beaten team who worked so desperately to resuscitate John Turner into a politician who could walk and talk without coughing, clearing his throat, barking out laughs, patting bums, licking his lips, swearing or rolling his eyes. They succeeded, but it still didn't work. Carol Reesor never planned to do their kind of overhaul. Her ambition when she first opened for business was to run a finishing school for young girls from good families. "When I set out to do this I had no intention of telling Cabinet ministers what kind of china to put in their offices," she admits. But that's what she ended up doing because politicians were the only ones who answered her ads.

Mrs. Reesor's courses run for two to four hours every week for four months and cost just under $3,000. Do the taxpayers foot the bill? What do you think? Cabinet ministers put the fees through their "discretionary spending" budget, nonaccountable funds used to defray little expenses. They get away with it because her school, Savoir Vivre Image Consultants, is registered with the Ontario Ministry of Education as an adult education program.

"People come to me for fine-tuning," she says. "My typical client is a thirty-five-year-old married male with at least one graduate degree. These are men who want to be fast-tracked." Her approach is motherly and abrupt, starting with hygiene. How often do you brush your teeth? she demands of her startled students. Wash your hair? Shower? Apparently, Mrs. Reesor's clients are never offended when she suggests they should do something about their teeth and hair and clothes. "A clinical psychologist told me the reason men are so accepting is that I'm just another coach. And they look upon all this as an adventure.

"I take them shopping and help them pick out shampoo. If they have bad skin, I take them to a dermatologist. I take them to my hairdresser, who can change their appearance with a good cut." Ten per cent of all parliamentarians in Ottawa, she confides, now have their hair permed and coloured. One of her clients, who normally has flat, lank hair, added two inches to his height with a soft, noncurly permanent. She told another MP that the cheap dye he was using was making his hair look flat and dead. "I told him it just wasn't good enough. But it didn't matter because he decided not to run again."

Clothes come next. Reesor is famous for her insistence on the navy suit as the mainstay of a successful man's wardrobe. She carts her clients off to the Rideau Centre ("Suburban stores are more expensive than stores in the centre of town") and dresses them, usually at Harry Rosen's. "Harry's been very good. If I have a busy minister who knows he is going to be on 'Canada AM' the next morning, one of the staff will send over a shirt and tie right away and the bill later. His staff are very discreet."

Reesor worries a lot about how politicians look to a camera when shot from the waist up. "What goes on around the neck is important. Most men buy shirts that are half a size too small and their necks always look too tight. And if the tie doesn't hit the top of his belt buckle, if, God forbid, it's two inches short and there's a chance he'll pop a button and expose two inches of flesh, well, Canadians would never get over it. Canadians hate flesh on men; the only flesh that is permitted from September to June is hands, wrists, neck and face. That's why men who wear short-sleeved shirts never get promoted."

These rules are for politicians operating in Ottawa. If she's trying to help a man fix up his image for another part of the country, she lets him become more casual, especially the farther west he goes. "In Alberta it's perfectly permissible to wear *good* cowboy boots, but he couldn't pull that off in Ottawa."

Once her politician looks good and smells good, it is time to tackle his communications skills. She teaches him first how to remember people's names. She warns him against what she calls "that terrible habit of older politicians, that double clasping of hands, often followed by a sincere grip of the arm." She has also had to teach the few women clients she's had to shake hands firmly, not with that clammy dead fish style so many women use.

Reesor sets the client a reading program of great books and important newspapers and magazines. "Syntax and a good vocabulary are important, and if they don't read they can't talk." She tries to break him of bad speech habits and giveaway words and phrases. "Civilized people," she snorts, "don't use 'at this point in time' and 'no problem' and 'basically'."

Reesor then instills the niceties of etiquette, what she calls "business and international protocol." She starts with tea at her house. "I teach them how to present a tea tray and tell them they are not allowed to use paper cups at the office. I go to a *vernissage* with them so they can learn how to look at pictures and introduce people and still balance a glass of wine and handle a business card. I take them through every kind of meal, so they learn how to handle silverware properly – things like sipping the soup out of the side of the spoon and pushing the spoon away from them and bringing it back to avoid drips on their flies."

Sometimes Reesor turns away potential clients because she thinks they are the genuine thing, "people who have an intrinsic sense of style that shouldn't be changed." Asked to identify politicians who need no finishing, she is quick with examples. "Someone like Marcel Masse, who is very well groomed and has excellent manners, doesn't need any help; nor would Cape Breton Liberal MP Russell MacLellan, who always looks good and is a gentleman and a scholar." Others are Toronto Liberal MP Jim Peterson, former communications minister Flora MacDonald and Employment and Immigration Minister Barbara McDougall. NDP president Johanna den Hertog "tests very well on television," and Halifax Liberal MP Mary Clancy is another woman Reesor would not dream of changing, despite the fact that Mrs. Clancy is overweight. "So what if she's not size 8? She's a handsome woman, a wonderful woman and I wouldn't do a damn thing about her."

Paul Martin, now, that's another matter. Reesor would like to have a go at this Liberal leadership hopeful. He needs, according to her, a new haircut and some voice training. "He's not getting his message across; his communications skills are poor."

If it weren't for the city's soft services sector made up of dressmakers, hairdressers, makeup artists, nannies, cleaning women, jewellers, decorators, speechwriters, chefs, doctors, aestheticians, florists, dentists, fitness experts, diet counsellors, caterers, party rental experts and clothing retailers, many Ottawans would be lost.

A woman can live all her life in Ottawa, unlike Toronto, and never need a long evening dress, but she will need a lot of cocktail outfits. While the city has several good designers, three stand out. Nicola Lang is a successful designer who makes classic day and evening clothes for most of the city's senior diplomatic and bureaucratic community. Some outfits are one-of-a-kind for special occasions, but she and her sister Sonia, her business manager, have also developed a ready-to-wear line, which they sell in Ottawa and in their own shop in Nantucket. By now, you may not be surprised to hear that the Lang sisters grew up in Rockcliffe, where Nicky, now married to a former Ottawa bureaucrat, David Low, still lives.

Another talented designer who has become as much part of the local social scene as Nicky Lang is Paddye Mann, an outspoken Newfoundlander with great flair and shrewd business acumen who runs her own couture business out of a picturesque stone house in nearby Pakenham. Mann's dramatic clothes are probably the most expensive you can buy in the area, but they are all custom-made from the best European silks and wools. She has a list of well-heeled clients in Toronto and other Canadian cities, most of them professional women between thirty-five and fifty-five. Her Ottawa clients include NCC chairman Jean Pigott, North South Institute president Maureen O'Neil and writer Sandra Gwyn, another Newfoundlander.

The third top dressmaker is Donna Kearns, who started in business as an antique lace and textile dealer and gradually built up a design studio. Six seamstresses labour over the pintucking and lace inserts that have become her trademark; another woman irons all the fragile silks, satins, linens and lawns used for her outfits. This is the place you'd send your daughter for her wedding dress if you wanted something exquisite to pass down to another generation. Maybe this is why the Montreal *Gazette*'s former lifestyles editor, Donna Nebenzahl, had her wedding suit made here and came up every weekend by train for fittings. Other clients include Diana Kirkwood and Popsy Johnston, who bought almost all her clothes here for her life in New York as wife of the Canadian consul general. The National Gallery's Shirley Thompson also comes to Donna Kearns for the dramatic clothes she likes to wear. Expensive call girls have counted on Kearns to keep them supplied with lacy teddies, camisoles and knickers, all slotted with red or black ribbons.

Roger Phillips, a Sassoon-trained Welshman who has been building up a clientele of top bureaucrats and businesswomen for the last fifteen years, is Ottawa's premier hairstylist. Every day his shop, Tag, on York Street in the market, is a hive of powerful women discreetly sharing office gossip. Phillips is himself too discreet to tell you that he usually gets invited to Government House to perform a quick "do" or comb-out on royalty or other state visitors. Carol Reesor likes to take her clients to The Parlour on St. Patrick, and when John Turner needs a haircut, he visits Yolande Cheff in her Wurtenburg Street salon, as do many other politicians. (Turner's bad back needs better help than Ottawa can offer, however, so he uses popular Toronto massage therapist Carroll Quinn, who travelled with him during the 1988 election campaign.) A few powerbrokers still go to Rinaldo's in Place de Ville; Rinaldo was the top hairdresser in Ottawa before Roger Phillips displaced him. His manicurist, Anna Casa Ramones, has captured Mila Mulroney with her skilled French manicures. The wives of the South American diplomats are among the biggest consumers of cosmetic services. When they're not playing canasta in each other's residences, you'll find them hanging around Danielle D'Amours' salon in L'Esplanade Laurier getting their legs waxed, their eyebrows plucked or their faces steamed.

It's all very well to look good, but Ottawa is a city that moves on its belly. Once, and quite rightly so, Ottawa had a reputation for dreadful food. The only places you could count on were French restaurants in Hull, places like Café Henry

Burger, still John Turner's favourite restaurant. Today, gusta-torially speaking, Hull is nowhere and Ottawa has many good restaurants and many gifted chefs.

One of the finest chefs in the city is Jean-Pierre Muller, the sturdy, no-nonsense Frenchman who owns Chez Jean Pierre. Chef to a string of eight U.S. ambassadors, Muller flourished during the Enderses' years at the embassy when Gaetana Enders, a demanding and often difficult boss, encouraged him to dazzling culinary feats. He used to keep her on a thousand-calorie-a-day diet, packing her exquisite low-cal lunches (with plenty of extra for her friends) for her cross-country ski picnics.

At that time the U.S. Embassy greenhouse was the only place in Ottawa where you could get fresh French tarragon or fresh basil in the middle of January. Muller's buddy the gardener brought him green offerings of tender lettuce and fresh peas and skinny asparagus each summer. Against village bylaws, he raised baby lambs on embassy grounds and then, very quietly, had them slaughtered. They would hang in neat little rows in the embassy cold room just off the kitchen. A nun across the river in Pointe Gatineau laboured with water-colours and fine camelhair brushes to create special menus that glowed like mediaeval illuminated manuscripts.

Then along came Reagan appointments Martha and Paul Robinson, who shut down the greenhouse, banished the lambs, scrapped the nun and even contracted out the garden-ing to a commercial service that had no time to cultivate a vegetable garden. In the embassy kitchen Muller flipped hamburgers, fried potatoes and did a slow burn. Finally, in complete exasperation, he quit (the Robinsons said they fired him for insubordination). He leaked to Allan Fotheringham his meticulously kept records of every meal prepared in the embassy to prove that all he ever cooked was steak, fries and hamburgers, and then stomped off to open his own restaurant, a modest establishment in an undistinguished apartment-hotel on Somerset Street. On opening night his friends, including

Yannick Vincent, Prime Minister Trudeau's chef (who was fired by the Mulroneys), all came in to help. Since then, his restaurant has flourished; just try to get a seat at noon without a reservation. Because Chez Jean Pierre is a little far from the Hill, people go there when they want privacy. This is also where you'll see some of the great mandarins and politicians of yesteryear like Robert Bryce, former deputy at Finance, eating with Jack Pickersgill.

Kurt Waldele's café at the National Arts Centre is the best people-watching restaurant in Ottawa at noon, and the food, given the size of the place and the frequency with which the tables turn over, is excellent. But Waldele's greatest fame comes from the state dinners and private meals he supervises for the Mulroneys, his best clients.

The Byward Market area is jammed with cafés and restaurants, but surprisingly few of them are any good. Probably the best is the café in the back of Domus, a housewares and kitchen shop where everyone in Ottawa seems to meet every Saturday morning and swap information. If you want to see the famous people taking it really easy, drop into Nate's on Rideau Street. For many years, this deli and steakhouse has been popular with politicians and journalists even though the food, well, lacks finesse.

Meals in Ottawa are less about food and more about power. The real action takes place at breakfast. It doesn't matter who you are, unless you are meeting Senator Keith Davey, you won't get Table 24 at the Four Seasons. Davey holds court there every morning and no one in the city is better informed than he is. If you want to catch him at it, be in the restaurant by 8 a.m. You'll often see Manitoba Senator Mira Spivak doing breakfast here; like Davey, she lives at the Four Seasons when she's in town. (The Four Seasons' Toronto head office despairs of the Ottawa hotel; they know it's a political institution now, just as the Château Grill was in the Trudeau-and-Coutts days, but because they have to give everyone "government rates" they don't make much money.)

If the Four Seasons is big at breakfast, the Westin is where some powerbrokers go at night. Its main restaurant, Les Saisons, is popular for its reasonably priced but elegant dinners. Former manager Tim Whitehead (now running Toronto's Royal York) was determined that the food should be the best in the city, and for hotel food, it probably is. He won over the new Tory government in 1984, and flocks of Cabinet ministers gather there every night.

For the most part you don't see a lot of powerful people at night; they've breakfasted and lunched so well, they're home with briefing books, eating boiled eggs and toast. Very late, though, when they get restless, you might find them in one of the city's excellent Chinese restaurants along Somerset Street or wolfing down lox and cream cheese at Bagel-Bagel. Sometimes you'll see a provincial premier or two, surrounded by aides, eating pizza at The Colonnade on Metcalfe in Centre Town. This is where Ontario's David Peterson and New Brunswick's Frank McKenna stoked up the night before a recent Ottawa meeting. In Rockcliffe Park, residents order in bland Chinese food from Tan-Ca-Luck at the foot of Springfield Road. Or they might phone for a pizza from Mario's on Beechwood, where you'll get no trendy thin-crust nonsense. This is he-man stuff, all thick and chewy and double cheese with the works.

Not surprisingly, the most interesting wining and dining takes place privately and gracefully in the elegant salons of embassy residences, official government buildings (such as the Lester Pearson Building or the House of Commons) and in official government residences such as 24 Sussex Drive and Stornoway and Rideau Hall.

Gerry Arial, who owns the Silver Rose on Laurier Street, a large shop he renovated for $185,000 two years ago, is Ottawa's society florist. Some critics find his arrangements too arch, too stiff, too wondrous when all they want is a floppy bowlful of roses and peonies and lilies, but for the grand occasions, Arial is a star. He decorated the Speakers' chambers in the House of Commons and Senate for the opening of Parliament in 1984, and in 1985 turned the Popeboat, which brought Pope John Paul II down the Rideau Canal, into a flower-covered extravaganza. He did all the flower arrangements for the television special "Little Gloria, Happy at Last" as well as for the 1984 World Figure Skating Championships. He lavishes blooms on tables and boxes at Arts Centre galas and state dinners and he's responsible for arranging the flowers at 9 Rideau Gate.

This is a big town for formal engraved invitations. "Pour mémoires" are sent even for informal dinner parties to follow up the initial phone invitations, and local printers keep busy with all the menus, cards, programs and other cream-coloured bits of paper which smooth the social round. One printer was badly stung by the Mulroneys' attempt to upgrade their paper arsenal. After receiving a present from Ronald and Nancy Reagan, which came wrapped in thick white paper embossed with the presidential seal, Mila Mulroney was eager to have the same thing for her presents. She asked Gary Grant at Sheffield Graphics in Ottawa to reproduce the Reagan paper, but instead with the coat of arms of Canada embossed into the paper. Grant subcontracted the job to another firm, M.O.M. Printing, because they were the only firm with the necessary equipment.

Eric Kanstrupp, who runs M.O.M. Printing, explained that his company does more than $10-million worth of business a year and that this was a small job. "They gave us a sample of Mrs. Reagan's paper," he said, "and we made up between five hundred and a thousand sheets for Mrs. Mulroney." The hitch was that just as he finished making her wrapping paper, Mulroney found out she was not entitled to use the coat of arms of Canada; protocol dictates that this right belongs only to the governor general. Her office refused to take delivery of the paper and refused to pay for it. After this story broke in Claire Hoy's column, the Mulroneys may have taken the paper after all. During research for a profile on Mila Mulroney in the spring of 1989, Montreal journalist Dominique Demers asked PMO officials about the paper and they said it was now being used by the Mulroneys.

Ottawa's backstairs world of drug dealers and hookers plays its own part in servicing the powerful. Drugs are all over Ottawa. Politicians, bureaucrats, diplomats and journalists are among the high-end users, and the drug of choice is cocaine. One well-informed source says the drug is brought onto the Hill by bicycle couriers, but others dispute this, saying the Hill security guards would find it if this were true. The drug of choice on the Hill is alcohol, say most people, and the Hill has its own branch of Alcoholics Anonymous to help people who become dependent.

"Many diplomats demand drugs," says another drug expert, "and they often bring their own into the country in their diplomatic pouches."

The most visible side of the skin trade – the strip clubs, table dancers, pornographic movie and video outlets and sex aids – flourishes on the other side of the river, in Hull and Gatineau. Three of the four movie houses in Hull, for example, places like the Pussycat and Cinéma l'Amour, are devoted exclusively to sex films, while five of the area's seven sex shops – the kind with whips, inflatable dolls, dildos and manacles – are in Hull and Gatineau. In these towns, late, late at night, you'll find Cabinet ministers and other politicians enjoying the booze, the girls, the ambiance. Former public works minister Roch LaSalle used to like to relax at the Lido, owned by his friend André Frechette and his partner Frank Bentivoglio. The Lido, which is open from 11 a.m. until 3 a.m., is just one of seven clubs owned by these men, according to *Citizen* reporter Tony Atherton, who, in 1986, put together an ambitious and fascinating series of stories about Ottawa's $37.5-million sex industry. The men also own the Lipstick, down the street from the Lido; between the two clubs, they rake in at least $3 million a year. They run an agency booking nude dancers from Montreal into strip clubs all over Ontario, the kind of business that made LaSalle's former right-hand man Frank Majeau and former Mafia killer Réal Simard famous.

Majeau and Simard ran an identical business, Prestige Entertainment, in Toronto in 1983 and used their dancers, according to Simard – Majeau always denied this – to bring cocaine into the clubs all over Toronto and western Ontario, from a Montreal distribution centre.

Ottawa has at least 120 escort services listed in the Yellow Pages, most of them owned by a ring of eight people. Almost all the services accept Visa, American Express and Master-Card; the prostitutes carry little card-processing machines in their purses. Most cards are routed through three restaurants, which pick up 20 per cent of the escort's earnings for providing the service. "The steady stream of affluent business-men, public servants and diplomats," Atherton wrote, "has made the Ottawa area a major centre for escort agencies, last year ranking third in the country for high-priced call girls." While street prostitutes were charging about $70 a trick, in 1986, according to Atherton, call girls could ask more. The escort service itself charges an hourly rate of between $20 and $60 per call, but what the woman charges her client is subject to negotiation.

Not surprisingly, stories about hookers are legion. One highly placed Rockcliffe source says that one of the city's most prosperous madams, who runs her escort service over the phone, lives in quiet elegance in the village. Another source states as gospel that at least two discreet brothels are run out of expensive apartment buildings in Sandy Hill. For the undis-criminating, there is always the sideshow of male and female prostitutes patrolling Murray and Mackenzie streets in Lower Town, although their presence has decreased with the growth of the escort services.

Some political aides should be more careful about their use of hookers. They shouldn't invite them for drinks in public places like the Press Club. Some Cabinet ministers should also cover their tracks better. A police source once reported that a minister habitually paid his favourite call girl with a personal cheque. At one point, the source explained, the woman had three cheques for $300 in her purse and decided to use them to pay her beeper service bill; like most Ottawa call girls, she used a message centre to keep track of her clients. She supposedly endorsed the cheques made out to her and turned them over to the message centre. An alert clerk in the centre noticed the signature on the cheques and photocopied them because the minister's name happened to be in the news. She passed along copies to the police.

At this point the story gets clouded. Police sources clammed up suddenly, so I contacted a friend who ran a beeper business also used by hookers to see if she had heard anything through the grapevine. She laughed off the story, saying not only that it was ridiculous but that she had not heard a whisper. We parted in a friendly fashion and I gave up. (Some years later, the minister was questioned about the incident during a court inquiry about another matter. He denied knowing anything about it.)

The next day I learned that this friend was not only dating the same minister's closest aide but had had dinner with him that evening, along with Patrick MacAdam and another senior Mulroney aide. The following day, Peter Maser, a colleague of mine from Southam News, received a call from his friend MacAdam, complaining that I was intruding into people's private lives.

Ottawa is a *very* small town.

Bibliography

Thomas Axworthy, "Of Secretaries to Princes": Journal of the Institute of Public Administration of Canada, July 1988.

David Bercuson, J.L. Granatstein and W.R. Young. *Sacred Trust? Brian Mulroney and the Conservative Party in Power.* Toronto: Doubleday, 1986.

Colin Campbell and George J. Szablowski. *The Super-Bureaucrats: Structure and Behaviour in Central Agencies.* Agincourt, Ont.: Gage, 1979.

Robert Fleming. *Canadian Legislatures.* Ottawa: Ampersand, 1988.

C.E.S. Franks. *The Parliament of Canada.* Toronto: University of Toronto Press, 1987.

Andrew B. Gollner and Daniel Salee, eds. *Canada Under Mulroney: An End of Term Report.* Montreal: Véhicule Press, 1988.

Katherine A. Graham, ed. *How Ottawa Spends: 1988/89, The Conservatives Heading Into the Stretch*. Ottawa: Carleton University Press, 1988.

J.L. Granatstein. *The Ottawa Men: The Civil Service Mandarins. 1937-1957*. Toronto: Oxford, 1982.

Sandra Gwyn. *The Private Capital*. Toronto: McClelland & Stewart, 1984.

Claire Hoy. *Friends in High Places: Politics and Patronage in the Mulroney Government*. Toronto: Key Porter, 1987.

Robert Jackson, Doreen Jackson and Nicolas Baxter-Moore, eds. *Contemporary Canadian Politics*. Scarborough, Ont.: Prentice-Hall, 1987.

Marc Lalonde. "The Prime Minister's Office" (paper delivered to the 1971 Conference of the Institute of Public Administration of Canada).

Robert Legget. *Rideau Waterway*. Toronto: University of Toronto Press, 1986.

Gary Levy. *Speakers of the House of Commons*. Ottawa: Library of Parliament, 1988.

James Littleton. *Target Nation: Canada and the Western Intelligence Network*. Toronto: Lester & Orpen Dennys/CBC Enterprises, 1986.

L. Ian MacDonald. *Mulroney: The Making of the Prime Minister*. Toronto: McClelland & Stewart, 1984.

Maureen McTeer. *Residences: Homes of Canada's Leaders*. Scarborough, Ont.: Prentice-Hall, 1982.

Patrick Martin, Allan Gregg and George Perlin. *Contenders: The Tory Quest for Power*. Scarborough, Ont.: Prentice-Hall, 1983.

W.A. Matheson. *The Prime Minister and the Cabinet*. Toronto: Methuen, 1976.

Nicole Morgan. *Nowhere to Go?* Ottawa: The Institute for Research on Public Policy, 1981.

————. *Implosion*. Ottawa: The Institute for Research on Public Policy, 1986.

————. *The Equality Game*. Ottawa: The Advisory Council on the Status of Women, 1988.

Brian Mulroney. *Where I Stand*. Toronto: McClelland & Stewart, 1983.

Rae Murphy, Robert Chodos and Nick Auf der Maur. *Brian Mulroney: The Boy from Baie Comeau*. Toronto: Lorimer, 1984.

Gordon Osbaldeston. *Keeping Deputy Ministers Accountable*. Scarborough, Ont.: McGraw-Hill Ryerson, 1989.

Sean O'Sullivan (with Rod McQueen). *Both My Houses: From Politics to Priesthood*. Toronto: Key Porter, 1986.

Timothy Plumptre. *Beyond the Bottom Line, Management in Government*. Ottawa: Institute for Research on Public Policy, 1988.

Gordon Robertson. "The Privy Council Office" (paper delivered to the 1971 Conference of the Institute of Public Administration of Canada).

John Sawatsky. *The Insiders: Government, Business and the Lobbyists*. Toronto: McClelland & Stewart, 1986.

Jeffrey Simpson. *Spoils of Power*. Don Mills, Ont.: Collins, 1988.

David Stafford. *Camp X: Canada's School for Secret Agents*. Toronto: Lester & Orpen Dennys, 1986.

John H. Taylor. *Ottawa, An Illustrated History*. Toronto/Ottawa: Lorimer/The Canadian Museum of Civilization, 1986.

Ernest Volkman and Blaine Baggett. *Secret Intelligence: The Inside Story of America's Espionage Empire*. Toronto: Doubleday, 1989.

Joseph Wearing. *Strained Relations: Canadian Parties and Voters*. Toronto: McClelland and Stewart, 1988.

Shirley E. Woods. *Her Excellency Jeanne Sauvé*. Toronto: Macmillan, 1986.

————. *Ottawa: The Capital of Canada*. Toronto: Doubleday, 1980.

Peter Wright. *Spycatcher: The Candid Autobiography of a Senior Intelligence Officer*. Don Mills, Ont.: Stoddart, 1987.

David Zussman, ed. *Shifting Sands: Managing People in Public Bureaucracies*. Toronto: The Institute of Public Administration of Canada, 1987.

Index

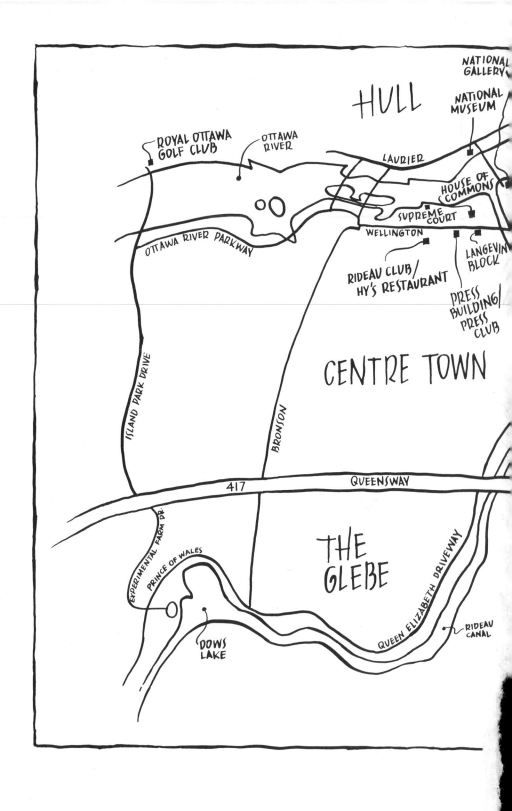